Bauwelt Fundamente 154

Edited by
Peter Neitzke

Advisory Board
Gerd Albers
Hildegard Barz-Malfatti
Elisabeth Blum
Eduard Führ
Thomas Sieverts
Jörn Walter

Mary Dellenbaugh,
Markus Kip, Majken Bieniok,
Agnes Katharina Müller,
Martin Schwegmann (eds.)

Urban Commons

Moving Beyond State and Market

Bauverlag
Gütersloh · Berlin

Birkhäuser
Basel

The Bauwelt Fundamente series was founded in 1963 by Ulrich Conrads, who served as series editor until volume 149 in 2013, from the early 1980s jointly with Peter Neitzke.

Front and back cover:
"Crossing Commons" by Agnes Katharina Müller and Markus Kip; Photographer Agnes Katharina Müller, April 2015, Alexanderplatz, Berlin

Library of Congress Cataloging-in-Publication data
A CIP catalog record for this book has been applied for at the Library of Congress.

Bibliographic information published by the German National Library
The German National Library lists this publication in the Deutsche Nationalbibliografie; detailed bibliographic data are available on the Internet at http://dnb.dnb.de.

This work is subject to copyright. All rights are reserved, whether the whole or part of the material is concerned, specifically the rights of translation, reprinting, re-use of illustrations, recitation, broadcasting, reproduction on microfilms or in other ways, and storage in databases. For any kind of use, permission of the copyright owner must be obtained.

This publication is also available as an e-book (ISBN PDF 978-3-03821-495-3; ISBN EPUB 978-3-03821-591-2)

© 2015 Birkhäuser Verlag GmbH, Basel
P.O. Box 44, 4009 Basel, Switzerland
Part of Walter de Gruyter GmbH, Berlin/Boston
and Bauverlag BV GmbH, Gütersloh, Berlin

bau│ │verlag

Printed on acid-free paper produced from chlorine-free pulp. TCF ∞

Printed in Germany

ISBN 978-3-03821-661-2

9 8 7 6 5 4 3 2 1

www.birkhauser.com

Contents

Preface 7

Markus Kip, Majken Bieniok, Mary Dellenbaugh, Agnes Katharina Müller, Martin Schwegmann
Seizing the (Every)Day: Welcome to the Urban Commons! 9

Perspectives

Brigitte Kratzwald
Urban Commons – Dissident Practices in Emancipatory Spaces 26

Markus Kip
Moving Beyond the City: Conceptualizing Urban Commons from a Critical Urban Studies Perspective 42

Majken Bieniok
The Complexity of Urban Commoning from a Psychological Perspective 60

Community

Tobias Kuttler, Angela Jain
Defending Space in a Changing Urban Landscape – A Study on Urban Commons in Hyderabad, India 72

Didi K. Han, Hajime Imamasa
Overcoming Privatized Housing in South Korea: Looking through the Lens of "Commons" and "the Common" 91

Manuel Lutz
Uncommon Claims to the Commons: Homeless Tent Cities in the US 101

Institutions

Daniel Opazo Ortiz
Creating and Appropriating Urban Spaces – The Public versus the Commons: Institutions, Traditions, and Struggles in the Production of Commons and Public Spaces in Chile 117

Ignacio Castillo Ulloa
Acting in Reality within the Cranny of the Real: Towards an Alternative Agency of Urban Commons 130

Agnes Katharina Müller
From Urban Commons to Urban Planning – or Vice Versa? "Planning" the Contested Gleisdreieck Territory 148

Melissa García Lamarca
Insurgent Acts of Being-in-Common and Housing in Spain: Making Urban Commons? 165

Resources

Ivo Balmer, Tobias Bernet
Housing as a Common Resource? Decommodification and Self-Organization in Housing – Examples from Germany and Switzerland 178

Sören Becker, Ross Beveridge, Matthias Naumann
Reconfiguring Energy Provision in Berlin. Commoning between Compromise and Contestation 196

AK Thompson
The Battle for Necropolis: Reclaiming the Past as Commons in the City of the Dead 214

Authors 236

Preface

This book is based on the conference *Urban Commons: Moving beyond State and Market* which took place at the Georg Simmel Center for Metropolitan Studies at the Humboldt University, Berlin on September 27 and 28, 2013. It is the product of a two-year-long process of revision and discussion. The result is a condensed publication about urban commons which provides both an overview on the state of affairs as well as an international range of specific case studies.

The editors of this book originally met in the Georg Simmel Center's doctoral colloquium, the Graduate Studies Group. This group consisted of PhD students from diverse disciplinary backgrounds such as architecture, psychology, geography, sociology, and planning, whose research all focused on cities and urban struggles. Nearing the end of our respective doctoral projects, the five of us met one night in summer 2012 to discuss topics and formats for further collaboration.

That night we decided to found the Urban Research Group and organize a conference on urban commons. After some reading and many discussions it occurred to us that this topic addressed a particularly current *zeitgeist*: the discourse on commons brings together valuable models of how to understand the city as a collective resource and offers possible approaches of how to use these resources, for example public space, collective housing and energy supply, in a way that shifts the focus from exchange value to use value.

The commons lens made it possible for us to dig deeper into many matters that were at stake both back in 2012 and today. In the shadow of the financial and euro crisis, the Arab Spring, the Occupy movements, intensifying gentrification in cities around the world (including Berlin), and a growing movement to remunicipalize former public services like water and energy supply, the debate around commons gave us both vital points of reference to address social and economic inequalities concretely in our cities and a lens to analyze and potentially create alternative models of urban resource use.

The conference "Urban Commons: Moving beyond State and Market," which was funded by the Fritz Thyssen Foundation, received considerable attention. Although we had to strictly limit acceptances, we were still able to host a geographically diverse group of researchers and case studies spanning the Americas, Europe,

Asia and Oceania, and including case studies in Germany, India, Chile, South Korea, Spain, Switzerland, and the United States.

We'd like to express our deep thanks to the other members of the Urban Research Group who worked with us to conceptually develop and organize the conference: Dr. Zofia Łapniewska and Katarzyna Puzon. We'd like to thank all of the participants at the conference, whose commentary and involvement created a stimulating atmosphere which motivated us to pursue this edited collection. In a way, they can be conceived as the first peer reviewers, giving critical responses to the various papers and ideas presented. In addition, we'd like to extend our gratitude to the authors who contributed to this volume for engaging our criticisms and requests in several rounds of revisions. Your dedication and effort, sometimes at short notice, were essential in this co-production. We'd also like to thank Peter Neitzke, whose unwavering faith that this publication would be relevant in the contemporary and future discourse on cities and societies was critical in the realization of this project. We were much saddened by his passing shortly before publication.

Finally, we'd like to acknowledge the support of the Georg Simmel Center and its spokesperson, Wolfgang Kaschuba, for hosting the conference; the intellectual and technical support that we received, as well as the use of space and resources for the conference, editorial meetings, and editorial work were instrumental in this endeavor.

We'd be remiss not to extend our gratitude to our partners, friends, and families for their understanding. What started as an intellectual side project turned into a major undertaking requiring countless hours of overtime and late-night meetings. Their support was crucial in allowing us to bring this project to its successful completion.

Agnes, Majken, Markus, Martin and Mary
Berlin 2015

Markus Kip, Majken Bieniok, Mary Dellenbaugh, Agnes Katharina Müller, Martin Schwegmann

Seizing the (Every)Day: Welcome to the Urban Commons!

As a result of recent global financial and political crises, more and more people have been seeking out alternative economic and political models beyond market and state. In the face of aggressive austerity measures, the struggle for urban resources has become an explicit struggle over the commons. Many urban movements today have lost confidence in the state as the trustworthy steward for collective consumption, and in the market as the optimal (and equitable) provider of goods and services. The concept of commons has therefore gained popularity, as it promises participatory self-governance against state tutelage as well as more equity in addressing human needs.[1] It is also for this reason that we see alternative forms of commoning for health care, food, housing, or public spaces emerging most prominently in places devastated by austerity reforms.

Originally, the concept of commons derived from the rural experience of shared natural resources such as pastures, fishing grounds, water, and so on; this concept has, however, also been applied to other areas of human production and reproduction. Charlotte Hess,[2] for example, has used the term "new commons" to mark collective governance mechanisms in the production of things such as "scientific knowledge, voluntary associations, climate change, community gardens, wikipedias, cultural treasures, plant seeds, and the electromagnetic spectrum." This rise of the new commons also coincides with an ongoing urbanization of the world population. It appears pedestrian to argue that cities are the foremost spaces (but clearly not the only ones) in which these new commons take shape. As such, the collective endeavor of the book has been to explore the link between these developments further. More specifically, this publication examines the struggle for urban commons and asks what, if anything, is specifically "urban" about them.

Research on urban commons has gained momentum in the last decade[3] and activists have increasingly taken up this notion to understand their problems in urban contexts. We, the editors, have witnessed the emergence of such commoning

Figure 1. Sidewalk in Berlin.

efforts in Berlin and elsewhere, which led us to wonder how these phenomena play into the political landscape and which urban research tools and methods might contribute to their understanding. These commoning efforts ranged from small- to large-scale and involved user groups of various sizes and compositions. As an initial approximation of the idea of the urban commons, we suggest that urban commons are about collectively appropriating and regulating the shared concerns of the everyday.

A first example presented itself when residents placed pots, boxes and old bathtubs on the sidewalk in front of their building in which to grow flowers and vegetables (Figure 1). This rather banal action was followed by a lively discussion within the neighborhood on whether those residents had the right to do so, and the aesthetic value of such actions. Is this an edible beautification of the streetscape for everyone to enjoy or an unsolicited privatization of public space? A few concerned citizens issued complaints to the local public affairs office *(Ordnungsamt)*, but, interestingly, the landlord never forwarded complaints to the tenants in the house. Did he like the initiative of his tenants, was he merely indifferent to it, or did he hope to increase the value of his housing asset through tenant-led beautification efforts?

The Tempelhofer Feld (the former city airport Berlin Tempelhof) might be considered a second example of a commons on a much larger scale, involving a larger area and more users (Figure 2). After it was closed, the former city airport was not immediately repurposed, and the unplanned open space became increasingly

Figure 2. Tempelhofer Feld.

popular among citizens who used it for various leisure activities such as biking, kite-surfing, picnicking, and gardening, or recognized its ecological value. As the real-estate market in Berlin began to recover from its post-2008 slump, the Berlin Senate made a plan to develop a part of this area and planned to allow private investors to construct upscale housing on its premises. Citizens' action committees like Squat Tempelhof and 100% Tempelhofer Feld were organized over the years; the local activists gained considerable public support in preserving the Feld in its unplanned, unbuilt state. The fight to preserve the Tempelhofer Feld as a common found its peak at the referendum *(Volksentscheid)* of 2014, which successfully blocked the Senate's plans.

The concept of commons may also be used as an analytical lens to understand the squatting practices of refugees in different German cities, like in Berlin at both Oranienplatz (Figure 3) and the Gerhart-Hauptmann-Schule between 2012 and 2014. The justification for these actions cannot be understood simply along the lines of public and private goods, services, and spaces. While a part of the protest certainly centers on survival and better housing conditions than in the German refugee camps *(Flüchtlingslager),* the squats are also a place from which to demand legal rights (for asylum), as well as the abolition of the *Flüchtlingslager* and compulsory residence *(Residenzpflicht)*. But indeed the protests are also about collective self-determination as a marginalized group, the creation of a space for public communication about these issues, and the forging of a sense of *common* humanity between

Figure 3. Refugee camp at Oranienplatz in Berlin, November 7, 2013.

citizens and non-citizens. Without many resources to count on, after a year of occupation the living conditions at Oranienplatz became pretty miserable, especially in winter. From one perspective, the self-organized refugee camps both at Oranienplatz and the Gerhart-Hauptmann-Schule became a cheap way for the state[4] to let itself off the hook of supporting refugees economically, while at the same time consciously ignoring the stressful living conditions so as to fuel internal infighting in the camp. Nevertheless, when the local state decided to clear both areas with police force, it still encountered heavy resistance and protest.

The emphasis on (political and economic) autonomy, the rejection of state tutelage, and the occupation of public spaces that can be found in these examples connects them with other global movements such as the Arab Spring, the *indignados* or the Occupy movement.[5] The urban context of these contestations is striking. However, in what way does an urban setting influence or condition commoning efforts? From an abstract perspective, urban space might involve both the facilitation and hindrance of commoning efforts. On the one hand, the diversity and density that characterize the urban structure create a fertile field to mobilize like-minded people or to create and test new social strategies. These are important assets for the development of new collective resource management forms at different scales. On the other hand, the anonymity, indifference, and narcissistic differentiation that are also often connected with urban lifestyles can function as significant barriers to such commoning efforts. In this sense, this collected work seeks to explore in greater detail how the historically and geographically specific urban condition has shaped the experience, development, and preservation of commons.

Bringing together a variety of case studies from different areas of the world, the aim of this volume is to examine the specific conditions surrounding urban commons, particularly how commons practices have developed in relation to state and capital while trying to push forward a political alternative beyond both. These intriguing cases have required us to question our previously held assumptions and imaginations of what commons are. Our book is premised on the idea that bringing theories of urban space and commons into dialogue with one another offers a new vantage point from which to consider the contentious constitution of the commons. In the following, we will highlight key aspects of the concept of the commons and the urban that set the foundation for the contributions in this book.

Defining commons

A wide spectrum of theoretical background literature defines commons in conspicuously similar ways. Most definitions present commons as a construct constituted of three main parts: (a) *common* resources, (b) institutions (i.e. *commoning* practices) and (c) the communities (called *commoners*) who are involved in the production and reproduction of commons.[6]

For example, Andreas Exner and Brigitte Kratzwald, two commons activists and researchers, stated that:

> commons [...] always consist of three elements, a resource (that may be material or immaterial), people who use the resource (often called commoners in the literature) and the process of negotiation on how to use that resource, thus the rules of appropriation.[7] [Translation: authors]

This parallels descriptions in the work of Silke Helfrich, the well-known researcher on commons in the German context, and Jörg Haas, a climate and energy expert, who describe commons as consisting of things (resources, objects, spaces), systems and practices (regulation, commoning), and the communities that are involved.[8] Using the same analytic triad, the political economist Massimo De Angelis outlines commons as follows:

> [C]onceptualizing the commons involves three things at the same time. First, all commons involve some sort of common pool resources,

> understood as non-commodified means of fulfilling people's needs. Second, the commons are necessarily created and sustained by communities [...]. Communities are sets of commoners who share these resources and who define for themselves the rules through which they are accessed and used. [...] [T]he third and most important element in terms of conceptualizing the commons is the verb "to common" – the social process that creates and reproduces the commons.[9]

Another definition of commons is given by geographer David Harvey, who sees commons:

> as an unstable and malleable social relation between a particular self-defined social group and those aspects of its actually existing or yet-to-be-created social and/or physical environment deemed crucial to its life and livelihood.[10]

Even if not enumerated, the three constituent parts can still be recognized in Harvey's definition: (a) "an unstable and malleable social relation," or "institution" we might say, (b) "a particular self-defined social group," in other words a "community" and (c) "aspects of its actually existing or yet-to-be-created social and/or physical environment," i.e. a "resource."

The three prongs can even be found in Elinor Ostrom's well-known "eight design principles" for common-pool resources.[11] The Nobel Prize winner in economics included two elements of the triad in her first principle calling for "clearly defined boundaries" which relate to the boundaries of the *resources* as well as the *community* of users.[12] The following seven principles focus on the third element, the *institutions* (commoning), in particular to "match rules governing use of common goods to local needs and conditions" (2), "ensure that those affected by the rules can participate in modifying the rules" (3), "make sure that the rule-making rights of community members are respected by outside authorities" (4), "develop a system, carried out by community members, for monitoring members' behavior" (5), "use graduated sanctions for rule violators" (6), and to "provide accessible, low-cost means for dispute resolution" (7). In her last principle, Ostrom advises to "build responsibility for governing the common resource in nested tiers from the lowest level up to the entire interconnected system" (8).[13]

Where Ostrom focuses on the institutional aspects, David Bollier, another commons scholar, elaborates on the resource characteristics and their effects on governing commons. Bollier categorizes common resources based on four main characteristics:

(1) Depletability, which is related to the question "can the resource be 'used up' or not?"[14] An example would be an urban garden (which can be depleted through overuse) versus radio transmissions (whose use by one person or group does not reduce the amount of the resource available for others);

(2) Excludability, related to the question "can access be restricted?" An example here would be a collectively run child-care facility (excludable) versus clean air (non-excludable);[15]

(3) Rivalrous use, with the related question "does one user's use of the resource take away from others'?"[16] Too many visitors to a public park may impair the enjoyment or utility of other users, who appreciate the park's silence (rivalrous). Squatting or participating in a road blockade, however, does not necessarily change the utility of such commons for other users (non-rivalrous) – to the contrary;

(4) Regulation, with the related question being "is the resource regulated? Are there rules governing the use of the resource?"[17] Providing households with electrical energy in self-governed fashion arguably involves a more explicit formulation of rules than hitting the dance floor at a neighborhood celebration.

In light of these four criteria, Ostrom's principles regarding institutions, and the complex nature of use and negotiation surrounding the group characteristics of the commoners, it is easy to understand why the commons debate is so complex.

In sum, the definitions of commons have led us to three important questions to ask in the examination of a potential commons with regard to the nature of the resource, the institution, and the user group(s), namely:
- What is the common resource?
- What are good practices and relevant relationships between commoners and different commons?
- Who belongs to the "we" of the community?

These three questions are relevant for both traditional commons such as fisheries, as well as the complex setting of urban commons discussed in this volume. The urban condition, as will be discussed in depth in the following section, may present particular complexities in the commons debate. For example, Elinor Ostrom's idea that clearly defined resource boundaries are a fundamental prerequisite for any commoning effort (as discussed in the eight principles above) may be challenged by the urban condition. Urban commons are not just local; they are often constituted by processes at several scales.

Defining the urban

As various authors note, "the urban" also entails promises framed as the right to the city that could form the basis of resistance to the enclosing forces of state and capital.[18] Lefebvre's idea of the right to the city in fact draws on an understanding of the city as an *oeuvre,* as an ongoing and collective work of art, created, used, and reshaped by its inhabitants, an idea with striking similarities to the idea of the commons. The more mainstream concept of "the urban" has a very different ideation of space. "The urban" is widely taken as a synonym for "the local," and the city is understood as an "entity,"[19] at times also including aspects of density and scale. Criticizing the global paradigm of urbanism, also referred to as the discourse of an "urban age," Brenner and Schmid argue that the range of variation, various measurement techniques, and local and national thresholds involved in international aggregate statistics of global urbanism make the definition of a space as a "city" more or less arbitrary.[20] Indeed, these definitions are based on the fundamental assumption that "global settlement space can and must be divided neatly into urban or rural containers."[21] Other accounts identify the city as having a specific form and shape, such as the density and height of built structures, or the presence and particular order of various functional areas (i.e. housing, business districts, commercial districts), famously divided into dwelling, work, leisure, and circulation (see also Le Corbusier's version of the Athens Charter published in 1943). Another strand of urban studies has latched onto the concept of global cities[22] as the epitome of what it means to be a city.

As urban scholars rooted in the critical lineage of urban studies, we conceive of the urban at a higher level of abstraction than the (local) city. The differentiation between "the city as a local entity" and "the urban" is not easy, but it is crucial particularly with respect to the challenge of the commons. Two particular insights on "the urban" can be derived from the existing literature in critical urban studies.

First, the urban has been conceived in terms of its multi-scalar constitution and its linkages to other spaces and places. This idea was predominantly drawn from a critique of political economy and conceives of urbanization as a global process that links various places and scales with each other, from the body to the global. Drawing on the work of Henri Lefebvre, Neil Brenner and Christian Schmid even claim that we are living in a situation of "planetary urbanization;"[23] urbanization is allegedly the prevailing mode of existence for our societies.

Second, the urban can also be understood as the realm of (modern) everyday activity. Imagined as a cultural process of mediating individual and everyday experiences with the requirements of capital accumulation and political hegemony, "the urban" functions as a prism to scrutinize how the logic of capital and state power seeps into the various experiences and tactics for coping with day-to-day life. The anonymity inherent with large and complex urban agglomerations may be at odds with the ideals of decentralized commons in which commoners know each other face-to-face. Several urbanists[24] however, value just these aspects of urban culture (i.e. anonymity), as they also embody liberation from forms of peer pressure and other kinds of social control, and function as a facilitator for diverse urban cultures.

Capturing the urban character of change and diversity, David Harvey succinctly states: "the city is the site where people of all sorts and classes mingle, however reluctantly and agonistically, to produce a common if perpetually changing and transitory life."[25]

Having conceptualized the wide range of dimensions of the urban, we might sum up "the urban" as a spatial organization of society. It is comprised of structural aspects, i.e. the acceleration and densification of connections, which are materially embodied in the development of the built environment, but also cultural aspects, i.e. ways of dealing with difference and complexity, which are based in the microphysics of the everyday encounter rather than sovereign planning. In order to circumvent the prevalent method of deriving theory from a set of urban experiences which are limited to the Global North, which view 'Third World' cities "as problems, requiring diagnosis and reform,"[26] we have made a concerted effort to also consider cities of both the Global North and Global South in our reflections. We have aimed for a perspective on "ordinary cities"[27] though we are also aware that the majority of our case studies are located in metropolitan centers.

The challenge of the urban commons is that any such commoning effort is subjected to the urban condition, albeit in different ways and to different degrees. On the one hand, urban commons have to deal with the challenge of devising strategic scales and boundaries for collective action. On the other hand, the ongoing urbanization of society, with its mobilities, ephemeralities, and diversity of subjectivities, constantly undermines and challenges boundaries. The question is: what kinds of institutions are needed in such a context of diversity and (at least partial) anonymity? And how should we think of the process of collaboration between these diverse urban actors? In the end, a shared set of common values and norms for any kind of social institutionalization seems inevitable.

Boundaries that create a sense of community at one moment may be perceived as a form of (unjustified) exclusion at another moment. Accusations of exclusivity thus might be raised against some commons. And clearly, any commons project that seeks to overcome state and market will need to consider these accusations seriously so as not to reproduce social divisions. Alternatively, boundaries could also be challenged from within; urban commoners might leave commoning endeavors, whether due to geographical mobility or because they lose a sense of identification with the community. A commons with a shrinking number of participants, however, is also likely to face challenges to reproduce itself. Committed participants may be desperately needed to keep up that neighborhood park or to hold (and renovate) that squat. Besides topographical mobility, commoners as urban actors are also likely to develop interests and identities in different directions. In this situation, urban commoners thus constantly need to negotiate and rearticulate the "we." Given such ongoing changes and developments, how can commoners still maintain collective interests and identities?

Another challenge of boundaries refers to the interrelation of different commons. Harvey pointed out that we should acknowledge the limits of horizontality as an organizational principle between commons.[28] In such a view, decentralization and autonomy are primary vehicles for producing greater inequality through neoliberalization, and therefore the interaction between autonomous (commons) units has to be regulated by rules which have to be established, asserted, enforced, and actively policed by a higher-order hierarchical authority.[29] Drawing on the work of Murray Bookchin, Harvey[30] has suggested a federated structure among various commons.

In each case, urban commons must be constantly vigilant in order to negotiate and revise their boundaries and institutional dynamics. In each instance, commons must keep the influences of state and market at bay while at the same time "leading the dance"[31] with them. Depending on externalities for accumulation, both capital and state have consciously latched onto urban life as a source of revitalization.[32] New forms of collaboration, social and cultural reproduction, technological innovations, fashion, and so on are important impulses for reinvigorating capital accumulation.[33] Initiatives to create "commons," such as networks of small entrepreneurs, subcultural producers, initiatives offering direct services to the marginalized and urban gardening, are welcomed and even facilitated by governments in order to (re-)valorize urban space and lessen the impacts of economic restructuring.[34] However, at the same time, the creative and reproductive potential of the urban commons is undermined by new attempts to exploit and control (i.e. enclose) them, which themselves are compounded by austerity politics.

The challenge of urban commons

Spelling out this challenge for the three dimensions of commons, we should note:
- Urban commoners' involvement in ongoing processes of mobility and social differentiation requires a rethinking of Ostrom's requirement for clear boundaries of commoners and their *communities*. Urban commoners thus should be thought of as engaging in constant boundary negotiation.
- Urban commons *institutions* thus confront the challenge of developing processes for such boundary-drawing and this negotiation of the relationships among commoners with different identities, mobilities, needs, and abilities. This task, in combination with the large-scale and multi-scalar constitution of the commons, increases the complexity for governance, making face-to-face relations virtually impossible.
- Urban commons *resources* should be considered from the perspective of the multiple scales involved in producing and consuming commons. Also, it should be carefully distinguished that an urban resource may mean different things to different people. Not taking resources as a "given" also requires closer scrutiny at the various ways in which resources are consumed, used or reproduced.

These are serious challenges of the urban commons for which we still lack any clear principles or rules. The fact that none are readily available, but will need to be developed in a process of negotiation, could be interpreted as inherently urban. The contributions in this collection tackle these challenges in different ways, offering different accounts of how urban commons have emerged, and been contested, enclosed and/or protected.

Overview of the contributions

The edited collection is divided into four sections. The *first section* provides a variety of conceptual perspectives on the urban commons. *Brigitte Kratzwald's* contribution considers urban commons as "dissident practices in emancipatory spaces." Kratzwald sets the conceptual foundation of commons for this volume and argues that cities have become hotbeds for political contestations around collective goods exacerbated by neoliberal austerity measures. Nevertheless, she also points out that "the theoretical discussion of urban commons is a relatively new phenomenon and must first create its own foundation." Assessing the historical emergence of the commons in rural England, she argues with Silke Helfrich that "common goods don't simply exist, they are created." In this vein, Kratzwald highlights the constant need for commons to reaffirm themselves vis-à-vis state and capital, and critically appraises Ostrom's principles for durable commons.

In his contribution, *Markus Kip* focuses on the concept of urban space by drawing on discussions from the field of critical urban studies. Considering the recent academic hype around "urban commons," he identifies the lack of an explicit take on what makes commons urban. Kip argues firstly that the negotiation of boundaries and solidarities requires greater analytic attention, as the multi-scalar constitution of urban space as well as processes of social differentiation present commoners with a constant challenge to establish a common ground for collective praxis. Secondly, he asserts that urban commons can only survive and prevail if their expansion matches that of capital.

Such expansion, however, is accompanied by several complexities, as *Majken Bieniok* outlines in her contribution. From a psychological perspective, Bieniok stresses the significance of social dilemmas, i.e. "situations in which the decision that has to be taken either supports the fulfillment of short-term self-interests or long-term collective interests." Psychological research provides interesting insights regarding the motivational, cognitive, and perceptual aspects involved in commoning efforts. Bieniok finds that the complexity characteristic of an urbanizing world poses difficulties for social cooperation and goes on to critically engage Vincent Ostrom's and David Harvey's proposals for cooperation among commons.

The following three sections are loosely grouped according to the three commons dimensions. Although each of these dimensions never exists in isolation from each other, the various contributions concentrate on the three dimensions to differing degrees.

The *second section* includes three contributions that offer insights and questions on the issue of community. In their study of the Begum Bazaar in Hyderabad, India, *Tobias Kuttler* and *Angela Jain* take a rather unconventional perspective on the negotiations of street space as a form of commoning. They found no strict group boundaries of commoners and no explicit sense of identity as a community. Kuttler and Jain's ethnographic research on appropriation and negotiation patterns suggests that "the creation of commons […] is realized successfully in the everyday appropriation of physical space and the production of social space." This real-existing commons, however, is marked by hierarchies and social inequalities and thus is far removed from the ideal model that Ostrom and others have conceived.

The contribution by *Didi Han* and *Hajime Imamasa* takes us to the recently established and currently expanding commune project *Bin-Zib,* with various "guest" houses in Seoul, South Korea. Han and Imamasa situate the emergence of this community in the context of the heated real-estate market in Seoul, which has created severe housing shortages and inequities. What is particularly striking about this community is its radical openness to newcomers and the absence of a "political ideology, program or bureaucratic structure." Beyond creating simply a housing commons, the residents also generate new forms of "being-in-common," through living arrangements and engagements with their social environment.

Manuel Lutz considers homeless tent cities in the US as an "uncommon" form of commons that has seen a dramatic increase post-2008. Although these tent cities may be described as "intentional communities," their intentionality relates primarily to shared resources and basic survival. In view of the larger political economic system that produces homelessness, one might suspect it to be a community-against-its-own-will. Lutz, however, emphasizes the agency and self-affirmation of these tent cities as communities resisting prevalent modes of governing the homeless. Against state modes of disciplining homeless people through shelters and specifically tailored services aimed at "rehabilitating" the homeless to become "housing ready," the mere existence of these communities already suggests that the real problem lies not in the homeless but in sub-standard housing.

The *third section* assembles contributions that offer intriguing insights into the practices of commoning and their contested institutionalization. *Daniel Opazo Ortiz* discusses the events around the *"toma de Peñalolén,"* the appropriation of land for an informal settlement in Santiago de Chile, Chile. A former private lot was taken over in 1999 by *pobladores* (slum dwellers), drawing on a long history of such praxis in Chile. Opazo suggests looking at this settlement as a commons that was cut short. In 2005, the state purchased the land and evicted the residents, with the official argument that such form of (citizen) appropriation is not constitutional. The state thereby discursively transformed "the *pobladores*' struggle for the right to the city and housing into an organized pressure group with a sort of 'privatizing agenda'."

The case study of *Ignacio Castillo Ulloa,* by contrast, exhibits a more successful outcome of a commons struggle. Using the works of Foucault and Lacan as theoretical scaffolding, Castillo scrutinizes how an urban movement in San José, Costa Rica was able to claim an elementary school, a public library, and a park for its own purposes. Although the neighborhood was relegated to the "excluded periphery" by state plans and dominated by centralized authorities and traditional political parties, Castillo advances the argument that this case of "radical commoning" became possible due to the "crannies of the Real." "The Real" of planning and control devices, as Castillo shows, has not been able to fully absorb (the lived) "reality" thus allowing for the "perennial possibility for counteraction, for the insurrection of local knowledges and languages, for the imagining an alternative future in present tense."

Agnes Katharina Müller looks at the contestations around the Gleisdreieck territory in Berlin. She tracks the legacy of these contestations from its former marginal location adjacent to the Berlin Wall to its post-reunification transformation into a coveted real-estate location. Throughout this history, various actors with different stakes in this territory formed coalitions to intervene against official plans. Müller proposes the consideration of these coalitions as commoning efforts that were able to disrupt official planning procedures to implement a more participatory "bottom-up" process. These coalitions were able to safeguard the Gleisdreieck territory as a common space to a certain extent, and pushed the municipal government to officially recognize it as such.

A case study on commoning as an "insurgent act" is also presented by *Melissa García Lamarca*. Looking at the 2007 bust of real-estate speculation in Spain and the resultant housing evictions, her chapter takes a closer look at a movement organizing against such evictions called the "Platform for Mortgage Affected People." Since 2009, the PAH has expanded to 200 branches nationwide, has successfully blocked 1,130 evictions, and "rehoused" 1,150 people in thirty recuperated buildings. García relates the movement's "being-in-common" to the "collective recuperation of housing, through the relationships built between the occupying group and their social and physical environment as they dwell together and organize themselves." Considering its future, she raises the tricky question of how such a movement can become both emancipatory and prevail in the long-run.

The *fourth section* centers on the resource dimension of urban commons. It starts off with *Ivo Balmer* and *Tobias Bernet's* examination of housing models in Germany and Switzerland from the perspective of commons. The authors scrutinize these models on the continuum formed by two criteria deemed crucial for the assessment of commons, namely the degree of decommodification and the degree of self-organization. Although public policy interventions in the housing sector are considered necessary and justified, Balmer and Bernet point to their political vulnerability in view of strategies of privatization. As an alternative, they favorably assess a "creative hack" of property rights in order to provide housing as a kind of common resource, namely the organization of collectively owned housing in the form of a private company.

Another central urban resource is the infrastructure related to electricity supply. *Sören Becker*, *Ross Beveridge* and *Matthias Naumann* follow the recent citizen campaigns to recommunalize Berlin's electricity network which was privatized in 1997. The issue of energy provision galvanized citizens' initiatives due to its relevance to various popular issues, including environmental protection, preservation of resources, democratic participation, and social equity. The two campaigns considered involved different commons politics; one was based on a cooperative ownership model, the other on a model of public control and accountability.

Last, but not least, *AK Thompson* concludes the volume with a fundamental and provocative consideration of the commons. "The Battle for Necropolis" expands the scope of what is ultimately at stake in any commoning effort. Thompson writes that, "it is precisely to the themes of *politics as war* and the *persistence of the dead* that we must turn if we hope to advance our struggles for the commons beyond their current state of wishful anticipation – a state that stimulates our longing for social transformation even as it thwarts the realization of our aims." In this fashion, Thompson unravels "the past" and "territory" as crucial resources that commoning projects need to claim if they want to have any political significance.

We hope that this volume inspires further rigorous discussion about the meaning and practice of collectively seizing the everyday. We are excited to be part of this commoning process.

Notes

1. David Bollier and Silke Helfrich, eds., The Wealth of the Commons: A World beyond Market and State (Amherst, MA: Levellers Press, 2013); http://wealthofthecommons.org/ (accessed January 26, 2015)
2. Charlotte Hess, "Mapping the New Commons", SSRN Scholarly Paper (Rochester, NY: Social Science Research Network, July 1, 2008); http://papers.ssrn.com/abstract=1356835.
3. See chapter by Kip, this volume.
4. "The state" is a generalization in this example and does not describe the often antagonizing forces on district, regional, and national level.
5. George Caffentzis and Silvia Federici, "Commons Against and Beyond Capitalism," *Upping the Anti*, no. 15 (September 2013): 83–97.
6. Yochai Benkler, "The Political Economy of Commons", in *Genes, Bytes and Emissions: To Whom Does the World Belong*, ed. Silke Helfrich (Berlin: Heinrich-Böll-Foundation, 2009), 1, 3. http://us.boell.org/2010/10/06/genes-bytes-and-emissions-whom-does-world-belong-economic-governance (accessed January 26, 2015)
7. Andreas Exner and Brigitte Kratzwald, *Solidarische Ökonomie & Commons: Eine Einführung* (Vienna: Mandelbaum, 2012), 23.
8. Silke Helfrich and Jörg Haas, "The Commons: A New Narrative for Our Times," in *Genes, Bytes and Emissions: To Whom Does the World Belong*, ed. Silke Helfrich (Berlin: Heinrich-Böll-Foundation, 2009), 1. http://us.boell.org/2010/10/06/genes-bytes-and-emissions-whom-does-world-belong-economic-governance (accessed January 26, 2015).
9. Massimo De Angelis and Stavros Stavrides, "On the Commons: A Public Interview with Massimo De Angelis and Stravos Stavrides," *An Architektur & e-flux journal*, no. 17 (August 2010): 4–7.
10. David Harvey, *Rebel Cities: From the Right to the City to the Urban Revolution* (London: Verso, 2012), 73.
11. Elinor Ostrom, *Governing the Commons: The Evolution of Institutions for Collective Action* (New York: Cambridge University Press, 1990).
12. Ostrom, *Governing the Commons*, 91.
13. Jay Walljasper, "Elinor Ostrom's 8 Principles for Managing A Commons," *On the Commons*, October 2, 2011, http://www.onthecommons.org/magazine/elinor-ostroms-8-principles-managing-commmons (accessed December 15, 2014).
14. David Bollier, "The Commons: A Neglected Sector of Wealth-Creation," in *Genes, Bytes and Emissions: To Whom Does the World Belong*, ed. Silke Helfrich (Berlin: Heinrich-Böll-Foundation, 2009), 5. http://us.boell.org/2010/10/06/genes-bytes-and-emissions-whom-does-world-belong-economic-governance (accessed January 26, 2015).
15. Ibid.
16. Ibid.
17. Benkler, "The Political Economy of Commons," 1.
18. See, for example, Henri Lefebvre, *Writings on Cities*, ed. and transl. Eleonore Kofman and Elizabeth Lebas (Oxford: Blackwell, 1996); Henri Lefebvre, *The Urban Revolution* (Minneapolis: University of Minnesota Press, 2003); and Andy Merrifield, *Dialectical Urbanism: Social Struggles in the Capitalist City* (New York: Monthly Review Press, 2002).
19. Peter J. Marcotullio and William Solecki, "What is a City? An Essential Definition for Sustainability," in *Urbanization and Sustainability: Linking Urban Ecology, Environmental Justice and Global Environmental Change* (Springer, 2013), 11–25.

20 Neil Brenner and Christian Schmid, "Planetary Urbanization," in *Urban Constellations*, ed. Matthew Gandy (Berlin: jovis, 2012), 10–13.
21 Ibid., 14.
22 Saskia Sassen, *The Global City: New York, London, Tokyo* (Princeton, NJ: Princeton University Press, 1991).
23 Brenner and Schmid, "Planetary Urbanization."
24 See, for example, Iris Marion Young, *Justice and the Politics of Difference* (Princeton, NJ: Princeton University Press, 1990).
25 Harvey, *Rebel Cities,* 67.
26 Ananya Roy, "The 21st-Century Metropolis: New Geographies of Theory," *Regional Studies*, 43, no. 6 (2009); 820.
27 Jennifer Robinson, *Ordinary Cities: Between Modernity and Development* (London: Routledge, 2006)
28 Harvey, *Rebel Cities*, 70.
29 Ibid., 83.
30 Ibid., 81.
31 John Holloway, *Crack Capitalism* (London: Pluto Press, 2010); see also contribution by Kratzwald, this volume.
32 Michael Hardt and Antonio Negri, *Commonwealth* (Cambridge, MA: Harvard University Press, 2009), 154–156.
33 Such a strategy is exemplified in Richard Florida's work on the "creative class." Richard L Florida, *Cities and the Creative Class* (New York: Routledge, 2005).
34 Margit Mayer, "The Onward Sweep of Social Capital: Causes and Consequences for Understanding Cities, Communities and Urban Movements," *International Journal of Urban and Regional Research* 27, no. 1 (March 1, 2003): 110–132.

Perspectives

Brigitte Kratzwald

Urban Commons – Dissident Practices in Emancipatory Spaces

1 Why urban commons?

How much sense does it make to talk specifically about "urban commons?" And why has this discussion been booming in the last few years? A specific focus on urban commons is sensible for several reasons. First, demographic development shows us that in just a few decades the majority of the world's population will live in cities, which will further intensify disputes about increasingly scarce spatial resources. Second, special forms of enclosure are emerging through the increasing exploitation of cities. The neoliberal restructuring of society is having a strong effect on cities and is most visible there; "societal utopias and alternatives are therefore always also alternatives for the organization of cities."[1] And finally, the theoretical discussion of urban commons is a relatively new phenomenon and must first create its own foundation.

Cities were centers of trade, and later centers of industry. They were and are the places where political and economic power is concentrated. Commoning practices have always been present in cities; however, in contrast to agricultural land, no handed-down rights or legal provisions exist with regard to urban commoning. In the cities, the rights of the merchants and craftsmen applied; the poor could expect at best alms, not rights. In the time of early capitalism, "poor laws" served to criminalize and repress the urban poor,[2] while their rural counterparts were able to a limited extent to attain a self-determined and dignified existence through the right to the commons, even when this theoretically existent claim was constantly undermined by landlords and rulers.

As the farmers moved to the cities in search of work following the enclosure of their commons by the nobility or the bourgeois government at the dawn of the industrial period, they took the practices of commoning with them. These however took new forms, adapted to the requirements of industrial capitalism. The first solidary insurance systems, as well as cooperatives for consumption, living, and housing estates, emerged through the self-organization of the industrial proletariat, and strengthened the political position of the workers' movement so that better working conditions and more political participation could be achieved.[3] In Fordism, Roosevelt's New Deal, and later the European welfare states, the state assumed the task of guaranteeing social and economic security, and made housing and infrastructure available. In this case, we can talk about a "state-ification" of the commons. Manuel Castells[4] clearly had this type of Fordist city in mind when he described cities as spaces of "collective consumption," where the public sector provides all the necessities. State and market should ensure welfare and security for all, and a liberal democracy was to guarantee equal rights for all; the combination of the two allowed the hope of a shining future. Commons seemed completely antiquated and appeared to no longer correspond to the requirements of modernity. In this way the idea of the commons disappeared from cities.

However, even then the rising quality of life was not available for everyone. Already in 1968, Henri Lefebvre expounded on the "Right to the City," the right to the participation in urban life, including for marginalized groups.[5] In the last few decades, the exclusions have become even more frequent and more intense. Urban space has been commodified and oriented towards exploitation more drastically under the auspices of neoliberal urban policies,[6] leading to a revitalization of the demands of the "Right to the City." Then as now, people stream into the cities looking for work, housing, and space to live. Capital, by contrast, expects profitable investment possibilities from cities. Urban administrations are faced with the challenge of serving both requirements; they are however pressured to serve the needs of capital in these times of systematically enforced budget shortfalls. This leads to a situation in which cities are more and more subjected to the logic of exploitation without consideration of the quality of life of the majority of their residents. Ever fewer can take part in Castells' collective consumption. The exploitation of the cities leads to new enclosures, and therefore to the situation that more people are excluded from access to space and resources due to a lack of financial capital, a condition which greatly limits their agency. Lack of future prospects and feelings of powerlessness and frustration, above all (but not only) among youths, are the result. People have the feeling that they have lost control over their lives. They no longer feel represented by politics or needed by the economy. They feel reduced to their role as consumer, at a time when their money gets them less and less.

It is at this point that the weaknesses of the welfare state system become completely visible: social security is coupled with wage labor, and therefore with economic growth. This type of security is thus only available to those who submit themselves to the logic of the system. In particular during times of economic crisis, when social security is most needed, it is not available. The citizens have delegated public issues to the state and thereby given up control over these issues. They have reduced their own role in the process to voting every few years for a party which they view as representing their interests. The government, however, has proved itself to be a bad trustee and manager of public property, and has tried to fill empty state coffers through their sale. These experiences of dispossession and exclusion have led to the revitalization of the discourse about and fight for the urban commons.

In light of neoliberal budget cuts, other forms of communal design of public space and goods have become interesting for urban administration as well. The term "commons" serves in this sense as a glittering, undefined and undefinable, and recurrently ambivalent projection screen for very different ideas and interests. Organizing cities as commons, urban planning as a process of commoning, and reflections about commons-friendly cities form the significant aspects of the discussion. While urban administrations and business see the self-organization of citizens in the first place as an economic relief and hope for a stabilization of the existing system of representative politics and the free market, marginalized and politically motivated groups seek a reappropriation of cities and public space for their residents. From the position of a radical criticism of the system, they attempt to develop alternatives to capitalism. Conflicts are inevitable, a characteristic which connects the new, urban commons with their historical counterpart.

2 Commons in historical England

In order to understand the potential and the ambivalence of the commons concept in today's political situation, it makes sense to first seek an understanding of its meaning and function in the pre-capitalist period. Although the concept can't be transferred one-to-one, it's still possible to identify principles and patterns that can be filled with content in today's world.

While the practice of commoning is as old as humanity itself, the moment for the beginning of historical commons research can be set at 1215.[7] In this year, King John II signed the Magna Carta in England. This legal act ended 150 years of constant conflict between the Norman conquerors and the British nobility and clergy. With his signature, King John, the descendant of the conqueror, was forced to recognize the existing "common law" from the time of the Norman Conquest, instead of introducing the Roman right from the continent in England. It's well known that the Magna Carta is the first example of the codification of political fundamental rights for all people, independent of status. In return, John II was recognized as king of England.

At the core, the Magna Carta is a contract between the nobility, the clergy, and the king, however the document also contained rules that affected the lives of "normal" people, that is: people who did not own land. That was the vast majority during the feudal period. So that the stipulation that all people are equal in the eyes of the law could be truly lived, the right to take what they needed from the commons was granted to them. The "common land" was legally the property of the aristocratic landowner, however they were only permitted to restrict access to certain aspects (in particular the hunt), while other aspects were required to remain accessible to the farmers for precisely regulated use types. These rules developed over decades relative to peoples' needs and the characteristics of the respective resources that they were permitted to use, for example pastures, fields, wood for fires or building, fish stocks, or forest fruits. The important realization here is: the right to the commons is something that the king must respect and not something that he can grant. It is not a favor; it is a right that is granted to every person at birth.[8]

Because the nobility's ability to dispose over their land was restricted, the commons were always contested. It was therefore for good reason that the right to defend the commons was set out in the Magna Carta, namely in order to prevent their enclosure and appropriation by the nobility and the clergy. Once a year during a public festival, the common land was paced off and all fences and walls that had been erected in the past year were permitted to be torn down. What would this process mean in today's city? What types of fences and walls have been put up in the last few years? Where would the perambulations lead us?

In London, this custom was revived a few years ago, as a basketball stadium for the Olympics was built on a piece of common land.[9] According to the law, in this case a comparable piece of land must be made into common land. This law was however simply overruled. Thus, the "New Lammas Land Defence Committee"[10] began to conduct perambulations and other events in order to increase the public's awareness of the existence of the commons and their importance.

3 Commons do not simply exist – they are created

An important lesson from history is that commons must be used and defended, otherwise they disappear. And they must constantly be reproduced; "common goods don't simply exist, they are created," writes Silke Helfrich.[11] Peter Linebaugh coined the phrase "there is no commons without commoning," as the practice of the creation, preservation, and use of commons is called. We often become conscious of the existence of commons only when they are threatened or have already disappeared. Commons are not things, per se. They are composed of three elements: a resource, i.e. the "common good," a group of people that use, tend, preserve, and reproduce this resource, and the rules that these people make to achieve these ends.

Commons and commoning are therefore both a set of social relationships and practices and the spaces in which they are negotiated. Historically, commons were not just important for the provision of basic supplies, they were also the place where people met, where they could negotiate their interests and reach agreements, but also where they could organize themselves when the landowners exercised their power excessively and restricted the rights of the commoners too much. The commons was the place from which resistance and rebellion against the landowners began.

The end of the story is well-known: the fight for the commons led to multiple civil wars,[12] and, at the end, to the first great wave of enclosures as a result of theestablishment of capitalism. The enclosure of the commons is however nowhere near complete; it is an ongoing process, as people continuously create new commons. Even though the knowledge of the commons disappeared from the public and scientific mainstream for a long time (at least in industrial countries), the practice could not be dispelled from the daily life of a large number of people. The fight for the commons is an intrinsic component of all systems of dominance, even capitalism.

Commons therefore were supposed to fulfill several functions in the feudal period: they ensured that everyone could satisfy their basic needs and wants, they prevented the overuse of resources, they made it possible for even the poorest to preserve their dignity and political rights, and they were a space of relative autonomy. Today we would say that they had economic and ecological goals, and that it was about human rights and democracy – even if that wasn't often implemented in that way in reality. Then as now, all these aspects are at stake, also in cities, which is why the term "urban commons" is well-suited to unite this plethora of contradictions and oppositions.

As both physical space and social practice "beyond state and market,"[13] commons can also be directly connected to discourses about "the right to the city as a collective re-appropriation of urban space, that is intended to lead to a transformed, renewed urban life oriented towards the use value of the city, and where 'exchange is not mediated by the exchange value, trade or profit'." These discourses are based "simultaneously on the city as a physical form and on the social relationships and practices that are interrelated with it."[14] Commons were a form of public space long before the term was used during the bourgeois revolutions. It is therefore not a contradiction to employ the concept of the commons in the defense of urban public spaces, and thereby to shift the term "public" in an emancipatory direction.

4 Commons and "public"[15]

In the last century, an understanding of "public" has become established which centers around the state. "Public" is often set equal with "national" or "governmental," owned by the state or government, or something that is provided by the state or a governmental institution such as a municipal or state government. The state is placed in an antagonistic position respective to the market economy, namely as an institution that compensates for or softens the negative effects of the market, and organizes various forms of social, economic, or legal security. This worked for a limited time in the European welfare states after World War II. Thus for a long time, the state was the recipient of social movements' demands. The state was supposed to enforce their rights, ensure social equilibrium, and manage and curate public property.

The state emerged, however, parallel to the capitalist market economy, and was responsible from the outset for ensuring the political framework for the market's functioning and growth. For this reason, the protection and promotion of private property is at the top of its agenda. From the very beginning, the state has existed in conflict with the idea of the commons. The state is responsible for the mitigation of social conflicts, either through social services or repression, usually a combination of the two. The state creates the political, social, and legal conditions for the functioning of the capitalist market. It ensures that people internalize the logic and the demands of the market system in their socialization to such an extent that it is even difficult to imagine, let alone implement, alternatives that do not follow the logic of the market. States have never been protectors of the commons. From the beginning governments belonged to the most important actors in enclosures, which themselves were a prerequisite for the success of capitalism. "Parliamentary enclosures" existed in early industrial England the same as today, when for example the EU passes laws that prohibit the passing on of seeds among farmers under threat of prosecution, or legally limits internet access.

In the meantime, many people have lost faith that the state wants to or is legitimized to act in their name, and to guarantee their rights. They turn against market and state. Some want to take matters into their own hands. They invoke the commons in this endeavor for very different things: water or energy supply, housing, health care, but also urban planning and the use of public space. But does it make sense to label all of these various things as commons? And is it enough to replace the term "public" with the term "commons?" What is the difference between the two, and what does it mean to regard "public" things, such as public services or public spaces, from the perspective of the commons?

Historically it was never the case that career politicians discharged public tasks and the citizens were solely concerned with their private responsibilities. For Aristotle, the human was per se a political animal, a social creature which created the community together with others. The Greek polis was created and existed because all free adult citizens participated in the governing and running of the state. Both took place in the public gathering of all citizens who constituted the state. Even the fact that women and slaves were excluded from this process at that point in history does not discredit the concept itself; it can still be employed today for the constitution of the "public." The same goes for cities or municipalities; "the Latin term municipium indicated a 'free town, a city whose citizens have the privileges of

Roman citizens but are governed by their own laws'." *Municipium* comes from *munus* "service performed for the community, duty, work," meaning "obligations," and *communis,* "bound together."[16] This describes pretty much exactly what the commons was for the farmers in England.

Perceiving state and "public" from the perspective of the commons means reclaiming the state and the public sphere. And this is exactly what people are doing today in many places. They are standing up, taking over responsibility and saying "this belongs to us – we want to decide what happens here." They demand that cities should be governed by their citizens. The city administrations can organize infrastructure and be in charge of management, but only in accord with the decisions of the citizens and under their control. One could say that through this process these infrastructures and goods truly become public goods, services, and spaces for the first time. The term "public" here therefore takes on an emancipatory twist.

One example of this change in perspective is the protest movement against the train station project "Stuttgart 21." The train station, one of the landmarks of Stuttgart, was slated to be torn down, and many trees in the "Schlosspark" (palace grounds) needed to be chopped down to make space for the new railway line. These trees were always "public property" in the sense that they belonged to the city. However, only when they were threatened, only when the workers came with chainsaws, did people suddenly realize: "These are our trees. If we don't care for them, if we don't fight for them, then no one will." That was the moment when the trees became a commons – unfortunately too late.

5 Principles for long-lasting commons institutions

Those who work with the concept of the commons and the question how they function can't avoid the commons researcher Elinor Ostrom and her team at Indiana University in Bloomington.[17] She asked two interesting questions: why do people cooperate and make arrangements that contradict the typical homo oeconomicus image of humanity? And how do they do it, which conditions are required for it to function?

The answer to the first question is relatively simple: people make commons, they communicate and cooperate, because then everyone can satisfy their needs better. When the right arrangements have been found, there is no contradiction between individual interests, because everyone profits. That is one of the essential principles, and why commons function and still don't require "better" people.

Regarding the "how," Elinor Ostrom established that there isn't one model for all, no blueprint by which commons function. Every commons functions differently. However, there are certain conditions whose presence significantly increases the chances that commons can exist long-term. Ostrom called them the "design principles for long-lasting commons." These eight principles, presented in the editors' introduction to this volume, are formulated from the perspective of an external observer, in order to ascertain similarities on a higher level of abstraction. In the following section, I will try to consider these principles from the perspective of someone who is involved, in order to make them usable for the practice of commoning.

5.1 The necessity of boundaries

Ostrom examined natural, physical commons, which are available in limited amounts and for which it is reasonable that both the resource and the user group should be clearly defined. Is that, however, applicable to knowledge, digital commons or urban commons?

From the perspective of the commoners, boundaries mean first and foremost knowing what the resource is that they use together with others and who "the others" are. With respect to knowledge, culture, or digital resources, it can be very useful to realize what exactly "the commons" is. In this way, a website with a creative commons license and its contents can be used freely, albeit under specific conditions. There could, however, be photos on the page that are copyrighted. It is therefore important to know where the boundaries are: how are they labeled, how can we ensure that they will be enforced? With regard to the user groups, there are also different approaches. Some websites such as Wikipedia can truly be used by everyone, both passively and actively. Anyone can write an article on Wikipedia. Other platforms, such as OpenStreetMap, require that users create an account with an email address in order to be able to make entries. The passive user group here is the whole of humanity (or at least those who are computer- and internet-savvy); the active user group is clearly defined, even if very large. That is significant, since boundaries play quite an important role, even in non-rivalrous resources.

How does this transfer to cities? What are the commonly used resources and who are the people that use them? Careful consideration shows that this is both not easy to establish and can change quickly. Here the weaknesses of Ostrom's research become visible. She investigated institutions which were relatively closed, and examined them during or after their establishment. What preceded the establishment, the conflicts and power relations that led to their formation, is not present. All of the struggles for commons in the course of the enforcement of capitalism, as described in detail by Linebaugh[18] or Polanyi,[19] do not play a role in institutional research. This is why these theories fall short, even if they are very helpful in some situations. Cities are in the midst of a rapid process of change, where the boundaries between private and public can shift daily. That is one of the causes and simultaneously the requirement for struggles for the urban commons. Boundaries are not fixed – they are fought over. They are changeable and are not thought of as lines, but rather spaces in which creative potential can develop. Stavros Stavrides uses the term "thresholds" to describe this phenomenon, and states that boundaries are there to be crossed. The shifting of borders as a central element of the struggles for commons – from both sides, through enclosures and reclaiming or the creation of new commons – is constitutive for commons from the perspective of social movements, and above all for urban commons; "the creation of an enclosure contains [...] the possibility at any moment of stepping out of this limitation into freedom."[20]

5.2 Congruence

Congruence comprises two aspects for Ostrom:

First: the relationship between that which a person brings into a commons and that which they take out of it must be felt as fair by everyone involved. This sounds easy, but is very difficult to achieve in reality, and often requires long negotiations, experiments, errors, failure, and new beginnings. Above all, this approach directly contradicts market logic, which prescribes that everything has an objective value which is expressed as its price; this price is the same for everyone and realized in the immediate trade with something of equivalent value. Exchange does exist within the commons, but it's neither exchange with something of equivalent value at fixed prices, nor is it between two people. The sum of all harvested resources must be sufficient to sustain the commons. The sum of all extracted resources should not be higher than what the commons yields (for limited resources), but should also, however, not be so low that the interest in the commons dwindles. In this case we're not talking about the efficiency principle, i.e. the concept of the highest yield for the lowest possible input. In this case, it's much more about each person contributing what they can and taking what they need, and therefore feeling fairly treated. This can hardly ever be the same for all involved. And it is exactly this fundamentally different logic that makes it difficult for people socialized in capitalism to imagine a functioning commons.

Secondly: in addition to the congruence between those involved, Ostrom also determined congruence between the extraction modality and the resource's characteristics, i.e. its cultural, climatological, and biological conditions. That is the reason why there are no two commons that function identically, simply because they are located in different locations and different people use them who must first develop their own form for dealing with this special resource. This congruence principle results in the fact that Ostrom's principles can be used not only for rivalrous, limited resources; non-limited, non-rivalrous resources can have use rules which are adjusted to their characteristics and still conform to Ostrom's principles.

5.3 Rules

This brings us to a further principle from Ostrom: commons have rules – they are not a no-man's-land where everyone can just do what they please. These rules are, however, neither uniform nor objective. They are not given from a higher authority, but rather developed and constantly changed by the people who use a resource correspondent to the above-mentioned congruence principles. The compliance with these rules is also enforced by the commoners themselves; sanctions can also be imposed when rules are broken.

These principles can play an important role for urban commons, as they highlight the necessity of self-determination for the proper functioning of civil society initiatives. This is, however, also a difficult challenge for urban governments, above all when – as is usually the case – it doesn't work from the beginning, or doesn't function the way that the urban government would like. Commoners are "unruly people," said Norbert Schindler,[21] who researched the enclosure of the agricultural commons in Austria. Peter Linebaugh says it similarly: "reciprocity, sense of self, willingness to argue, long memory, collective celebration, and mutual aid are traits of the commoner."[22]

5.4 Dealing with conflicts and recognition from external authorities

The last two principles are significant in the context of urban commons. On the one hand, easily accessible conflict resolution mechanisms are needed. From the perspective of involved parties, that means first and foremost finding an adequate way of dealing with conflicts within the group. Just as frequent, and often more difficult to resolve, are conflicts between the people who are trying to create a commons and their environment, which is oriented towards privatization and commodification. This could be an important task for municipalities who take citizen participation seriously. And that segues seamlessly to Ostrom's last principle about the recognition from outside by the state; for urban commons, this would be the municipal government or administration. Even extremely radical, anarchistic initiatives can survive over longer periods of time only if they are at least tolerated by the urban government.

From an institutional-theory perspective, it's rather simple: the principles formulated by Ostrom make it possible to create institutions that foster cooperation, participation, and taking responsibility, and guarantee access to the means for livelihood. This perspective is concerned with questions like:
– Who has access to this resource?
– Is no one excluded from the use of essential resources?
– Who makes decisions about which resources are necessary for a good life?
– Does everyone consider the relationship between what they receive and what they contribute to be fair? What happens when that's not the case? Are there appropriate solutions for these types of conflicts?
– Is the commons protected enough against privatization, destruction, and exploitation?

These and similar goals can be achieved through various legal forms and property regimes; usually this involves a combination of different legal forms and institutions.

"Beyond state and market" does not mean that no governmental institutions or urban administrations can or may take part. It means much more that the role of the public institutions changes when they take part in commons arrangements. Urban administrations or public institutions can manage various things as a trustee respective to the decisions that the citizens have reached. They do not, however, have the right to sell these things. If conflicts arise, governments and administrations can assume mediation tasks, or provide space or financial assistance. Local businesses can also be part of these types of arrangements, as long as they obey all of the agreed-upon rules.

This can function when politics and administration have a real interest in people organizing their world themselves. These are however exceptions, as this simultaneously means a loss of power and influence for politics, and that the situation can always develop differently than planned. It's much more common to have pseudo-participation processes, where citizens are instrumentalized to dress up or legitimize decisions already reached by politicians, or where the results of neoliberal faults are outsourced to the citizens.[23]

Even when they exhibit a high degree of self-organization, this form of commons is particularly easy to integrate into the system, and the image of the active citizen who takes responsibility for the community is very compatible with the liberal understanding of the state. When a neglected district is brought back to life through self-organization, it becomes attractive for investors and becomes threatened by enclosures again.[24] If the participants try to call the system into question, their livelihoods are threatened under various pretenses, or they are criminalized.

The current power structures are stacked against the preservation and creation of commons. Commons are, even today, threatened by enclosure, destruction, criminalization, or appropriation within capitalist power structures. Now as in the past, they are fiercely contested; "capitalist urbanization perpetually tends to destroy the city as a social, political and livable commons."[25] For the analysis of the struggle for commons, Ostrom's research doesn't offer a sufficient basis. Instead, it is necessary to address hegemonic processes and power structures.

6 Commons and capital

The ambivalence of the commons in capitalism stems from one of capitalism's biggest contradictions: capital cannot reproduce itself. In order to survive, it needs resources from outside. This is one reason why, in opposition to other opinions, capitalism can never be a totality; several modes of production exist simultaneously in every society. The sources from which capital takes what it needs so that the production of added value can function are unpaid work (usually from women), natural resources, and commons.[26] Capital is very successful in making commons and other resources outside of itself useful for its own ends.

On the other hand, as already mentioned, the production, use, and tending of commons creates a certain amount of independence from the dominant system for people. We cannot escape this ambivalence. There are not good and bad commons, correct and incorrect commons. Commons permit the participants more self-determination precisely because they are useful within the capitalist system. The decision can therefore only be made by the participants in each individual case: does the commons in which they take part increase their autonomy? Can they transfer resources from the system into the commons? Or is it the other way around, and their commons supplies capital with cheap or free resources? Usually both are the case, and then the decision is about which aspect dominates and who has the larger benefit. There is no objective answer to this question.

We can suitably deal with this ambivalence only when we do not view commons as a static concept, but rather "as an unstable and malleable social relation between a particular self-defined social group and those aspects of its actually existing or yet-to-be-created social and/or physical environment deemed crucial to its life and livelihood."[27] Especially temporary commons such as protest camps, squatted houses or spaces created by the Occupy movement can play an important role here, in contrast to the frequently voiced critique that they don't bring about lasting change or, like the anti-globalization movement, have failed.

These temporarily occurring forms of self-organization are important spaces for learning and experiencing, in which we can overcome the barriers that we have acquired through the socialization in a liberal legal system organized around private property, wage labor, competition, and representative democracy, and that prevent us from thinking about alternatives. Getting involved in conflicts that go above and beyond the bourgeois consensus and the mechanisms of representative politics and make the participants into immediate political individuals changes people, even when the struggles are chalked up as failures.[28] In these processes, the involved experience "that they are capable of meaningful and self-conscious productions."[29]

This type of handling is most successful in spaces that lie outside of the sphere of influence of the market and politics, or lack importance for them, for example empty houses, abandoned lots, or closed factories.[30] While such spaces sometimes exist in the margins of the global megacities, and make it possible for people to develop their own economic forms,[31] they have to be created constantly in the cities of the Global North, which are often planned down to the last detail.

John Holloway said that capital appropriates the alternatives that people develop over and over again (this doesn't just apply to commons); the only way to stop it is to stay in motion. He describes it as a dance, as something joyful and happy. Artists and urban commons activists do just that. They keep appearing in new places with constantly new ideas, in order to call the status quo into question, to define public space and the possibilities for its use in new ways, and to make it possible for people to design their lives and environments themselves. Commons can therefore be understood as dissident practices in emancipatory spaces, which lead to the creation of new modes of production and social relationships. They are spaces of resistant creativity, in which alternatives to capitalism can be physically experienced and lived.

Notes

1. Andrej Holm and Dirk Gebhardt, eds., *Initiativen für ein Recht auf Stadt. Theorie und Praxis städtischer Aneignung* (Hamburg: VSA Verlag, 2011), 9 [translation: Mary Dellenbaugh].
2. Giovanna Procacci, "Social Economy and the Government of Poverty," in *The Foucault Effect. Studies in Governmentality,* eds. Graham Burchell, Colin Gordon, and Peter Miller, 151–167 (Chicago: University of Chicago Press, 1991).
3. Andreas Exner and Brigitte Kratzwald, *Solidarische Ökonomie und Commons* (Vienna: Mandelbaum Verlag, 2012), 54.
4. Manuel Castells, "Collective Consumption and Urban Contradictions in Advanced Capitalism," in *The Castells Reader on Cities and Social Theory,* ed. Ida Susser, 107–129 (Oxford: Blackwell, 2001).
5. Henri Lefebvre, *Le droit à la ville* (Paris: Anthropos, 2009).
6. Holm and Gebhardt, *Initiativen für ein Recht auf Stadt,* 9.
7. Peter Linebaugh, *The Magna Carta Manifesto. Liberties and Commons for All* (Berkeley/Los Angeles/London: University of California Press, 2008).

8   Ugo Mattei, "First Thoughts for a Phenomenology of the Commons," in *The Wealth of the Commons. A World Beyond Market & State,* eds., David Bollier and Silke Helfrich (Amherst, MA: Levellers Press, 2012); http://wealthofthecommons.org/contents (accessed January 26, 2015).
9   http://www.metamute.org/editorial/articles/lammas-land-and-olympic-dreams (accessed January 26, 2015).
10   http://www.lammaslands.org.uk/ (accessed January 26, 2015).
11   Silke Helfrich, "Common Goods Don't Simply Exist – They Are Created," in *The Wealth of the Commons. A World Beyond Market & State,* eds. David Bollier and Silke Helfrich.
12   The English Civil War of the seventeenth century which finished the monarchy and established democracy dealt also with questions of enclosures. This issue was especially highlighted by the movements of the Diggers and the Levellers, but also the German "Bauernkriege" of the sixteenth century, all of which concerned land-use rights and enclosures.
13   Elinor Ostrom, *Governing the Commons: The Evolution of Institutions for Collective Action* (New York: Cambridge University Press, 1990).
14   Holm and Gebhardt, *Initiativen für ein Recht auf Stadt,* 8 [translations: Mary Dellenbaugh].
15   Brigitte Kratzwald, "Rethinking the Social Welfare State in Light of the Commons," in *The Wealth of the Commons,* eds. David Bollier and Silke Helfrich.
16   Online Etymology Dictionary "municipal (adj.)". http://www.etymonline.com/index.php?term=municipal (accessed January 26, 2015).
17   Ostrom, *Governing the Commons.*
18   Linebaugh, *The Magna Carta Manifesto.*
19   Karl Polanyi, *The Great Transformation: The Political and Economic Origins of our Time* (Boston: Beacon Press 2001).
20   Stavros Stavrides, *Towards the City of Thresholds* (professional dreamers. 2010), 14. http://www.professionaldreamers.net/_prowp/wp-content/uploads/978-88-904295-3-8.pdf (accessed January 26, 2015).
21   Norbert Schindler, *Widerspenstige Leute. Studien zur Volkskultur in der frühen Neuzeit* (Frankfurt am Main: Fischer Verlag, 1992).
22   Linebaugh, *The Magna Carta Manifesto,* 103.
23   Massimo De Angelis, "Crises, Capitalism and Cooperation: Does Capital Need a Commons Fix?" in *The Wealth of the Commons,* eds. David Bollier and Silke Helfrich.
24   David Harvey, *Rebel Cities. From the Right to the City to the Urban Revolution* (London: Verso, 2012), 74.
25   Ibid., 80.
26   De Angelis, "Crises, Capitalism and Cooperation."
27   Harvey, *Rebel Cities,* 73.
28   AK Thompson, *Black Bloc White Riot. Anti-Globalization and the Genealogy of Dissent* (Edinburgh/Oakland/Baltimore: AK Press, 2010), 19.
29   Ibid., 24.
30   Friederike Habermann, *Der homo oeconomicus und das Andere. Hegemonie, Identität und Emanzipation* (Baden-Baden: Nomos, 2008), 93.
31   As shown for several cities in Latin America by Raul Zibechi, *Territorien des Widerstands. Eine politische Kartografie der urbanen Peripherien Lateinamerikas* (Berlin: Assoziation A, 2011).

Markus Kip

Moving Beyond the City: Conceptualizing Urban Commons from a Critical Urban Studies Perspective

A hype goes to town

The idea of commons has been attracting greater interest in academic and activist circles over the past decade; recently, the idea of the "urban commons" has become a focal point. For historian Peter Linebaugh, urbanization implies an increasing enclosure of "rural" commons such as pastures, prairies, woodlands, or seashores, leading to a point where "the commoners of the world can no longer retire to the forest or run to the hills."[1] While struggles for rural commons may thus have decreased in significance,[2] the struggle for the urban commons is alive and well. The recent cycle of urban contestations spanning the "Arab Spring," anti-austerity actions in Southern Europe, the battle for Taksim Square, and the Occupy movement clearly contributed to the interest in the relationship between city and commons.[3] Grasping hope at the sight of these struggles, Linebaugh exclaims: "unprecedented as the task may historically be, the city itself must be commonized."[4]

Other authors emphasize that the city is already a commons and call for the city to be reclaimed as such. According to Lefebvre, "[t]he city is itself 'oeuvre,' a feature which contrasts with the irreversible tendency towards money and commerce, towards exchange and products. Indeed, the oeuvre is use value and the product is exchange values."[5] His description as an *oeuvre* points to the city's character as a creative work-in-progress, a work of art made up of the everyday routines of all who are part of the city. David Harvey elaborates on this idea:

> The human qualities of the city emerge from our practices in the diverse spaces of the city [...]. Through their daily activities and struggles, individuals and social groups create the social world of the city and, in doing so, create something common as a framework within which we all can dwell.[6]

Hardt and Negri's declaration of "the metropolis as a factory for the production of the common"[7] invokes the same idea of the city as a collective oeuvre:

> The city, of course, is not just a built environment consisting of buildings and streets and subways and parks and waste systems and communications cables but also a living dynamic of cultural practices, intellectual circuits, affective networks, and social institutions. These elements of the common contained in the city are not only the prerequisite for biopolitical production but also its result; the city is the source of the common and the receptacle into which it flows.[8]

These accounts present the city as a key location in the struggle for the commons, if not the Promised Land for commons-based politics. And so, it is not surprising that the hype around the commons thus finally came to town. In recent years the notion of urban commons[9] has become a phenomenon, with publications in various disciplines including law,[10] history,[11] geography,[12] sociology,[13] anthropology,[14] economics,[15] political science,[16] urban planning,[17] architecture,[18] and even the performing arts.[19] It is important to note though that these publications largely resist disciplinary categorizations and my attributions rely chiefly on the institutional affiliations of authors. More significant is the fact that the discussion has established a truly transdisciplinary field.[20] The literature on urban commons has multiplied rapidly, in particular over the past three years. I was able to dig up forty-three publications with an explicit take on urban commons in languages that I comprehend; forty of these were in English. Altogether thirty-seven contributions were published since 2011 (thirty-two in English), thus leaving only six publications before 2011. Compared with traditional commons in rural settings discussed by Hardin and Ostrom, this literature discusses urban commons such as public space, sidewalks, access to parks and recreation areas, infrastructure like public transport, the provision of roads, the supply of energy or water, an environment that is free of waste, air pollution, or noise, or even public culture as a new kind of commons. The vast majority of these contributions, however, take notions of "urban" and "city" for granted. "Urban commons" thus mostly refer to a commons that exists in a physical space located in the territory of a city.

The tricky issue is: what exactly makes these commons urban? Do urban commons have anything in common other than being located within the perimeters of the city? If not, "urban commons" would amount to nothing more than a fashionable label – a hype – without, however, adding anything conceptual to the idea of the commons. If yes – urban commons are to be conceptualized as a specific kind of commons – then in what ways does urban space condition the appropriation and governance of these commons? While the literature provides several implicit hints towards answering this question, I will draw here on literature from the field of critical urban studies to present an explicitly urban perspective on the commons. I want to stress the "urban challenges" to predominant conceptualizations of the commons as outlined in the introduction to this volume. In particular, I would like to make two points: first, urban commons require us to take the negotiation of boundaries and solidarities seriously. Mobility and social differentiation in an urbanizing world constantly challenge commoners to re-establish the common ground of their collective praxis as well as their relationship to their environment. Secondly, just as urbanization keeps expanding and capital latches onto new externalities, urban commons can only survive if they keep expanding as well.

My argument proceeds in four steps. First, I will draw on Parker and Johansson's discussion of the challenges of the urban commons as a useful starting point. Studying the existing work on "urban commons," they distill the specifically urban challenges of commons. In the second part, I will reconstruct the discussion around the urban within critical urban studies. Two main conceptualizations of the urban will be presented, both of which draw on the work of Henri Lefebvre. In the third part, I will offer a synthesis of these two strands and conceptualize the urban as a dialectical process of ontological openness and strategic enclosure. The fourth part will then apply these ideas to define the challenges that define what makes urban commons *urban*.

So far, so (common) good? Conceptualizing urban commons

Ida Susser and Stéphane Tonnelat's[21] article can be taken as an example for a conceptualization of urban commons in which the "urban" simply designates a location in the (territorially defined) city. The "three urban commons" they are discussing – labor and public services, public space, and art – are so broadly interpreted that it is hard to consider them specific for cities. Susser and Tonnelat, however, define the urban characteristic of the commons not in terms of a specific quality but quantity. Simply put, certain commons are urban because they "are numerous in the cities."[22] On this basis the authors derive an ideal-type quality of urban life and specify Lefebvre's right to the city by differentiating it into three rights: "the right to urban everyday life, the right to simultaneity and encounters, and the right to creative activity."[23] Without a clear conception of the city or the urban, however, this account raises the question how urban commons compare with "non-urban" commons, and whether there is any difference.

By contrast, the contributions of Peter Parker and Magnus Johansson seek to carve out a specifically urban quality of commons.[24] In their extensive review of available literature on commons in city settings, the authors find three features that distinguish urban commons from the "traditional commons," such as fisheries, watersheds, agricultural land, and woodlands, that Elinor Ostrom and her colleagues and followers have focused on. The first distinctive feature is urban commons' *large scale* and the resulting *lack of salience* for individuals. In contrast to Ostrom's case studies involving a few hundred persons, commons in the city can involve hundreds of thousands, if not more. While in the former case commoners are acutely aware of the commons resource and their role in maintaining it (irrigation, shared pasture, etc.), in the latter, the urban residents are often not even aware of an entity such as the ecosystem, water and electric supply, road usage and qualities such as silence being a "common." In the face of a large number of users, payoffs for individuals who invest in commons' upkeep are small. Modeling the problem this way invites comparison with Garrett Hardin's[25] tragedy of the commons. While in some cases norms (around recycling, for example) may prevent such a tragedy, Parker and Johansson suggest that, in many other cases, large-scale regulation is likely to require greater formalization of rules and decision-making.

A second feature of urban commons, according to Parker and Johansson, is the *contested character of the urban commons*. Whereas the utility of the commons for traditional commons is rather obvious and usually shared by everyone in the group (the pasture is for feeding the cattle, the irrigation system for watering the fields etc.), this cannot be assumed for commons in an urban context. Several kinds of social differentiation and division, such as class, gender, ethnicity, race, or occupation, create different relationships to common resources, leading to diverse groups appreciating the various aspects of these resources differently. A community garden, for example, might be for some a location for the production of food and for others a space of community and communication. It can be a place to sleep at night for homeless persons or an asset for revalorizing real estate in the neighborhood for urban developers. The mobility and different temporal outlooks of urban residents also require us to take the different stakes in and commitments to commons seriously. Establishing a community garden means something quite different for long-term residents in comparison with those who are only temporary residents.

For urban commons to cope with this diversity, Parker and Johansson consider *cross-sectoral collaboration* as a third feature. Urban infrastructure is discussed as a resource with various stakeholders, including citizens, private companies, and public authorities. Since such provision requires a long-term perspective and significant investment volumes, a difficult coordination of investments, contributions, regulatory capacities, and resulting privileges may be necessary. Parker and Johansson thus see the need for cross-sector collaboration between citizens, non-profits, governmental authorities, and others in order to provide and govern such commons. It is therefore assumed that the role of the state as a facilitator will be enhanced, with its primary role being as the regulating and monitoring authority in urban commoning.[26]

The problem with Parker and Johansson's account, I contend, is their underlying idea of the city and the urban as defined by a territorially bounded entity. Urban commons are specified by the criteria that "the resource in question should be available primarily on a citywide or smaller scale." This idea, unfortunately, stops short of conceiving urban commons as phenomena with significance beyond the city.

The understanding of the urban as a quality of a territorially defined city persists tenaciously in everyday thinking and much of scholarly writing,[27] including the vast majority of pieces on urban commons referred to above. Clearly a reason for this is that such notions help us to make sense of the widely experienced difference between spaces within the city and those outside of it, i.e. in the countryside or in the suburbs. As an analytical category, however, this conception has severe limitations. Already in 1938, Louis Wirth[28] pointed out that we cannot take the notion of the city, and hence, the urban, for granted and attach it to a clearly delimited object. Wirth argued that using criteria such as density, size of population, or settlement area amounts to an arbitrary means to conceive of the city. Today, urbanization patterns also increasingly challenge the seemingly self-evident distinction between city and countryside, urban and rural spaces. Some parts of a "large city" may look or *feel* like a village, whereas some villages with important marketplaces, for example, might bring images of the urban to mind. What about peasant farmers marching to the capital city to deliver their demands: Is this protest "urban?" And what about cultural practices developed in rural regions over generations, now continued by migrants who live in the city? Urban or not?

Two tales of the urban

In order to go beyond the aforementioned limits of the conception of the city as a "local entity," two main approaches have been developed within urban studies. Henri Lefebvre's work constitutes a springboard for both, as he conceived of the city as *échelle* (scale) and *niveau* (level). Thus, one of Lefebvre's takes focuses on the urban as a produced scale and opens a window onto its interrelation with various other scales – from the body to the global. *Niveau*, by contrast, concentrates on cultural aspects of the city as a space of mediation, mitigating between the everyday and the logic of commodification.

The multi-scalarity of the urban

Brenner and Schmid[29] suggest a shift away from the city as an entity defined by rigid and homogeneous metrics to the *theorization* of "the urban" on a higher conceptual level, an approach already suggested by Wirth in his caution not to mistake "urbanism" for the "physical entity of the city."[30] Indeed, Wirth shows a near prescience of future developments when he writes:

> The technological developments in transportation and communication which virtually mark a new epoch in human history have accentuated the role of cities as dominant elements in our civilization and have enormously extended the urban mode of living beyond the confines of the city itself."[31]

Lefebvre picked up and expanded upon this insight, arguing that the "urban problematic" has become generalized within society, leading him to speak of an "urban society."[32] For Lefebvre, the urban condition has long gone beyond the boundaries of the city and brings together distant spaces, events, and people across the globe. Both megacities and less densely settled "rural" spaces are subject to the urbanization process which links their development intimately to places elsewhere.

Lefebvre describes the "urban revolution" as an ongoing process of increasing connectivity, linkages, and flows at particular hubs, i.e. cities. Consequently, the urban should not be conceived as a self-contained space with its own dynamic[33] but as a node in a globalizing network of flows (of capital, commodities, people, practices, images etc.), as Castells promulgated in his later work.[34] These flows, which constitute the city at any particular moment, go not only beyond the territorial limits of the municipality, but often also those of the nation-state.

An emphasis on flows and connectivity has highlighted the "command and control" function of global cities as strategic hubs in the globalization of capital and labor.[35] Setting off an avalanche of research, "global cities" soon came to be reconfigured as the epitome of the urban, while neglecting that "ordinary cities," particularly those of the Global South, are also shaped by globalizing flows and connections.[36] Contrary to the prevailing focus on capital and commodities to understand connectivities, scholars like Ong emphasize the significance of migration and transnational social spaces in these dynamics, coining the process with the term "worlding."[37]

In these developments, authors like Michael Peter Smith see the emergence of a "transnational urbanism" as:

> a marker of the criss-crossing transnational circuits of communication and cross-cutting local, translocal, and transnational social practices that "come together" in particular places at particular times and enter into the contested politics of place-making, the social construction of power differentials, and the making of individual, group, national, and transnational identities, and their corresponding fields of difference.[38]

Transnational flows of commodities, communication, and people, however, have not leveled the global playing field. On the contrary, critical geographers have emphasized the role of scales in organizing inequality and uneven development. For Neil Smith, scales are not pre-given or an a priori:

> Geographical scale is socially produced as simultaneously a platform and container of certain kinds of social activity. Far from neutral and fixed, therefore, geographical scales are the product of economic, political and social activities and relationships; as such they are as changeable as those relationships themselves… Scale is the geographical organizer and expression of collective social action.[39]

Brenner claims that the urban scale plays a key strategic role in the current globally occurring rescaling of statehood and the production of a neoliberal global economy.[40] Today, the city-scale, conceived as a "structured coherence" of urban labor markets[41] or as the "100-mile-city,"[42] becomes a key site for national strategies of economic competitiveness. Cities are charged with the tasks of facilitating entrepreneurialism among the urban citizens, creating favorable conditions for transnational investments, reducing social expenses by activating neighborhood self-help, all the while producing greater revenues for the national budget.[43] In this process, "grassroots" organizations and commoning endeavors are enlisted to supplant the managerial role of the state.[44]

The urban as a space of mediation

Focusing on Lefebvre's notion of the urban as *niveau,* authors like Stefan Kipfer, Rob Shields, or Andy Merrifield[45] emphasize a cultural perspective distinct from Brenner's perspective on the political economy. Legacies of early twentieth-century scholars like Georg Simmel or Louis Wirth can be traced in this account emphasizing the experiential and cultural characteristics in constituting "city life." In his famous essay "The Metropolis and Mental Life," Simmel describes the experience of city life as an "intensification of nervous stimulation which results from the swift and uninterrupted change of outer and inner stimuli."[46] Social and psychological reactions against this condition foster differentiation and extravagance thus feeding into a self-reinforcing dynamic.

According to Simmel, an emerging urban culture of anonymity entails both alienating and liberating aspects. Urban inhabitants thus, on the one side, tend to adopt a blasé attitude, an indifference and "hidden aversion" towards strangers[47] leading to a cynical outlook on social relations. Clearly, Simmel sees a distinct connection between this attitude and the economic base as he writes: "cynicism and a blasé attitude – both of which are the results of the reduction of the concrete values of life to the mediating value of money."[48] On the other side, anonymity liberates the individual from forms of peer pressure and other kinds of social control and facilitates the development of diverse urban cultures. Iris Marion Young takes this idea further, emphasizing four desirable ideals inherent in urban life: (1) "social differentiation without exclusion," (2) variety, (3) publicity, and (4) "eroticism […] in the wide sense of an attraction to the other, the pleasure and excitement of being drawn out of one's secure routine to encounter the novel, strange, and surprising."[49]

Just like Simmel, Wirth, Young and co., Lefebvre conceives of difference as a defining quality of the urban experience; "the urban can be defined as a place where differences know one another and through their mutual recognition, test one another, and in this way are strengthened or weakened."[50] The emergence and multiplication of social milieus and subcultures and the individualization of lifestyles are thus part and parcel of urbanization. It is in this urban milieu of diversity that innovation and creativity are fostered, and new forms of production and reproduction developed. According to Lefebvre, the capitalist city plays a key role in making such new developments commensurable with the logic of capital.

Lefebvre distinguishes between the levels of personal experience (what he calls the "private order" P) and capital accumulation (the "global order" G); the urban (mediation M) exists halfway between them, functioning as a space of everyday experience and commodification. In order to fulfill this role of mediation between different actors, Lefebvre considers centrality as an implicit ideal within urban space: "the fact that any point can become central is the meaning of urban space-time."[51] Shields argues that the urban amounts to a theoretical ideal and virtuality, whose potential exists in the city, and is, using Lefebvre's terminology, a "concrete abstraction."[52] However, since not every point can become central simultaneously, urban politics is about negotiating these different claims to centrality. On the one end of the spectrum of responses, spaces of commodity consumption such as shopping malls or business districts seek to create an ambience of social encounter and opportunities, all the while relying on various forms of exclusion against marginalized groups.[53] On the other end, the urban may also facilitate collective resistance among the excluded insofar as they realize their commonality of being marginalized. Again, Lefebvre: "the right to the city legitimizes the refusal to allow oneself to be removed from urban reality by a discriminatory and segregative organization… [and] proclaims the inevitable crisis of city centers based upon segregation."[54]

Urban mediation itself is subject to scalar production and only a "fleeting form."[55] Kipfer describes it as a "possible prism to understand, connect, and act on the fragmented and homogenized aspects of the modern world, the contradictions and possibilities of everyday life."[56] The urban in this sense thus can be understood as the arena constituted by "daily interactions," as Susser and Tonnelat suggest, that:

> manifest each individual's practical integration in the shared territories of the city, [enabling] people also [to] develop sentiments of affiliation to a largely anonymous collective at the scale of the city. Becoming a New Yorker, or a Parisian, is […] the ongoing and

demanding work of rubbing shoulders with strangers, no matter how we may like it.[57]

The urban experience may thus foster reflexivity of the self and expand the right to the city by a right to difference. This development, however, is not automatic.

Dialectics of the urban: Strategic enclosures and ontological openness

I propose to combine these concepts of the urban as a multi-scalar space and as a space of mediation. Drawing on both approaches, I argue that they both capture important aspects of the urban that we should think of as dialectically related. As I will show, each approach has a peculiar take on conceiving of the urban which involves both ontological openness and strategic enclosure. Enclosure and openness do not operate on the same plane; the former relates to social perceptions and strategy, the latter to material and normative dynamics. Once we bring the two approaches together, we can understand the urban phenomena as the result of their dialectical dance.

Strategic enclosure means that the urban organizes space by delimiting it from other spaces. It is an enclosure insofar as some relationships between actors and spaces are eclipsed, i.e. virtually cut off. The scaling debate suggests that the urban scale comes to appear as a "container for certain kinds of social activity," to repeat Neil Smith's formulation above. Social and political activities not associated with the urban scale are thus bracketed as being of a different kind. A similar enclosure is also indicated by the perspective on cultural mediation that draws a line between mundane and urban events, on the one side, and extraordinary ones on the other. It is important to note that such enclosures of the urban are only temporary. Both the production of scale and the experience of the everyday are politically contingent processes and thus subject to considerable historical and geographical variation.

Temporary enclosure is not simply a *disabling* condition (by relegating certain relationships and activities to the background) but also an *enabling* one. The experiential delimitation of urban space is a sine qua non for the socialization of individuals. By learning to act within its horizon, individuals restructure and expand these spatial foundations. In spite of Lefebvre's insistence on urban society as having outlived the city-countryside opposition, his call for the "right to the *city*" may be understood as the recognition that the city remains a central scope of everyday experience and a strategic space for articulating common interests, demands, and activities. The desire to shape one's own everyday environment often finds the urban scale as an appropriate starting point for collective mobilization around a "local problem." In this vein, it makes sense to reconsider Castells'[58] idea of the urban as the arena of struggle around public goods and collective consumption such as housing, public infrastructure (water, electricity, roads, transportation systems, etc.), education, child care, health care, parks, spaces for leisure and cultural activity, and so on.

The *ontological openness* relates to the urban as a space that is open towards and builds connections with other spaces. In this sense, Vasudevan describes the city as the product of "an ever thickening and indeterminate intersection of bodies, materials, spaces and things."[59] We have already seen that the "urban scale" can be deconstructed as a product of powerful processes that are driven by capital, communication, migration, and cultural dynamics operating on various scales and, in spite of all limitations, with a tendency towards engaging and producing new spaces.[60] The urban aspect of mediation also points to such a moment of openness, namely an inherent right to be different.

Strategic enclosure and ontological openness are dialectically related in the urban. On the one side, ongoing urbanization and "worlding" consistently test temporary enclosures and, in several cases, eventually undermine their effectiveness. The resulting change in functionality of such enclosures may then in turn also initiate a change in social perception and require new responses and a redrawing of how enclosures are bounded. For example, flows of migration challenge the idea of who the stakeholders of housing are, who has a right to housing and how and what equity means under new transnational circumstances. A similar challenge is posed by the privatization and financialization of public housing. In these contexts, housing activists may realize that the resolution to the "housing problem" can't be fully resolved at the city level, since it involves transnational networks of migration and finance capital. Following financial flows or decision-making powers, activists may create a map of the multi-scalar constitution of the city and begin to understand what connections need to be made beyond the city. In this process, local struggles may be connected with other spaces that are affected by the same corporations, state actors, or legal configurations. This is what happened to the "Right to the City Alliance" in the US. Having realized that the different city-based struggles are thwarted by the same regulations at the national level, a "national" platform has been devised to facilitate cooperation in view of common interest and targets.[61] More recently, in Poland, urban movements have also begun to build a broad coalition towards influencing national politics. Kacper Pobłocki, a spokesperson of this coalition, declares: "now we understand that waging many separated local struggles is pointless and that we need to change the law and this can be done only at the national level."[62] Going even further, there have been also efforts to foster a global alliance for the "Right to the City."[63]

The presented dialectic, however, does not imply a teleology of the urban towards greater *political* openness. The opposite development is possible as well: as local inhabitants realize the significance of other actors or processes at different scales and spaces, they may insist on enforcing boundaries more decisively against intruders or outside influences. Also, greater political openness does not necessarily create conditions conducive to commoning. A diversification of interests may also throw a delicate negotiation of commitment and self-interest in commons projects out of balance and dissolve commoning efforts. Thus, which way the dialectic between enclosure and openness develops is ultimately to be decided by social praxis, and therefore an important object for critical study.

Conclusion: The challenge of the urban commons

To conclude, I want to highlight two peculiar "urban challenges" to the commons: first, the ongoing need to negotiate boundaries and solidarities and, secondly, the exigency for urban commons to expand in order to match and outdo capitalist urbanization.

Once we take the thesis of the urbanization of society seriously, we have to think of commons as part of this process, not outside of it. The idea of urban commons thus recognizes the fact that commoning efforts are not pure and distinct spaces. Urban commoners are always already part of other processes and spaces that influence, inform, foster, or compete with their involvement in a particular commoning project. Rather than positing clear boundaries that define a particular resource and boundaries between commoners and non-commoners, urban commons require us to be attentive to the ongoing negotiations and fluctuations of such boundaries.

As already noted by Parker and Johansson, the mobility of urban individuals as well as the contested character of defining a commons resource create a certain volatility of commons boundaries. In this respect, it might be useful to rethink Ostrom's principle of user-group boundaries as processes that determine how membership may be acquired or lost.[64] According to Stavros Stavrides, however, it is not only boundaries that are modified under urban conditions, but also commoners' subjectivities: "emerging subjects of commoning actions transform themselves by always being open to 'newcomers,' by becoming always newcomers themselves."[65]

An "internal" challenge to urban commoners can also be described by relying on Simmel's elaboration on urban culture. From this perspective, urban commoners, as any other urban subject, are part of an ongoing process of social differentiation, constructing new personal identities and interests that may develop in divergent directions. To ensure ongoing collaboration among commoners under such conditions, ideals of homogeneity need to be replaced by multiplicity, and commonalities of interest cannot be taken for granted, but need to be re-established incessantly.[66] While an ethics of multiplicity sounds nice, the tough question is: what arrangements are conducive to institutionalizing such ethics as a social practice?

As the composition of identities and interests becomes more complex, another institutional challenge comes into view: is it possible for everyone in large and complex groups to be involved in negotiating the different, and sometimes conflicting, interests and needs among commoners?[67] While horizontality and participation are essential features of commons, at what point are formalizations and "bureaucratic" divisions of labor warranted so that commoners are able to do things beyond discussions? The challenge of complexity, however, is not only about negotiating boundaries and instituting solidarities.

The second urban challenge to the commons relates to the expansive and multi-scalar course of urbanization. Parker and Johannsson, as presented above, highlight that the large-scale character of urban commons poses specific problems to governance. This issue becomes even more difficult once we take the multi-scalar organization of the urban into consideration. In this respect, urban commoning means recognizing that various resources of the commons are not controlled by the commoners, but by external processes (i.e. even a squat needs food, tools, and repair materials). The urban politics of commons thus necessitates the tracking of these external resources and finding ways to make them compatible with the commoning work – or else risk death or starvation. This quirk increases the likelihood for commons to be colonized by market or state logics. Capitalist urbanization, as we have seen with Lefebvre, infiltrates and seeps into the various pores of the everyday. It increases the pressure of valorization on the entire environment by bringing it into competition with newly accessed markets, capital, or labor. In order to avoid cutthroat competition, commons therefore constantly need to expand their networks of collaboration with other commons to match this process of commodification.

Commons expansion, however, is a politically contingent matter. A status as a commons does not guarantee that two different commoning efforts will collaborate productively with each other. Countering any romanticized idea of the commons, Stavrides interjects that "we need to abandon a view of autonomy that fantasizes uncontaminated enclaves of emancipation."[68] Surely, there is no blueprint for how real-existing commons are to work together. In order to prevent commons from entering into competition with each other, Harvey proposes a federated structure (akin to Murray Bookchin's ideas) to coordinate activities, claims, and interests into a coherent opposition to capital. The "downside" of such federation is a greater complexity of coordination and regulation which, again, seems to make a certain degree of formalization and differentiation inevitable. A large-scale collaboration among urban commoning efforts also seems expedient in order to avoid the risk of becoming appendices to a workfare state that is premised on the activation and co-optation of community organizations. The challenge in this process is for commons not to become dependent on the state, but rather, in reverse, to be continually able to push the state to do certain things.[69] This reminds me of how Peter Linebaugh described the relationship between commoners and the king in The Magna Carta:[70] the rights of the commoners were not granted by the king, but rather the king was forced to accept them as already existing practices.

Notes

1. Peter Linebaugh, "The City and the Commons: A Story for Our Times," in *Stop, Thief! The Commons, Enclosures, and Resistance* (Oakland, CA: PM Press, 2014), 40.
2. An important edited collection that challenges such generalization is Alexander Reid Ross, ed., *Grabbing Back: Essays against the Global Land Grab* (Oakland, CA: AK Press, 2014).
3. George Caffentzis and Silvia Federici, "Commons Against and Beyond Capitalism," *Upping the Anti* 15 (September 2013): 83–97; Ozan Karaman, "Defending Future Commons: the Gezi Experience," *Antipode Intervention,* 2013, http://wp.me/p16RPC-M5 (accessed December 15, 2014); Linebaugh, "The City and the Commons," 24.
4. Linebaugh, "The City and the Commons," 40.

5   Henri Lefebvre, *Writings on Cities,* trans. Eleonore Kofman und Elizabeth Lebas (Oxford: Blackwell, 1996), 66.
6   David Harvey, "The Future of the Commons," *Radical History Review,* no. 109 (2011): 103–104.
7   Michael Hardt and Antonio Negri, *Commonwealth* (Cambridge, MA: Harvard University Press, 2009), 250.
8   Ibid., 154.
9   I am limiting this overview to explicit mentions of the term "urban commons."
10 Sheila Foster, "Collective Action and the Urban Commons," *Notre Dame Law Review* 87 (2011): 57–134; Nicole Stelle Garnett, "Managing the Urban Commons," *U. Pa. L. Rev.* 160 (2012): 1995–2027; Alison Young, "Cities in the City: Street Art, Enchantment, and the Urban Commons," *Law & Literature* 26, no. 2 (2014): 145–61.
11 Linebaugh, "The City and the Commons: A Story for Our Times"; Jesús A. Solórzano Telechea, "The Politics of the Urban Commons in Northern Atlantic Spain in the Later Middle Ages," *Urban History* 41, no. 2 (May 2014): 183–203; Geoff D. Zylstra, "Struggle over the Streets: Industrialization and the Fight over the Corporate Control of Street Space in Philadelphia, 1830–1860," *Journal of Urban Technology* 20, no. 3 (July 1, 2013): 3–19; Alvaro Sevilla-Buitrago, "Central Park Against the Streets: The Enclosure of Public Space Cultures in Mid-Nineteenth Century New York," *Social & Cultural Geography* 15, no. 2 (December 2013): 151–71.
12 David Harvey, "The Creation of the Urban Commons," in *Rebel Cities: From the Right to the City to the Urban Revolution* (London: Verso, 2012); Nicholas Blomley, "Enclosure, Common Right and the Property of the Poor," *Social & Legal Studies* 17, no. 3 (September 2008): 311–31; Tim Simpson, "Macau Metropolis and Mental Life: Interior Urbanism and the Chinese Imaginary," *International Journal of Urban and Regional Research* 38, no. 3 (May 2014): 823–42; Ursula Lang, "The Common Life of Yards," *Urban Geography* 35, no. 6 (June 13, 2014): 852–69; Stuart Hodkinson, "The New Urban Enclosures," *City* 16, no. 5 (2012): 500–518; Efrat Eizenberg, "Actually Existing Commons: Three Moments of Space of Community Gardens in New York City," *Antipode* 44, no. 3 (2012): 764–82; Alexander Vasudevan, "The Autonomous City Towards a Critical Geography of Occupation," *Progress in Human Geography,* April 30, 2014; Shin Lee and Chris Webster, "Enclosure of the Urban Commons," *GeoJournal* 66, no. 1–2 (2006): 27–42; Renaud Le Goix, Chris Webster, et al., "Gated Communities, Sustainable Cities and a Tragedy of the Urban Commons," *Critical Planning* 13 (Summer 2006): 41–64; G. Ling, C. S. Ho, and H. M. Ali, "Institutional Property Rights Structure, Common Pool Resource (CPR), Tragedy of the Urban Commons: A Review," *IOP Conference Series: Earth and Environmental Science* 18, no. 1 (February 25, 2014): 1–5; Amita Baviskar and Vinay Gidwani, "Urban Commons," *Economic and Political Weekly* XLVI, no. 50 (December 10, 2011); Anant Maringanti "No Estoppel: Claiming Right to the City via the Commons," *Economic and Political Weekly* XLVI, no. 50 (December 10, 2011).
13 Patrick Bresnihan and Michael Byrne, "Escape into the City: Everyday Practices of Commoning and the Production of Urban Space in Dublin," *Antipode* (July 1, 2014); Adrian Parr, "Urban Debt, Neoliberalism and the Politics of the Commons," *Theory, Culture & Society* (June 16, 2014); Derese Getachew Kassa, "A Tragedy of the 'Urban Commons'? A case study of 2 Public Places in Addis Ababa," 2008, http://dlc.dlib.indiana.edu/dlc/handle/10535/792 (accessed December 15, 2014).
14 Andrew Newman, "Gatekeepers of the Urban Commons? Vigilant Citizenship and Neoliberal Space in Multiethnic Paris," *Antipode* 45, no. 4 (2013): 947–64; Ida Susser and Stéphane Tonnelat, "Transformative Cities: The Three Urban Commons," *Focaal* 66 (2013): 105–32.
15 Johan Colding et al., "Urban Green Commons: Insights on Urban Common Property Systems," *Global Environmental Change* 23, no. 5 (October 2013): 1039–51; Daniel Tumminelli O'Brien, "Manag-

ing the Urban Commons: The Relative Influence of Individual and Social Incentives on the Treatment of Public Space," *Human Nature* 23, no. 4 (December 2012): 467–89.

16. Richard Pithouse, "An Urban Commons? Notes from South Africa," *Community Development Journal* 49, suppl. no. 1 (January 1, 2014): 31–43.

17. Spike Boydell and Glen Searle, "Understanding Property Rights in the Contemporary Urban Commons," *Urban Policy and Research* 32, no. 3 (July 3, 2014): 323–40; Natalia Radywyl and Che Biggs, "Reclaiming the Commons for Urban Transformation," *Journal of Cleaner Production* 50 (2013): 159–70; Orlando Alves dos Santos Jr., "Urban Common Space, Heterotopia and the Right to the City: Reflections on the Ideas of Henri Lefebvre and David Harvey," *urbe. Revista Brasileira de Gestão Urbana* 6, no. 2 (August 2014): 146–57; Sumitaka Harada, "Komonzu Kara No Toshi Saisei: Chiiki Kyodo Kanri to Ho No Aratana Yakuwari (Urban Commons and City Revitalization: Community Management of the Commons and New Functions of the Law)," *Social Science Japan Journal* 17, no. 2 (January 7, 2014): 247–51; Peter Parker and Magnus Johansson, "Challenges and Potentials in Collaborative Management of Urban Commons," in *Multi-Faceted Nature of Collaboration in the Contemporary World*, eds. Tamara Besednjak Valic, Dolores Modic, and Urša Lamut (Vega Press, Ltd, 2012), 92–113; Peter Parker and Magnus Johansson, "The Uses and Abuses of Elinor Ostrom's Concept of Commons in Urban Theorizing," Paper presented at the Conference of the European Urban Research Association, Copenhagen, 2011, http://dspace.mah.se/handle/2043/12212 (accessed December 15, 2014); Ian McShane, "Trojan Horse or Adaptive Institutions? Some Reflections on Urban Commons in Australia," *Urban Policy and Research* 28, no. 1 (March 2010): 101–16; Krystyna Stave and Leslie Armijo, "The Las Vegas Wash: A Changing Urban Commons in a Changing Urban Context," in *Eighth Biennial Conference of the International Association for the Study of Common Property*, 2000, http://digitalscholarship.unlv.edu/sea_fac_articles/210 (accessed December 15, 2014); Merle Breyer, "Owning by Doing: In Search of the Urban Commons" (Master of Sustainable Urban Planning and Design, Royal Institute of Technology, 2013), http://www.diva-portal.org/smash/record.jsf?pid=diva2:740911 (accessed December 15, 2014).

18. Stavros Stavrides , "Emerging Common Spaces as a Challenge to the City of Crisis," *City* 18, no. 4–5 (2014): 546–50; Jorge Vergara Vidal, "Bienes comunes urbanos una aproximación inicial," *Diseño urbano y paisaje* 9, no. 23 (2012); Francesca Ferguson, *Make_Shift City: Die Neuverhandlung des Urbanen* (Berlin: Jovis, 2014); Andrea Baier, *Stadt der Commonisten: neue urbane Räume des Do it yourself* (Bielefeld: Transcript, 2013); Georg Franck, "Die urbane Allmende: Zur Herausforderung der Baukultur durch die nachhaltige Stadt," *Merkur* 65, no. 746 (2011): 567–82; an entire volume of the magazine *uncube* (#20, 2014) was dedicated to "urban commons."

19. Marissia Fragkou and Philip Hager, "Staging London: Participation and Citizenship on the Way to the 2012 Olympic Games," *Contemporary Theatre Review* 23, no. 4 (November 1, 2013): 532–41.

20. Several conferences and projects in different parts of the world have taken place on the topic of the urban commons such as the International Summer School: *Commoning the City*, June 22–29, 2014, Academy of Fine Arts Vienna; The Conference: *Commoning the City,* April 11, 2013 Royal Institute of Art, Stockholm; The Common(s) Course: *Commoning the City & Withdrawing from the Community of Money*, September 2013 – April 2014, 16 Beaver St., New York City; *Mapping the Commons, A Research Lab on Urban Commons,* a network involving scholars in Brazil, Turkey, Greece, and Spain (mappingthecommons.net), and, of course, the conference *Urban Commons: Moving Beyond State and Market*, September 27&28, 2013, Georg-Simmel-Zentrum at the Humboldt University in Berlin.

21. Susser and Tonnelat, "Transformative Cities: The Three Urban Commons."

22. Ibid., 109.

23. Ibid., 108.

24 Parker and Johansson, "Challenges and Potentials in Collaborative Management of Urban Commons"; Parker and Johansson, "The Uses and Abuses of Elinor Ostrom's Concept of Commons in Urban Theorizing."
25 Garrett Hardin, "The Tragedy of the Commons," *Science* 162, no. 3859 (1968): 1243–48.
26 Parker and Johansson, "Challenges and Potentials in Collaborative Management of Urban Commons," 100–101.
27 See, for example, Peter J. Marcotullio and William Solecki, "What is a City? An Essential Definition for Sustainability," in *Urbanization and Sustainability: Linking Urban Ecology, Environmental Justice and Global Environmental Change* (New York: Springer, 2013), 11–25.
28 Louis Wirth, "Urbanism as a Way of Life," *American Journal of Sociology* XLIV, no. 1 (July 1938): 1–24.
29 Neil Brenner and Christian Schmid, "Planetary Urbanization," in *Urban Constellations,* ed. Matthew Gandy (Berlin: Jovis, 2012), 10–13.
30 Marcotullio and Solecki, "What is a City?"
31 Wirth, "Urbanism as a Way of Life," 4–5.
32 Henri Lefebvre, *The Urban Revolution* (Minneapolis: University of Minnesota Press, 2003).
33 The concept of the "intrinsic logic" of cities has been developed by Martina Löw, "The Intrinsic Logic of Cities: Towards a New Theory on Urbanism," *Urban Research and Practice* 5, no. 3 (2012): 303–15.
34 Manuel Castells, *The Rise of the Network Society. Vol. 1: The Information Age: Economy, Society and Culture* (Oxford: Blackwell, 1996).
35 Saskia Sassen, *The Global City: New York, London, Tokyo* (Princeton, NJ: Princeton University Press, 1991).
36 Jennifer Robinson, *Ordinary Cities: Between Modernity and Development* (London; New York: Routledge, 2006).
37 Aihwa Ong, "Introduction: Worlding Cities, or the Art of Being Global," in *Worlding Cities: Asian Experiments and the Art of Being Global,* eds. Ananya Roy and Aihwa Ong (Chichester: Wiley-Blackwell, 2011), 1–26.
38 Michael P. Smith, *Transnational Urbanism: Locating Globalization* (Malden, MA: Blackwell Publishers, 2001), 5.
39 Smith quoted in Neil Brenner, "The Urban Question as a Scale Question: Reflections on Henri Lefebvre, Urban Theory and the Politics of Scale," *International Journal of Urban and Regional Research* 24, no. 2 (2000): 267.
40 Neil Brenner*, New State Spaces: Urban Governance and the Rescaling of Statehood* (Oxford/New York: Oxford University Press, 2004).
41 David Harvey, *The Urban Experience* (Baltimore: Johns Hopkins University Press, 1989).
42 Deyan Sudjic, *The 100 Mile City* (London: Flamingo, 1993).
43 Brenner, *New State Spaces: Urban Governance and the Rescaling of Statehood.*
44 Margit Mayer, "The Onward Sweep of Social Capital: Causes and Consequences for Understanding Cities, Communities and Urban Movements," *International Journal of Urban and Regional Research* 27, no. 1 (March 1, 2003): 110–32.
45 Stefan Kipfer, "Why the Urban Question Still Matters: Reflections on Rescaling and the Promise of the Urban," in *Leviathan Undone? Towards a Political Economy of Scale,* eds. Rianne Mahon and Roger Keil (Vancouver: UBC Press, 2009), 67–86; Rob Shields, "The Urban Question as Cargo Cult: Opportunities for a New Urban Pedagogy," *International Journal of Urban and Regional Research* 32, no. 3 (2008): 712–718; Andy Merrifield, *Dialectical Urbanism* (New York: Monthly Review Press, 2014).
46 Georg Simmel, "The Metropolis and Mental Life," in *The Sociology of Georg Simmel,* ed. Kurt H. Wolf (New York: Free Press, 1950), 409.

47 Ibid., 413–416.
48 Georg Simmel, *The Philosophy of Money* (London/Boston: Routledge & Kegan Paul, 1978), 255.
49 Iris Marion Young, *Justice and the Politics of Difference* (Princeton, NJ: Princeton University Press, 1990), 239.
50 Lefebvre, *The Urban Revolution,* 96.
51 Ibid., 116.
52 Shields, "The Urban Question as Cargo Cult," 716.
53 Margaret Kohn, *Brave New Neighborhoods* (New York: Routledge, 2004); Don Mitchell, *The Right to the City: Social Justice and the Fight for Public Space* (New York: Guilford Press, 2003).
54 Lefebvre, *Writings on Cities,* 195.
55 Kipfer, "Why the Urban Question Still Matters," 73.
56 Ibid., 81.
57 Susser and Tonnelat, "Transformative Cities: The Three Urban Commons," 113.
58 Margit Mayer, "Manuel Castells' The City and the Grassroots," *International Journal of Urban and Regional Research* 30, no. 1 (2006): 202–206.
59 Vasudevan, "The Autonomous City: Towards a Critical Geography of Occupation," 6.
60 Hardt and Negri, for example, consider the multitude as the agent of an ever widening sociability. Michael Hardt and Antonio Negri, *Empire* (Cambridge, MA: Harvard University Press, 2000).
61 http://www.righttothecity.org/index.php/about (accessed December 15, 2014).
62 Henry Foy, "Young Rebels Upset Politics in Central and Eastern Europe," *Financial Times*, November 11, 2014.
63 See, for example, the International Meeting on the Right to the City, in São Paulo, Brazil, November 12–14, 2014.
64 For examples of how this might function see also the contribution in this volume by Kuttler and Jain.
65 Stavrides, "Emerging Common Spaces as a Challenge to the City of Crisis," 548.
66 Ibid., 547.
67 See also Majken Bieniok's contribution in this volume.
68 Stavrides, "Emerging Common Spaces as a Challenge to the City of Crisis," 547.
69 Pithouse, "An Urban Commons?"
70 Peter Linebaugh, *The Magna Carta Manifesto: Liberties and Commons for All* (Berkeley: University of California Press, 2009).

Majken Bieniok[1]

The Complexity of Urban Commoning from a Psychological Perspective

Urban life and commons

Urbanization is on the rise globally, therefore issues related to cities and the urban are becoming increasingly important.[2] People are moving to cities with the expectation of improving their living conditions. In spite of negative aspects of urban life such as pollution or vanishing public open spaces, urban agglomerations remain attractive for a number of reasons, broadly including personal development opportunities (jobs and business) and access to services (education, medical care, housing and entertainment). Many human needs can be satisfied in cities. Research has showed that needs can be grouped into three basic categories: (a) *physically-oriented needs* – physical needs (air, light, water, nutrition, excretion, sex), motion & mobility, repose & regeneration, safety & protection as well as physical & mental health; (b) *socially oriented needs* – social connectedness, relationship & partnership, various contacts & communication, love, care & acceptance, privacy & intimacy, as well as pleasure & emotional expression; (c) *self-oriented needs* – meaning, reasonableness, order & aesthetics, self-fulfillment & creativity, self-acceptance, identity & self-esteem, knowledge, learning experience & novelty-seeking, autonomy & self-determination, control & active shaping of the social and environmental surroundings.[3] Every individual has an individual set of priorities, i.e. how he or she ranks social activities, cultural engagement, leisure etc.

People also connect the decision to live an urban life with the expectation of more personal freedom and a tolerant and open-minded environment. In general, the preferred features of an urban life refer to aspects such as "social potential & vision," "diversity," "internationality," "opportunities," and "density, size & segmentation."[4] These features may be provided by the urban environment.

Urban agglomerations are complex systems which can be conceived as commons in many different ways. For example, while any city (or network of cities) as a whole may be interpreted as being commons (i.e. a shared urban resource), the city may also be conceived as consisting of several commons of a smaller scale(s) (from urban districts and neighborhoods down to little urban gardening projects) or in any other way, depending on the historical and social narrative with which urbanity is being conceived. Urban commons can be of different scales, ranging from a house project or a neighborhood to the whole city or even a worldwide network of cities. However, the very notion of larger-scale commons raises many serious conceptual and empirical dilemmas.

Based on current discourse, this article aims to sketch some of these dilemmas and point out several major questions related both to urban commons and to the adaptation of commons terminology to large-scale enterprises in general.

Complex social dilemmas and principles for commoning

Commons are traditionally associated with the idea of cognitive or social dilemmas and the danger of being misused and exploited. Hardin uses the famous rural example of the herdsman and his cattle to describe the tragedy of the commons.[5] The overuse of the limited resources (fields) for grazing could substantially contribute to the personal income and livelihood of the herdsman's family[6] while the costs for this overuse are distributed across the whole community. This is a perfect example of a social dilemma, defined, generally speaking, as a situation in which the decision to be made either supports the fulfillment of short-term self-interests or long-term collective interests. These long-term interests include the long-term benefits for the individual, although this may not always be immediately obvious to him or her. The obvious short-term interest may include saving money, personal energy, and/or time.

Another example of commons misuse is free-riding. For example, citizens may not contribute to the "democratic process" because they don't want to make the effort of promoting a social issue, but still benefit from the effort of others and may even invest the spared energy in their own personal good. Free-riding seems to be an effective way to spare one's own effort while gaining the same expected outcome as, or one even better than, the others'.

The personal decision for either the common interests or the short-term-oriented individual interest therefore depends on the comparison between investment and benefits. The decision can be either intrinsically motivated e.g. by moral values, self-concept, or pleasure, or extrinsically motivated e.g. by money, incentives, and lower costs of investment. An additional variable that is taken into account while making a decision is the point in time at which the "payoff," especially of extrinsically motivated benefits, will occur. According to the principle of delay discounting or temporal discounting, the amount of discounting increases with the length of the delay interval. That means that the same outcome may "count" less if its "pay-out" is postponed into the future, and people often choose smaller benefits that are available immediately, over larger benefits that are available later.[7, 8, 9]

The dimensions in which social dilemmas occur can range from very small groups of people to the largest possible group – humanity. Structures like neighborhoods or cities and countries fall somewhere in between. One of the first psychologists defining social dilemmas was Dawes.[10] He defined two characteristics of social dilemmas. The first characteristic was that each individual receives a higher payoff for a socially defecting choice (e.g. having additional children, using all the energy available, polluting his or her neighbors) than for a socially cooperative one, no matter what the other individuals in society do. The second characteristic was that all individuals are better off if all cooperate than if all defect.[11] Acting defectively may result in a tragedy through overuse especially when it comes to limited common goods.[12] In a commons dilemma, individuals decide how much they take from the common resource and may not consider the full social costs of their activities. The resulting behavior, either egoistic or cooperative, also depends on the complexity of the context. The higher the complexity, the more vulnerable processes of cooperation are to individual defectors.

The complexity of social dilemmas depends for example on the number and stakes of the people involved, power asymmetries, the amount and complexity of information needed, perception processes, the sense of control over the situation, and knowledge of the optimal use of the resource or the consequences of non-optimal use.

Therefore, to understand urban commoning better, the psychological effects of the individual human nature and social circumstances in which they become relevant, like changing group-size, are worth consideration. Various effects of group size may be seen in the following examples:

- In groups up to ~150 people, it is still possible for all participants to know each others' faces personally, maintain stable relationships, and build a cohesive group to reach common goals;
- Increase in group size decreases cooperation and discourages a sense of belonging and self-efficacy;
- The anticipation of immediate (personal) consequences and the benefits of acting egoistically both increase with group size and with the expectation or occurrence of single (one-time) contacts between group members (as opposed to repeated, i.e. multiple contacts between group members);
- Group norms of behavior (for reciprocity or being loyal to group members) change with group size, e.g. with an increasing group size, the development of trust and the sense of family get lost, giving rise to the development of more self-oriented exchange relationships (the relationship shifts from a communal to an exchange relationship);
- Making the choice in public and not in an anonymous setting of a larger group of people increases the amount of cooperative (compared with defecting) activities;
- Social loafing, diffusion of responsibility, groupthink, and problems in communication or information-transfer into and within the group increase as the group size increases.[13, 14, 15, 16, 17, 18]

Stressing the importance of these aspects, Kopelman, Weber, and Messick identified nine types of variables that influence cooperation in commons dilemmas: social motives, gender, payoff structure, uncertainty, power and status, group size, communication, causes, and frames.[19] These variables may be sorted into two groups: *psychological individual differences* (stable personality traits) and *situational factors* (the environment) including both the task (social and decision structure) and the perception of the task. The term 'situational factors' refers to the Ostrom principles to which we'll come back later.

As indicated by the same group of researchers (Weber, Kopelman, and Messick) two years later, the perceptional component is essential for decision making in social dilemmas. In their "appropriateness framework" they suggest that people making decisions ask themselves (explicitly or implicitly), "What does a person like me do in a situation like this?" which leads them to the identification of three significant factors: (a) recognition and classification of the kind of situation encountered,

(b) the identity of the individual making the decision, and (c) the application of rules or heuristics in guiding behavioral choice.[20] Confirming these results, Van Lange et al. discuss similar variables in their literature review.[21] They add structural variables like uncertainty about information and psychological variables like social values, trust, consideration of future consequences, priming processes, emotions, dynamic interaction processes, changing partners, and reciprocal strategies to the list.

One strategy to organize commons in a sustainable way was presented by Ostrom.[22] She directly referred to aspects of power distribution, communication, interaction, trust, and the identity of the commoners. Elinor Ostrom indicated eight principles or demands that have to be fulfilled so as to direct the decision-making process in a collective, beneficial direction. She indicated that defining of individual group rules and boundaries, monitoring, sanctions, and rewards applied on a local level, and matching the local needs may help to organize commons.[23] Ostrom also indicated additional factors for a cooperative solution in a social dilemma such as effective communication, internal trust, and reciprocity.

Meta-analytical studies seem to reinforce Ostrom's principles and stress the importance of reward and punishment; they highlight that this approach may be particularly effective when administered by actual participants in the cooperative venture.[24] In addition, cooperative behavior is more likely if the group remains together for further activities and if the group members trust each other. In his meta-analysis, Klöckner identified more concrete predictors of behavior that support Ostrom's principles.[25] Briefly summarized, he found out that: (a) intentions are predicted by attitudes, personal and social norms, and perceived behavioral control, (b) personal norms are predicted by social norms, perceived behavioral control, awareness of consequences, ascription of responsibility as well as a specific (in his case ecological) world view and self-transcendence values, and (c) self-enhancement values have a negative impact on personal norms. According to his model, it would be necessary, in order to change behavior, to focus on de-habitualizing behavior, strengthening social support, empowerment, and increasing self-efficacy through concrete information about how to act cooperatively and in a self-determined way.

However, if the complexity of the situation grows (number of persons involved over ~150, no face-to-face communication, less trust, no experiences in autonomous groups, less available norms, socialization in hierarchical structures …) and the perceived self-efficacy decreases, it is more likely that experts will be asked, leaders will be elected or institutions and institutionalized government strategies will be installed to find the right decisions or to govern the commons. This is especially the case when the group has failed to achieve optimal outcomes in public goods dilemmas.[26] Centralization of decision-making and delegation of responsibility provide a promising solution to handle the huge amount of specific or complex information, the time investment, and the number of people and opinions involved, although there might be other solutions (e.g. a decentralized society). An additional strategy – a mental coping strategy – would be to rely on heuristics and superficial information processing because of limited mental resources or restricted access to information resources.[27]

A crucial effect of this process may be that commons may not be perceived and run as commons anymore. In the final consequence they may cease to "be" commons. This also opens the door for processes of privatization, commodification, and privileging of a few at costs to the community. Once privatized and perceived as private goods, it may be extremely difficult to reverse the process.

In addition, the former commons may not fit the definitions of commons anymore. The current characterization of commons in the English-language Wikipedia demonstrates this effect: "Commons refers to the cultural and natural resources accessible to all members of a society, including natural materials such as air, water, and a habitable earth. These resources are held in common, not owned privately."[28] At this point, a further tragedy of the commons becomes visible. Commons, suffering from unequal power distribution after they are for example privatized or nationalized through the delegated authorities initially elected by the community in order to administrate the commons for the community, can per definition no longer be perceived as commons, as for example in the case of gated communities. Beside the fact that the public is not able to enter or use the space of a gated community and that this fact in itself restricts the freedom of movement, the public is generally expected not to be aware of or interested in what is going on inside a community of this kind – it's private. In this case, different social rules and norms are applied, for example not getting involved. Moreover, as a regular citizen, you're no longer part of the in-group of users. You are excluded, and you do not share the same interests as the gated community members. As a matter of fact, your and their interests now contradict each other.

The crucial importance of perceiving something as common and the ability to differ between private and common interests may be demonstrated through the example of the private project Elbphilharmonie Hamburg (concert hall in the

HafenCity of Hamburg). From the beginning on, the alleged "commons idea" of this private project was stressed in public representation. The applied marketing strategy referred for example to the spatial design of avoiding an indoor hierarchy in the concert hall and offering a public plaza within the project. Moreover, the commons idea was used as a legitimizing tool to garner public funding for a public-private-partnership prestige-object based on a private initiation by A. Gérard and his wife J. Marko. A few players functioned as initial major donors, which motivated the public administration to also participate with donations and gifts. A huge funding campaign accompanied the whole process, using slogans like "We are building…" to underline the commons-based idea of the project and get public funds for an exclusive private circle.[29, 30] This example demonstrates how public resources can be used for private benefit by "commons-washing" a planned private project. At the same time, this strategy may also serve to prevent the community from claiming a good, in this case the concert hall, as their common good.

As can also be seen in this example, a second important aspect of perceiving the commons is the idea of perceiving oneself as part of a community – the "we." Communities mainly consist of the social bonds between people, the attachment to places or distinct urban areas, or related political, symbolic, and cultural implications. Sarason, for example, defined the idea of the sense of community as follows: "the sense that one was part of a readily available mutually supportive network of relationship."[31, 32] According to Mannarini et al., the sense of community is related to various positive outcomes, such as well-being and life satisfaction, sense of safety and security, social and political participation, and even the individual ability to use problem-focused coping strategies.[33] Public spaces like parks or squares, which are the most common spaces for commoning, may foster the sense of community by facilitating casual encounters between people and helping to build place identity.[34] Uzzell et al. state that place-related social identity is expressed through both collective social relations and individual and collective relations to place.[35] To form place identity, two major aspects must be met: first, a perceived distinctiveness, for example of one urban place/area compared with other areas in the city, and second, its role in the individual and collective interactions.[36, 37] From the descriptions above, urban commoning seems to be linked to, or better based on, both social and place identity.

If a city, a decentralized network of cities and several interacting smaller-scale urban enterprises can be considered commons, then the question may arise how these various commons scales should be organized.

The organization of commons

"Autonomy & self-determination" and "control & active shaping of the social and environmental surrounding" are basic human needs[38] which are directly linked to the praxis of commoning and the organization of interaction. There are three types of interaction: (1) interaction between individuals inside the group of commoners (in-group), (2) between the in-group and the "out-group" or society, and (3) between commoners of different groups.

Ostrom already indicated the importance of the right interactions and describes the relevant conditions for commons endeavors to be successful (see the eight principles).[39] She seems to perceive the aspects of autonomy, self-determination, and control as mainly related to the processes and internal interaction of the in-group and less to relations between the in-group and its surroundings. In her principles, she only indicates that the rights of rulemaking should be respected by outside authorities in order to sustain the commons. In her last principle, she mentions that commons have nested tiers, referring to the interaction of different groups of commoners, but not automatically implying hierarchically structured systems. Vincent Ostrom,[40] for example, postulates a polycentric order of smaller units (i.e. of single commons) in which "many elements are capable of making mutual adjustments ordering their relationships with one another within a general system of rules where each element acts with independence of other elements."

Dennis R. Fox shares this emphasis of decentralization and explains that "only by such a process can we avert major global crises while we simultaneously expand human dignity and meet human needs."[41] For Fox "only a decentralized society has any chance at all of surviving in a form that is fully acceptable to most human beings." According to Fox, the way members of different autonomous communities perceive themselves and manage to balance between individual autonomy and sense of community has to be worked out in the future: "It is only *after* utopia is made a goal that the long and difficult undertaking of defining the content for a new society can begin […]."[42] In his view, autonomy, self-determination, and self-control are not only an internal in-group matter but a more general notion of how to form a society with sovereign independence or independencies. There would be no state regulating the interaction and limiting the rights of the society members in a top-down manner like Harvey suggests.[43] Society members would have to develop their own rules of interaction (self-government) without hierarchies (which is a direct threat to any form of coercive government) and find ways to handle the problem of coping with complexity.

Harvey picks up Elinor Ostrom's idea of nested commons and refers to it within the context of a society as a whole. He argues that good collective governmental solutions, like those which were described by Ostrom for small-scale commons, cannot be applied in global social systems without using hierarchical organizations with "nested" structures. According to Harvey, one should acknowledge the limits of horizontality as a hegemonic organizational principle and be prepared to go far beyond it if necessary.[44] He stresses that short-term moneyed interests may compromise horizontally organized commons. However, he does not tackle the question whether short-term moneyed interests are possible within horizontally structured systems. Harvey asserts that decentralization and autonomy are the primary vehicles for producing greater inequality through neoliberalization, and therefore that the interaction between autonomous units has to be regulated by rules which have to be established, asserted, enforced, and actively policed by a higher-order hierarchical authority.[45] Again, he does not address the question whether neoliberal enterprises are possible within a horizontally structured system. In this perception of commoning, autonomy, self-determination, and self-control end where interactions of the in-group with their surroundings take place. Additionally, he does not seem to take into account the option that there may be solutions for these kinds of problems of which we are not or cannot be aware right now.

Conclusion

In the previous parts of this article, some psychologically relevant issues of commoning such as
- different scales of commons,
- social behavior, norms, and dilemmas,
- motivational aspects,
- cognitive processes and informational complexity,
- perceptual aspects, community and identity, and
- social self-organization

have been described.

This brief overview of the main psychology-related commons issues shows that this topic, at least in the larger sense, brings up difficult and complex questions with far-reaching sociological, economic, political, and psychological implications. Concluding this article, we would like to suggest a partial list of these questions:

First: What can be learned and concluded from research and experiences of small-scale commons with respect to larger-scale, more comprehensive commons projects which incorporate society as a whole? Is there any correlation between small-scale and large-scale commoning, or do these two issues constitute two different fields altogether?

Second: Is there a way to define what the term commons, in its large-scale sense, includes (i.e. does it include all available resources and facilities (e.g. knowledge) or just a part of them, like water and lands)? In large-scale commoning like urban commons, is it possible and necessary to establish a system of defining the commons beyond perceptual manipulation?

Third: What kind of social institutional structure is the most adequate for establishing and running large-scale commoning? Do the two levels (establishing and running) require two different institutional structures? Who is entitled to make decisions about the creation of institutions before a commons-based society is established?

Fourth: Can and should we speculate what the major problems of a commons-based society would be, once such a society is established?

It seems that recognizing these questions as significant is a prerequisite for any future discussion about commons as a foundation for a society.

Notes

1 I would like to thank Hans-Hermann Albers and Tore Dobberstein for the inspiring discussions about commoning which influenced this article.
2 *United Nations, World Urbanization Prospects: The 2007 Revision* (New York: United Nations, Department of Economic and Social Affairs, Population Division, 2008).
3 Majken Bieniok, Reinhard Beyer and Elke van der Meer, *Die ideale Metropole – Ein Konzept in der Theorie und Praxis*, Empirische Evaluationsmethoden, 15, (2011): 45–64, Berlin, ZeE Verlag .
4 Ibid.
5 Garrett Hardin, "The Tragedy of the Commons," *Science,* vol. 162, no. 3859 (December 13, 1968): 1243–1248.
6 Ibid., 1968.

7 George Ainslie, *Picoeconomics: The Strategic Interaction of Successive Motivational States within the Person* (Cambridge, UK: Cambridge University Press, 1992).
8 Leonard Green and Joel Myerson, "A Discounting Framework for Choice with Delayed and Probabilistic Rewards," *Psychological Bulletin* 130 (2004): 769–792.
9 Howard Rachlin, *The Science of Self-Control* (Cambridge, MA: Harvard University Press, 2000).
10 Robyn M. Dawes, "Social Dilemmas," *Annual Review of Psychology* 31 (1980): 169–193.
11 Ibid. 169.
12 Hardin, "The Tragedy of the Commons."
13 Paul B. Paulus, Jared Kenworthy, and Hamit Coskun, "Group Dynamics," in *Encyclopedia of Human Behavior*, 2nd ed. (2012): 276–282.
14 Paul A. M. Van Lange, Jeff Joireman, Craig D. Parks, and Eric Van Dijk, "The Psychology of Social Dilemmas: A Review," *Organizational Behavior and Human Decision Processes*, vol. 120, no. 2 (2013): 125–141.
15 Robin I. M. Dunbar, "The Social Brain Hypothesis," *Evolutionary Anthropology*, vol. 6, no. 5 (1998): 178–190.
16 Dawes, "Social Dilemmas," 169–193.
17 Michael Taylor, *Anarchy and Cooperation* (London: Wiley, 1976).
18 Margaret S. Clark and Judson Mills, "Interpersonal Attraction in Exchange and Communal Relationships," *Journal of Personality and Social Psychology* 37 (1979): 12–24.
19 Shirli Kopelman, Mark Weber, and David Messick, "Factors Influencing Cooperation in Commons Dilemmas: A Review of Experimental Psychological Research," in E. Ostrom et al., eds., *The Drama of the Commons* (Washington DC: National Academies Press (2002): 113–156.
20 Mark Weber, Shirli Kopelman, and David Messick, "A Conceptual Review of Decision Making in Social Dilemmas: Applying a Logic of Appropriateness," *Personality and Social Psychology Review* 8 (2004): 281–307.
21 Van Lange et al., "The Psychology of Social Dilemmas: A Review," 178–190.
22 Elinor Ostrom, *Governing the Commons: The Evolution of Institutions for Collective Action* (New York: Cambridge University Press, 1990).
23 See the introduction to this volume.
24 Cf. Daniel Balliet, Laetitia B. Mulder, and Paul A. M. Van Lange, "Reward, Punishment, and Cooperation: A Meta-Analysis," *Psychological Bulletin*, 137 (2011): 594–615; Daniel Balliet and Paul A. M. Van Lange, "Trust, Punishment, and Cooperation Across 18 Societies: A Meta-Analysis," *Perspectives on Psychological Science*, vol. 8, no. 4 (2013): 363–379.
25 Christian A. Klöckner, A Comprehensive Model of the Psychology of Environmental Behaviour – A Meta-Analysis, *Global Environmental Change*, 23 (2013): 1028–1038.
26 Van Lange et al., "The Psychology of Social Dilemmas: A Review," 178–190.
27 Alexander Todorov, Shelly Chaiken, and Marlone Henderson, "The Heuristic-Systematic Model of Social Information Processing," in *The Persuasion Handbook: Developments in Theory and Practice* (London: Sage, 2002), 195–212.
28 http://en.wikipedia.org/wiki/Commons (accessed September 9, 2014).
29 http://de.wikipedia.org/wiki/Elbphilharmonie (accessed October 10, 2013).
30 Hans-Hermann Albers, *Corporate Urban Responsibility – Die gesellschaftliche Verantwortung von Unternehmen in der Stadtentwicklung*, 221ff (Frankfurt am Main: Campus Verlag, 2011).
31 Seymour B. Sarason, *The Psychological Sense of Community: Prospects for a Community Psychology* (San Francisco, CA: Jossey-Bass, 1974).
32 Ibid., 1.

33 Terri Mannarini, Stefano Tartaglia, Angela Fedi, and Katiuscia Greganti, "Image of Neighborhood, Self-Image and Sense of Community," *Journal of Environmental Psychology* 26 (2006): 202–214.
34 Emily Talen, "Measuring the Public Realm: A Preliminary Assessment of the Link between Public Space and Sense of Community," *Journal of Architectural and Planning Research* 17 (2000): 344–360.
35 David Uzzell, Enric Pol, and David Badenas, "Place Identification, Social Cohesion, and Environmental Sustainability," *Environment and Behavior* 34 (2002): 26–53.
36 Kalevi M. Korpela, "Place Identity as a Product of Environmental Self-Regulation," *Journal of Environmental Psychology* 9 (1989): 241–256.
37 Uzzell et al., "Place Identification, Social Cohesion, and Environmental Sustainability," 26–53.
38 Majken Bieniok, *Das Konzept der idealen Metropole in Theorie und Praxis am Beispiel von Berlin* (Berlin: Verlag Peter Lang, 2012).
39 Ostrom, *Governing the Commons*.
40 Vincent Ostrom, "Polycentricity-Part 1," in Michael McGinnis, ed., *Polycentricity and Local Public Economies* (Ann Arbor: University of Michigan Press, 1999).
41 Dennis R. Fox, "Psychology, Ideology, Utopia, and the Commons," *American Psychologist* 40 (1985): 48–58; http://www.dennisfox.net/papers/commons.html, accessed January 22, 2015.
42 http://www.dennisfox.net/papers/commons.html.
43 David Harvey, *Rebel Cities, From the Right to the City to the Urban Revolution,* Verso, 2012.
44 Ibid., 70.
45 Ibid., 83.

Community

Tobias Kuttler and Angela Jain

Defending Space in a Changing Urban Landscape –
A Study on Urban Commons in Hyderabad, India

Introduction

The processes of privatizing and commodifying collective resources that accompany recent urbanization have evoked literature that focuses on the *urban commons*. In the case of India, scholars emphasize that the destruction of collective resources is threatening the livelihoods and social safety of urban populations.[1] Urban street space plays a crucial role for many urban dwellers in South Asia, particularly the urban poor, as the streets of the city provide them with the basis for generating income.[2] Furthermore the streets are the place where they conduct most of their daily social activities.[3] In this article, we will develop an understanding of commoning that builds upon Henri Lefebvre's theory of the production of space. Commoning, we argue, is a spatial production process consisting of the appropriation of physical space, negotiation of different concepts of space, and the production of social meaning. To elaborate this argument, we will analyze how urban dwellers, through their appropriations of street space and the production of social space, create an urban common. Thereby, we follow the understanding of David Harvey that the aim of creating collective and non-commodified spheres that are off-limits to the logic of global capitalist enclosure lies "at the heart of the practice of commoning."[4] Thus, we consider the particular common that is discussed here as a form of resistance and a defense of space.

This analysis of commoning in and around urban space challenges fundamental assumptions of how commons are successfully created. The way of creating commons that is traced here neither involves a clearly self-defined group nor strictly defined boundaries of a particular resource in the form Elinor Ostrom has suggested.[5] There is no particular group that practices commoning around the resource of street space. However, the absence of designated commoners and mutually defined resource boundaries does not mean that successful commoning is not possible. We suggest that the creation of commons – understood as collective and non-commodified spheres that oppose capitalist enclosure – is realized successfully in the everyday appropriation of physical space and the production of social space.

Placing the analysis of spatial appropriation and production within the framework of the commons provides the opportunity to recognize the agency of the ordinary and to contribute to an understanding of urbanization and conceptualization of "the Urban" in the Global South (see the editors' introduction to this volume). By drawing on the concept of the commons, we seek to highlight how urban space is produced by social practices of negotiating and appropriating the materialities of the city. Focusing on the spatial production process, we reject the assumption that globalization and the commodification of spaces are the overwhelming forces that shape urban realities today. The privilege of a supposed globalizing force over the local and ordinary in much of globalization literature is contested by recent approaches in urban studies that focus on place-based narratives, social processes, and everyday practice.[6] These approaches countervail the "marginalization of intellectual production on globalization produced in the 'peripheries' of the world"[7] in attempts to understand contemporary urbanization in the Global South.

Among these approaches, those that examine how material infrastructures are interlinked with the social production and restructuration of urban space, and how they relate to the experience of urban life, are particularly useful for the study of the urban commons. Jonathan Anjaria and Colin McFarlane highlight how people, for example in a collective effort to generate income, "actively move through, practice, cope with, seek to dominate and learn how to live in the city,"[8] thereby making use of the urban materialities and producing as well as contesting urban space. Focusing on how "expanded spaces of economic and cultural operation become available to residents of limited means,"[9] AbdouMaliq Simone emphasizes concretely the collaborative aspect in what he calls "people as infrastructure":

> A specific […] collaborative practice is constituted through the capacity of individual actors to circulate across and become familiar with a broad range of spatial, residential, economic, and transactional positions.[10]

In doing this, they "engage complex combinations of objects, spaces, persons, and practices."[11] The conjunction of these elements creates a "coherent platform for social transaction and livelihood."[12] As he points out, these forms of collaboration do not proceed within the boundaries of specific communities or self-defined groups, instead they "rehearse new ways […] to construct a sense of commonality."[13] A crucial characteristic is that these practices are rather invisible to governing and planning agencies, as their spatial logic is based on "(im)mobility, ephemerality, contingency and fungibility"[14] and the outcomes of the collaborations are "radically open, flexible, and provisional."[15] From these theoretical considerations it can be concluded that – for our examination of urban space as commons – it is necessary to keep in mind that "restructuring of urban landscapes, and social and cultural changes in cities, are […] 'messy', difficult, contingent and open to contested interpretations and applications."[16] These interpretations and applications are forms of resistance against the separation of public spaces for the creation of enclosed elite spaces, for example high quality infrastructure for fast transportation that is available to urban elites but excludes the ordinary dwellers.[17] Castells states: "While the space of flows has been created by and around dominant activities and social groups, it can be penetrated by resistance, and diversified in its meaning."[18] This resistance takes shape in the agency of the ordinary people, who by their everyday spatial practice convert and thereby reappropriate spaces for their own purposes.[19]

With these considerations as starting point, we chose to make a densely populated inner-city commercial area – Begum Bazaar in the South Indian city of Hyderabad – the object of our study on the urban commons. Such localities, characterized by a multiplicity of uses that take place in the street, can be found in any Indian city, varying in size and density. They build a sharp contrast to the neatly separated uses and functions of modern residential neighborhoods and high-tech districts.

Local space in the globalizing city of Hyderabad

The urban landscape of Hyderabad, as in many South Asian cities, has experienced a profound change. In the late 1990s, the government of the former state of Andhra Pradesh adopted an economic growth strategy that focused on global growth sectors of IT and the development of infrastructure.[20] The restructuring of the city has produced two different poles of urban reality within close proximity of each other but socially and economically far apart: The high-rise residential buildings and malls of Cyberabad in contrast to the Old City of Hyderabad. The expansion of private-sector involvement into financing, building, and maintaining urban infrastructure has played a crucial role in realizing policy-makers' vision of Hyderabad as a "world-class city."[21] This development was accompanied by reforms in urban governance and expansion of private-sector involvement in formerly public services such as administration, education, and health care.[22] It can be concluded that regional politics and planning have been "redirected to accommodate new globally mobile populations while neglecting the needs of established communities of Hyderabad."[23]

Particularly the restructuring of the transportation infrastructure has been a key component of Hyderabad's economic development strategy. Like in most Indian cities, recent development of transportation infrastructure has mainly focused on the needs of private motorized transportation.[24] Highways, flyovers, and the vehicles themselves are now a dominant characteristic of every Indian city. Referring to post-war Germany, Katharina Manderscheid has called automobility the "hegemonic dispositif of spatial constitution."[25] This observation can also be made for present-day urban India.

The dominance of the private motorized vehicle has drastic implications for urban societies. Large parts of urban space prioritize fast transportation, some even exclude non-motorized forms of mobility. Thus, spaces of slow mobility and spaces that are used for other activities vanish. Those who socially and economically depend on the use of street space are denied access to it. This observation makes clear that "roads not only connect but also disconnect populations, citizens and subjects."[26] However, in many parts of the city, street space is still a shared space, where the conditions for free movement of cars and larger transportation vehicles are limited.

Begum Bazaar, a historic wholesale market area in the centre of Hyderabad, is such a place. It was established in the eighteenth century by merchants who migrated from northern India to Hyderabad.[27] Since then, Begum Bazaar has been and still is attracting migrants from all over India. In the last hundred years, the street layout has not considerably changed, as historical maps indicate,[28] but over the last decade many old buildings of two or three stories have been replaced by new ones with up to six stories. The ground floors of the buildings are mostly occupied by wholesale and retail businesses, with small storefronts towards the streets. The upper floors are used for storage of goods and as residential space. In the narrow streets, vending activities and the provision of repair services are widespread.

Figure 1. Private vehicles do not match the spatial dimensions of the narrow streets in the market area, thus drivers have a tough time when moving in Begum Bazaar.

The street vendors and service providers build the basis for the local supply of residents, retail and wholesale customers, shop owners, and employees. Apart from these economic activities, many social, cultural, and political activities regularly take place in the street. Walking is still the dominant form of moving inside the market area, followed by motorized scooters and bicycles. Goods are mostly transported by unmotorized tricycles and small motor rickshaws, while private vehicles are yet relatively rare.

Conceptualizing the commons

How can the commons of urban space be conceptualized in the case of a particular locality in an Indian city? And how do the commons become effective as a mode of resistance against incorporation into the circuits of neoliberal capitalism?

The commons of urban space do not exist a priori, but are created in a very particular relationship between a group of people and its environment. Thus, instead of analyzing the product – the commons – we shift the perspective towards how this particular relationship is established in a "social practice of commoning."[29] Building upon Lefebvre and his theory about the production of space,[30] we argue that it is essentially a process involving three modes of spatial production: 1) the practices of everyday life as "specific spatial competence and performance"[31] based on the perception and appropriation of physical space, 2) the abstraction and conceptualization of space and the negotiation of different concepts of space, and 3) the lived space, which implies the production of meaning by "making symbolic use"[32] of the objects of physical space.

Furthermore, we consider physical street space of the locality of Begum Bazaar as the material starting point of our analysis about how urban commons have been historically shaped by the practice of appropriating spaces, negotiating different concepts of space, and making meaning of space. Street space in this particular setting is an economic resource and bearer of social protection and embeddedness that counteracts the multiple forms of capitalist enclosure of space as a *defensive common*.

However, we argue that the commons of defense are not a commons of social change, i.e. a framework for the empowerment of the poor. It is a "common without community"[33] that does not necessarily create a just city, just like other practices of resistance that are initiated by or involve the poor, such as insurgent citizenship, do not necessarily create a just city.[34]

Spatial practice: Appropriation of physical space[35]

Street space is a scarce and hence very valuable resource in Begum Bazaar. Almost every economic activity in the area depends on the availability of street space. This dependence is either direct or indirect: street vendors, goods carriers, cattle drovers, waste pickers, and other laborers physically operate in street space, thus are directly involved in negotiations about the use of space. When the possibility to use street space is lost, more effort is needed to generate income. Others, especially the business owners, do not directly interfere in the negotiations about space. However, their businesses largely depend on services such as the transportation of goods which are carried out in open space.

As street space in general is accessible to everyone, the streets of Begum Bazaar are also a resource that can be used by everyone. Those wanting to appropriate space need to arrange their claims with those of others. In the following, four major mechanisms are analyzed more closely: appropriation by a) transferring and inheriting the right to use space, b) negotiation, c) state complicity and disobedience, and d) religious practice and political representation.

Appropriation by transferring and inheriting the right to use space

In her research about access to street space in Dhaka, Kirsten Hackenbroch has pointed out that affiliation to a family or a specific tribal, caste, or religious association enables members of these families or associations to access space.[36] The permission to use certain spaces is granted by heads of families or leaders of associations in oral agreements. Similar mechanisms can be observed in Begum Bazaar. The process of transferring and inheriting the right to use spaces is rooted in Begum Bazaar's long history of migration. The businesses that were established by migrants were mostly family enterprises, employing family members in executive positions.[37] Thereby income opportunities for future generations were created, i.e. for migrants that settled later in Begum Bazaar from the same geographical origin or similar religious or caste background.[38] Still today, networks of distinct families, castes, religions, or geographical origins play an important role, as the example of a tea vendor illustrates:

> The shop is here since 1983, from Indira Gandhi's time there is the permission. I got the shop fifteen years ago from a man in my village in Karnataka, where I stayed before I came to Hyderabad. He had died and so I took the chance and succeeded him.[39]

Another street vendor, originally from Pune, gained permission to use a spot by drawing on his religious affiliation:

> With the help of the community[40] president I chose this place here. We have our own Ganesh celebration here, Ganesh is important for people from Pune. I requested the president, and I got the place.[41]

Inherited or granted rights to use a certain spot in the area are often the basis for business or livelihood activities. In this case, appropriation of space is relatively uncontested and a regular income is secured. Vendors do not need to negotiate occupation of "their" spot with other potential appropriators on a daily basis. To further manifest the right to appropriate a certain spot, vendors build fixed and stable stalls that are not removed during the night.

Appropriation by negotiation

In case the right to use space is not transferred or granted in oral agreements, access to space is negotiated among users. Actors who start to engage in street vending or in the transportation of goods most certainly invade spaces that someone else has already claimed. Thus the appropriation of space is conflictual, as shown in the case of a street vendor who refused to let another street vendor establish a vending cart next to his business:

> There is a man here selling plastic toys for eight days now. I daily tell him to leave, but he comes back daily. I already threw his things on the street once.[42]

Although evicted at first, new actors can try to come to an arrangement, as the example of another street vendor shows. Initially he placed his stall in front of a shop with a large storefront. The owner of the shop forced him to leave the spot because he perceived the stall as a disturbance during business hours with high customer frequency.[43] In order to avoid conflict with the shop owner, the street vendor decided to place his cart at the right margin of the shop's front and only in the evenings, thereby achieving limited and less favorable but nevertheless regular access to space:

> The shop here has some objection that I put my vending cart here. I don't come in the morning, only in the evenings. In other daytimes I am moving in the streets. I don't need to give money to him, it is just an understanding.[44]

The case of a tricycle driver shows that, in case regular access to space could not yet be established, additional effort needs to be employed to generate income:

> I am the new one, so most of the shop owners don't want that I place my rickshaw in front of their shops. I go around in the street, that's how I get my orders. The other drivers have been working here for a very long time that's why no one can object [to] them.[45]

Appropriation by state complicity and disobedience

Formal regulations for street vending exist[46] but are not strictly executed.[47] Nevertheless, arrangements need to be made to cope with these regulations because the threat of unexpected police inspections, raids, and evictions always exists, as several interviewees indicated. The usual way to avoid this and secure undisturbed activity is paying bribes to the police or city officials.[48] Coordination and operation of livelihood activities proceed "in an environment of state complicity,"[49] thus are

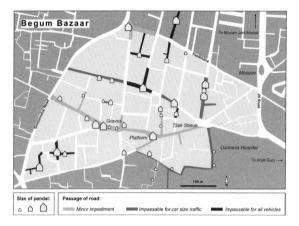

Figure 2. One of the most ecstatically celebrated festivals in Begum Bazaar, Ganesh Chaturthi, lasts eleven days. Temporary wooden temples (pandals) are erected in many streets and block junctions, which forces traffic to take alternative routes for almost three weeks.

not conducted "outside the state," but are linked to the state in a "hybrid relation, [...] permeating each other in [...] the production of space."[50]

Apart from bribing, there may be further rules that vendors need to follow, as an entrepreneur who owns two food stalls in Begum Bazaar explains:

> I am here daily 3.30pm–12pm. I manage[51] the traffic police. But at this spot they do not allow me to place my food stall before 3.30pm, because in the morning VIPs – ministers and judges – drive down on JN Road. I do not take any risk.[52]

Other actors handle regulations by disobeying or ignoring them. Although shop owners are not allowed to use street space in front of their shops to display goods, as this reduces space for parking and the movement of vehicles in narrow streets, it is common practice to do so. "There is no use to raise fines against the shop owners, the goods are out on the street again in the next morning."[53]

Appropriation by religious and political representation

Street spaces are frequently appropriated for political, religious, and other cultural performances and representations. Two modes of appropriation can be distinguished: one that alters physical space permanently due to the construction of buildings, and one that shapes spaces temporarily as happens during religious festivals or political rallies. The building of temples, mosques, and other religious

Figure 3. The pandals of Ganesh Chaturthi change the physical landscape and the perception of spatial relations.

structures is often an incremental process that involves the appropriation of street space and is often accompanied by negotiations and conflicts between religious groups and the state.[54] The construction of religious buildings is, on the one hand, an expression of people's desire to perform their religious duties close to where they live and work, and, on the other hand, marks the respective territories of the religious groups' influence.[55]

Temporal forms of spatial appropriation are religious festivals, functions, worship ceremonies *(pujas)* and specific parts of wedding celebrations (the *baraatis*). They are performed in public and use parts of the streets for a certain period of time (see Figure 3). Evidence from the interviews indicates that these appropriations of street space are largely approved in Begum Bazaar as most of them are long established practices.[56]

Interim conclusion: The rhythms of the market

The above analysis of four mechanisms of spatial appropriation shows that these mechanisms should not be seen as ruling each other out. Rather they can be or must be combined by actors who want to use street space. Comparatively few actors possess the privilege to occupy a fixed spot during the whole day. A road corner can be occupied by two or three different users or user groups during the day, for example for cattle feeding in the morning, for parked vehicles at noon and for food vending in the afternoon and evening.

These daily rhythms illustrate an important principle of the kind of commons we propose here: the mechanisms described above allow a maximum of users to make use of physical space for one purpose or another. They do not demarcate strict territorial boundaries or rely on particular groups as the sole appropriators of space, both considered inevitable by Elinor Ostrom to create successful commons.[57] Rather these mechanisms constitute a hierarchy among the appropriators, determining access to the most beneficial positions in space. The appropriation of physical space, as the first dimension of the process of commoning, is thus a collective, but highly hierarchical sphere.

In the following subchapter we discuss how space is conceived by actors who operate in street space, and how these concepts interfere with spatial rationalities that are imposed by actors who operate "outside" the market area.

Abstraction of space: Negotiating different concepts of space

As the use of physical space is contested and negotiated, different concepts and notions of space also challenge each other. People's notions of street space are not necessarily of universally accessible and open public space, as such an understanding is based on a "particular configuration of commonness that emerged in the capitalist-democratic West."[58] Before the idea of public space was introduced into colonial India by the British administration,[59] the outside world was perceived as inhospitable in contrast to the security and purity of the home environment, a distinction that was especially relevant for members of higher caste.[60] This perception was reinforced in colonial times as the outside was the dominant sphere of the colonial ruler.[61] However, parts of the urban middle class have been responsive to the modern colonial city and its promise of freedom.[62] Considering this historic evolution, a consensus about a universal notion of space in the Indian city is impossible. The concept of public space is only one of many different notions of space.

Today, the modes of appropriating street space described above are in conflict with the state's project to create regularized and formalized public spaces which allow a separation of uses and undisturbed movement of vehicles and people. A commercial environment like Begum Bazaar is perceived as chaotic by the city administration. The planning agencies respond to this by issuing new spatial restrictions for street vendors[63] and zoning regulations,[64] which are counteracted by users of street spaces who disobey or circumvent these rules as described above. Similar opposition can be observed in the case of traffic regulations. An attempt to regulate traffic and improve access for motorized vehicles by implementing a one-way regulation was thwarted by shopkeepers and eventually aborted after one week.[65] Furthermore, the cellar spaces in new buildings are often not used to provide parking space – as mandated by the building permit – but are leased as commercial space. These practices can be seen as a denial of rules that are not produced locally. But Kaviraj suggests they have also "conceptual implications," meaning that people have different conceptions of space: those who impose the rules have the concept of a modern, orderly, and civilized city, while others violate these rules because they have a different concept of space.[66] The act of disobedience thus means a denial of representations of space in the form of "ideal totalities" as they are created by technocrats, urban planners, and architects.[67]

The process of negotiating different abstractions of space is a crucial component of the practice of commoning. Although not the concerted effort of a particular group, it is a collective effort to oppose concepts of space that aim to enclose spaces for the use of global capitalist exploitation.

The lived space: Micro-spaces of social significance

The third dimension of commoning is the production of meaning. The process of establishing and maintaining access to space requires constant communication, interaction, and reaction. These actions create *micro-spaces of social significance:* distinct local settings that embed the actors as active subjects and provide protection and security through small networks of dependencies, responsibilities, and solidarities. For Harvey, such settings constitute the social quality of the city: "through their daily activities and struggles, individuals and social groups create the social world of the city, and thereby create something common as a framework within which all can dwell."⁶⁸

These micro-spaces of significance are constituted around the materialities that have evolved from the appropriation of physical space, for example a tea, cigarette, or food stall. They exist at almost every street corner in the bazaar. Each of these stalls is the anchor for a social network and creates a social space around it. Different stalls attract different groups of individuals, also at different times of the day. For example, a specific tobacco stall is mostly frequented by rickshaw drivers who park their vehicles nearby. During their breaks they linger at the stalls, drink tea, smoke, and chat. These customers come regularly and visit the stall several times a day. Thus the core of a social space consists of a small group of people – the vendors, regular customers, friends – whose claim to occupy a certain place is relatively uncontested. However, the social delimitations of these micro-spaces are dynamic. People can enter them by establishing a relationship with the core group. When asked about the character of these relationships, the interviewees used terms in Telugu, Hindi or Urdu that can be most adequately subsumed under the word "familiarity." These terms denote a close acquaintanceship with another person or group of people that is established over a period of time and is connoted with reliability and trustworthiness. The actors thus develop a very specific personal knowledge about who to cooperate, interact, and do business with. One owner of a tobacco stall termed these relationships as "somewhat friends."⁶⁹

The third process of commoning illustrates that cooperation for producing the commons is not only aimed at organizing a particular resource for economic reasons. The production of a sense of social belonging as well as a social form of control – seen from the neighborhood perspective – is a crucial element of the commons we describe here.

The defensive common

Commoning, we have argued, is a process of spatial production that consists of appropriation of physical space, negotiation of different concepts of space, and the production of social meaning. The dynamic process of material and social inclusion and the constant negotiations on the boundaries of spaces have created a collective and non-commodified common. This common forms a reliable platform for acting and surviving in the streets. From the perspective of governance and macro-planning, this spatiality is a challenge because the ephemeral arrangements, the alterations between mobility and immobility, and the involvement of a multiplicity of different actors cannot be controlled. This spatiality is illegible to those who understand urban space as an abstract concept, i.e. a generalized and totalized idea of space, but neglect spatial practice and the lived space. This illegibility makes the commons less penetrable by external macro-forces such as masterplanning, automobilization, and commodification. Furthermore, these commons literally leave no "room" for the macro-enclosures of neoliberal urban politics that seek to restructure the city by putting spaces in order and "purifying" them. In their physical dimension, these commons inhibit the invasion of private motorized vehicles in the area, withstanding the takeover of street space for the prime use of (private) mobility. In the abstract dimension, they are a form of resistance against the constitution of "automobile landscapes" that the hegemonic practice of motorized mobility has already created outside the market area.[70]

Furthermore, the defensive common can be sustained in the long run without official recognition by the state. This contrasts with Ostrom's principle that, for a successful common, governments need to acknowledge the rule-making right of other actors as legitimate.[71] But the practices of everyday spatial appropriation involve occupation of private and public land that is considered illegal by law in most of the Global South. Consequently, these practices cannot be officially recognized as legitimate by the state; if they were officially recognized, the system of legally held property and concepts of citizenship would be threatened.[72] However, spatial claims are often de facto acknowledged by the state.[73]

From defensive commons to the commons of equity?

The defensive commons of Begum Bazaar are strongly hierarchical and consolidate long-established power structures and social inequalities. As illustrated, local elites, i.e. the leaders of religious or caste associations, organize access to space to a certain degree by employing their powers and thereby advantaging certain individuals while disadvantaging others. Hence, these commons miss the aspiration for empowerment and change towards "deep democracy" that would empower the urban poor.[74] For example, the poorest in Begum Bazaar, impoverished rural migrants working as waste pickers, have almost no possibility for upward social mobility due to their occupation.[75] The amount of time and physical labor they need to invest in order to secure their survival is much higher than of others. Furthermore, it is also they who are most deprived by environmental degradation such as noise, air, and water pollution.

How can the specific qualities of the defensive commons be utilized in a way that empowers the urban poor in their claims for recognition, equity, and participation? The path towards "deep democracy" requires forms of horizontal exchange and learning across localities,[76] possibly in the form of the "nested enterprises" that Elinor Ostrom proposes.[77] But also forms of vertical exchange and learning are required: the inherent knowledge of spatial practice needs to respond to the instruments that are employed by the state in order to restructure the urban landscape and mitigate the current urban crisis. These instruments – formalization, restriction, division of functions up to eviction, dispossession, and dislocation – are based on experts' totalitarian and simplified conceptions of space. Nevertheless, expert knowledge of formal urban planning and governance legitimates enforcement of these instruments, often without consideration or proper knowledge of actual spatial practice and the lived space.[78] That these concepts are perceived as legitimate and others are not illustrates that "in modern life, the mental field dominates over others."[79] "For an 'urban revolution', such an ideological component should be uncovered and the actual interdependence between mental field and spatial practice strengthened."[80] A deep understanding of this interdependence is certainly an important element of an ethic of the commons that is aware of social injustice and refuses to create new forms.

Notes

1. Vinay Gidwani and Amita Baviskar, "Urban Commons," *Economic & Political Weekly* 46, no. 50 (2011): 42; Anant Maringanti, "No Estoppel: Claiming Right to the City via the Commons," *Economic & Political Weekly* 46, no. 50 (2011): 65.
2. Kirsten Hackenbroch, *The Spatiality of Livelihoods: Negotiations of Access to Public Space in Dhaka, Bangladesh* (Stuttgart: Franz Steiner Verlag, 2013), 31.
3. Ibid., 31–32.
4. David Harvey, *Rebel Cities: From the Right to the City to the Urban Revolution* (London: Verso Books, 2012), 73.

5. Elinor Ostrom, *Governing the Commons: the Evolution of Institutions for Collective Action* (New York: Cambridge University Press, 1990), 90–102.
6. For a reconsideration of *place* see for example Henrike Donner and Geert De Neve, "Space, Place and Globalisation," in *The Meaning of the Local: Politics of Place in Urban India,* Henrike Donner and Geert De Neve, eds. (New York: UCL Press, 2006). Recent preoccupation with urban social processes and everyday practice has been fueled by the concept of Urban Assemblage, see for example Colin McFarlane, *Learning the City: Knowledge and Translocal Assemblage* (Hoboken: John Wiley & Sons, 2011). For a critique see Neil Brenner, "Theses on Urbanization," *Public Culture* 25, no. 1 (2013): 85–114.
7. Arturo Escobar, "Culture Sits in Places: Reflections on Globalism and Subaltern Strategies of Localization," *Political Geography* 20, no. 2 (2001): 170.
8. Jonathan Shapiro Anjaria and Colin McFarlane, "Conceptualising the City in South Asia," in *Urban Navigations: Politics, Space and the City in South Asia,* Jonathan Shapiro Anjaria and Colin McFarlane, eds. (New Delhi: Routledge, 2011), 7.
9. AbdouMaliq Simone, "People as Infrastructure: Intersecting Fragments in Johannesburg," *Public Culture* 16, no. 3 (2004): 407.
10. Ibid., 408.
11. Ibid.
12. Ibid., 410.
13. Ibid., 427.
14. Swati Chattopadhyay, *Unlearning the City* (Minneapolis: University of Minnesota Press, 2012), 248.
15. Simone, "People as Infrastructure," 408.
16. Stephen Graham and Simon Marvin, *Splintering Urbanism: Networked Infrastructures, Technological Mobilities and the Urban Condition* (London/New York: Routledge, 2001), 388.
17. Ibid., 34–35, 281–284.
18. Manuel Castells, "Grassrooting the Space of Flows," *Urban Geography* 20, no. 4 (1999): 297; cited in Graham and Marvin, *Splintering Urbanism,* 388.
19. Michel de Certeau, *The Practice of Everyday Life* (Berkeley / Los Angeles: University of California Press, 1984), 96. Like AbdouMaliq Simone, de Certeau highlights that these spatial tactics remain largely invisible to the authorities. James C. Scott argues that invisibility is a strategy of spatial politics in itself. These *infrapolitics* have the logic "to leave few traces in the wake of its passage. By covering its tracks it [...] minimizes the risks its practitioners run." James C. Scott, *Domination and the Arts of Resistance: Hidden Transcripts* (New Haven: Yale University Press, 1990), 200.
20. Loraine Kennedy, "New Forms of Governance in Hyderabad: How Urban Reforms are Redefining Actors in the City," in *New Forms of Urban Governance in India: Shifts, Models, Networks and Contestations,* Isabelle Suzanne Antoinette Baud and Joop De Wit, eds. (New Delhi: Sage, 2008), 257.
21. Loraine Kennedy, "Regional Industrial Policies Driving Peri-Urban Dynamics in Hyderabad, India," *Cities* 24, no. 2 (2007): 100.
22. Sangeeta Kamat, "Neoliberalism, Urbanism and the Education Economy: Producing Hyderabad as a 'Global City'," *Discourse: Studies in the Cultural Politics of Education* 32, no. 2 (2011): 194–195; N. Purendra Prasad and P. Raghavendra, "Healthcare Models in the Era of Medical Neo-Liberalism," *Economic & Political Weekly* 47, no. 43 (2012): 119; Kennedy, "New Forms of Governance in Hyderabad," 257, 267.
23. Kamat, "Neoliberalism, Urbanism and the Education Economy," 188.
24. Madhav G. Badhami, "The Urban Transport Challenge in India: Considerations, Implications and Strategies*," International Development Planning Review* 27, no. 2 (2005): 178; Angela Jain et al., *Participative Processes in the Field of Traffic and Transport (*Bremen: Europäischer Hochschulverlag, 2013), 2–4.

25   Katharina Manderscheid, "Automobilität als raumkonstituierendes Dispositiv der Moderne," in *Die Ordnung der Räume,* Henning Füller and Boris Michel, eds. (Münster: Westfälisches Dampfboot, 2012), 168.
26   Nikhil Anand, "Disconnecting Experience: Making World-Class Roads in Mumbai," *Economic and Political Weekly* 41, no. 31 (2006): 3422.
27   Early migrants were most notably Marwaris, Agarwals, Jains, and Goswamis, who were encouraged by the rulers of Hyderabad to settle here (Karen Leonard, "From Goswami Rajas to Goswami Caste in Hyderabad," *Contributions to Indian Sociology* 47, no. 1 (2013): 2; Alka Patel, "Mercantile Architectural Patronage in Hyderabad, late 18th–19th Centuries," in *Indo-Muslim Cultures in Transition,* Alka Patel and Karen Leonard, eds. (Leiden: Brill, 2012), 142.
28   Leonard Munn, "Sheet no. 4, City Area," digitized content from the MIT Libraries' Collection, 1915, http://dome.mit.edu/handle/1721.3/45464 (accessed Aug 22, 2013).
29   Harvey, *Rebel Cities,* 73.
30   Henri Lefebvre, *The Production of Space* (Oxford: Blackwell, 1991), 36–39.
31   Ibid., 38.
32   Ibid., 39.
33   Maringanti, "No Estoppel: Claiming Right to the City via the Commons," 66.
34   Ananya Roy, "Why India Cannot Plan its Cities: Informality, Insurgence, and the Idiom of Urbanization," *Planning Theory* 8, no. 1 (2009): 85–86.
35   The data used for this paper was collected during a seven-month period of field work in Hyderabad from August 2012 until February 2013. Multiple methods were employed, including narrative interviews with inhabitants, street vendors, business owners, rickshaw drivers, and so on; expert interviews with representatives of the city authorities; mapping, rhythm analysis, and observation accompanied by many informal discussions and conversations. At the end of the research period a public exhibition was conducted in the street about the negotiation of street space. This intervention revealed further useful insight about how space is organized and conceptualized and which strategies the actors employ.
36   Hackenbroch, *Spatiality of Livelihoods,* 255–257, 259–262.
37   Karen Leonard, "Family Firms in Hyderabad: Gujarati, Goswami, and Marwari Patterns of Adoption, Marriage, and Inheritance," *Comparative Studies in Society and History* 53, no. 4 (2011): 830–831.
38   Karen Leonard, "The Hyderabad Political System and its Participants," *The Journal of Asian Studies* 30, no. 3 (1971): 574.
39   Interview with Tea Vendor from Karnataka, October 25, 2012.
40   "Community" is used here in the sense of religious or caste association.
41   Interview with Vendor of Sugar Cane Juice, October 28, 2012.
42   Interview with Street Vendor selling Shopping Bags, November 7, 2012.
43   Interview with Owner of Vessel Shop 1, November 8, 2012.
44   Interview with Street Vendor of Corn, November 15, 2012.
45   Interview with Tricycle Driver, November 25, 2012.
46   Greater Hyderabad Municipal Corporation (GHMC), "Policy on Simplification of Regulation of Street Vending/Hawking in MCH area," *Hyderabad: GHMC,* 2006. http://www.ghmc.gov.in/approvedplans/hawkers_notification.pdf (accessed Aug 22, 2013).
47   Information about the frequency of police patrolling in the area from the interviewees differs considerably, but there were no reports about recent evictions or raids.
48   Jonathan Shapiro Anjaria, "Street Hawkers and Public Space in Mumbai," *Economic and Political Weekly* 41, no. 21 (2006): 2140–2144; Ritajyoti Bandyopadhyay, "Hawkers' Movement in Kolkata, 1975–2007," *Economic and Political Weekly* 44, no. 17 (2009): 119; Sharit Bhowmik, "Legal Protection for Street Ven-

49. Kate Meagher, "Crisis, Informalization and the Urban Informal Sector in Sub-Saharan Africa," *Development and Change* 26, no. 2 (1995): 277.
50. Kirsten Hackenbroch, "Urban Informality and Negotiated Space: Negotiations of Access to Public Space in Dhaka, Bangladesh," *disP – The Planning Review* 47, no. 187 (2011): 60.
51. This expression used by several street vending entrepreneurs in the interviews to circumscribe the practice of paying bribes.
52. Interview with Owner of two Dosa Stalls at JN Road, November 8, 2012.
53. Interview with Additional Director Heritage and Conservation to Greater Hyderabad Municipal Corporation, February 25, 2013.
54. Achyut Yagnik, *Communal Riots in Hyderabad – What the People Say* (Ahmedabad: SETU Centre for Social Knowledge and Action, 1984), 13; Ursula Rao, "Contested Spaces. Temple Building and the Re-creation of Religious Boundaries in Contemporary Urban India," in *On the Margins of Religion*, Frances Pine and Joao Pina-Cabral, eds. (Oxford: Berghahn, 2008), 82–83.
55. Rao, "Contested Spaces. Temple Building and the Recreation of Religious Boundaries in Contemporary Urban India," 83.
56. However, there are indicators that the spatial practice of religious groups is one of the reasons for recurring conflicts between these groups, see Ratna Naidu, *Old Cities, New Predicaments: A Study of Hyderabad* (New Delhi: Sage Publications, 1990), 205–206 and Sudhir Kakar, *The Colors of Violence: Cultural Identities, Religion, and Conflict* (Chicago: University of Chicago Press, 1996), 13–14.
57. Ostrom, *Governing the Commons*, 90–91.
58. Sudipta Kaviraj, "Filth and the Public Sphere: Concepts and Practices about Space in Calcutta," *Public Culture* 10, no. 1 (1997): 86.
59. William J. Glover, "Construing Urban Space as 'Public' in Colonial India: Some Notes from the Punjab," *Journal of Punjab Studies* 14, no. 2 (2007): 212.
60. Sara Dickey, "Permeable Homes: Domestic Service, Household Space, and the Vulnerability of Class Boundaries in Urban India," *American Ethnologist* 27, no. 2 (2000): 470.
61. Partha Chatterjee, *The Nation and its Fragments: Colonial and Postcolonial Histories* (Princeton: Princeton University Press, 1993), 121.
62. Kaviraj, "Filth and the Public Sphere," 94.
63. Greater Hyderabad Municipal Corporation (GHMC), "Policy on Simplification of Regulation of Street Vending/Hawking in MCH area," *Hyderabad: GHMC*, 2006; http://www.ghmc.gov.in/approvedplans/hawkers_notification.pdf (accessed Aug 22, 2013).
64. Hyderabad Metropolitan Development Authority (HMDA), "Metropolitan Development Plan-2031 for Hyderabad Metropolitan Region," *Hyderabad: HMDA*, 2013; http://220.227.252.236/ehmr/PDFDownload/45X42_1,00,000%20scale%20PLU.pdf (accessed Aug 22, 2013).
65. Interview with Street Vendor of Shopping Bags, November 7, 2012 and Interview with Owner of Vessel Shop 2, November 19, 2012.
66. Kaviraj, "Filth and the Public Sphere," 84.
67. Elisa T. Bertuzzo, *Fragmented Dhaka: Analysing Everyday Life with Henri Lefebvre's Theory of Production of Space* (Stuttgart: Franz Steiner Verlag, 2009), 31.
68. Harvey, *Rebel Cities*, 75.
69. Interview with Owner of Paan Stall, November 2, 2012.
70. Manderscheid, "Automobilität als raumkonstituierendes Dispositiv der Moderne," 159.
71. Ostrom, *Governing the Commons*, 101.

72 Partha Chatterjee, *The Politics of the Governed: Reflections on Popular Politics in Most of the World* (New York: Columbia University Press, 2004), 136–137.
73 This can happen for a multiplicity of reasons, e.g. because of fragmented rationalities of state institutions (see Seth Schindler, "A New Delhi Every Day: Multiplicities of Governance Regimes in a Transforming Metropolis," *Urban Geography* 35, no. 3 (2014): 404).
74 Arjun Appadurai, "Deep Democracy: Urban Governmentality and the Horizon of Politics," *Environment and Urbanization* 13, no. 2 (2001): 42–43.
75 Marijk Huysman, "Waste Picking as a Survival Strategy for Women in Indian Cities," *Environment and Urbanization* 6, no. 2 (1994): 155.
76 Appadurai, "Deep Democracy: Urban Governmentality and the Horizon of Politics," 42.
77 Ostrom, *Governing the Commons,* 101.
78 Clearly, these instruments have also been used purposely by state agencies to transfer prime land to real-estate firms and project developers for surplus extraction, see, among others, Swapna Banerjee-Guha, "Revisiting Accumulation by Dispossession: Neoliberalising Mumbai," in *Accumulation by Dispossession. Transformative Cities in the New Global Order,* Swapna Banerjee-Guha, ed. (Los Angeles: Sage, 2010), 214–216; and Solomon Benjamin, "Occupancy Urbanism: Radicalizing Politics and Economy beyond Policy and Programs," *International Journal of Urban and Regional Research* 32, no. 3 (2008): 721.
79 Bertuzzo, *Fragmented Dhaka,* 31.
80 Ibid.

Didi K. Han, Hajime Imamasa

Overcoming Privatized Housing in South Korea: Looking through the Lens of "Commons" and "the Common"

Introduction

Bin-Zib is an urban commoning movement based in Seoul, South Korea. It was founded seven years ago when three former student activists in their early thirties decided to create an urban community fundamentally opposed to the notion of the house as private property. Sharing a three-bedroom apartment with others, the activists envisioned a house in which all residents, regardless of their length of stay, including themselves, are regarded as "guests." The name *Bin-Zib,* doubly signifying "empty house" and/or "guests' house" in Korean, was coined to represent the community's radical openness and unconditional hospitality. *Bin-Zib* has grown considerably in size as well as influence: today they operate a network of houses, a community café, and a community bank supporting not only *Bin-Zib* but also other alternative communities in and outside of Seoul. In the following pages, we first present a brief historical overview of urbanization centered around Seoul and the development of *Bin-Zib*. Then we examine *Bin-Zib* through the lens of "commons" and "the common," trying to understand how *Bin-Zib* operates. Finally, we discuss *Bin-Zib* as an attempt to devise a new usage for the city, and create different values and relations in order to live together with others.[1]

Seoul's urban expansion and *Bin-Zib*[2]

With a population of twenty-five million, the greater metropolitan area surrounding Seoul is home to fifty percent of the entire population of the country.[3] Although Korea was an agrarian nation merely a few decades ago, today urbanity has become the general condition of the country. The countless high-rise apartment complexes towering over the land testify to this. However, perhaps more significant is the way in which these apartments tower over people's lives. The apartments have become not only the commonly coveted housing form but also the most tradable commodity based on their investment value.

The development of apartments was initiated by the state and state-sponsored conglomerates in response to the shortage of housing that the city encountered as rapid industrialization caused explosive urban population growth. According to Kwak, the influx of rural migrants created expansive shanty towns in Seoul, and its population grew from 3,250,000 in 1963 to more than ten million in 1998.[4] While large-scale apartment projects provide housing to the emerging middle class, the bulldozing of the slums that made this construction possible exposed the brutal realities of South Korean society.

Neoliberalism has taken root in South Korea in the years following the IMF-mandated restructuring of South Korean economy in 1997.[5] The function of the metropolis as the economic dynamo of the country has shifted its focus away from manufacturing to the financialization of land and housing.[6] While the construction of apartment complexes in the 1980s had more to do with providing desirable, modern middle-class housing for the protagonists of the Fordist economy, the massive redevelopment projects that built more luxurious apartment buildings in the capital area in the years following 1997 were concerned with their investment value. Speculative investment in real estate in Korea has caused a serious housing problem in Seoul. From 1963 to 2007, the land prices of Seoul rose 1,176 times, whereas the price of consumption products rose forty-three times, and actual income of city workers increased only fifteen times.[7] While this trend has benefitted property owners, it has made urban living excruciatingly difficult for poor renters. Before the 1990s, lower income groups lived in shanty towns or old neighborhoods, where people were able to rely on the social relations found in their community to address, however inadequately, the general conditions of economic poverty. Most of these communities, however, no longer exist. Since the late 1980s, residential space for the poor has become invisible and fragmented in Seoul, depriving the urban poor not only of economic needs but also social relations.[8] More than 200,000 people in Seoul are unable to afford the rent for adequate housing, residing instead in precarious places.

It was against this backdrop that three former student activists in their early thirties started a communal living experiment in the middle of Seoul in 2008. They rented an apartment and communalized it, inviting other people to live there without claiming exclusive rights to the *jeonse* (key money) that they had paid to acquire the house.[9] To raise the $120,000 in key money used to rent the place, they collected

$40,000 among themselves and took out a loan for the remaining $80,000. Everyone paid an equal amount of *bundamgeum* (shared expenses), regardless of how much (if any) they contributed to the key money fund.[10] This financial arrangement, initially made among activism-minded friends, also reflected their Marxian vision to create the common, to which the residents would contribute according to their abilities and/or will.

As the number of 'guests' increased, so did the number of rented houses. Three more *Bin-Zib*s were set up within a year. The commoning effort of *Bin-Zib* expanded in scale, with the establishment of two communal sub-entities or institutional components. The first of these was a communal fund/bank named *Bin-Go*. Not limiting its membership to the residents of *Bin-Zib*, *Bin-Go* receives funding from anyone who agrees with the basic values of *Bin-Zib*, grants loans to *Bin-Zib* houses, and adjusts the amount of shared expenses between the houses accordingly.

In the operation of *Bin-Go*, a person who puts her money in *Bin-Go* earns 3 percent interest in her account.[11] *Bin-Go* then grants loans to each house at 6 percent interest. The remaining 3 percent interest is then utilized as a shared fund for setting up more *Bin-Zib*s, as well as supporting social movements and like-minded communities. Most importantly, *Bin-Go* was able to create a situation in which every member of *Bin-Zib* had the same rights regardless of how much money the person contributed. This also helped *Bin-Zib* develop resilience against various fiscal problems. One resident put it succinctly: "even though people are continuously moving in and out, and housing contracts are also being made and terminated, we've been able to deal with fiscal problems smoothly through *Bin-Go*."[12]

The other institution of *Bin-Zib* is a coffee shop named *Bin*-Café. Several long-term residents of *Bin-Zib* established it in 2010 as a space to generate fun and creative activities while earning money. Although the initial proposal failed to get community-wide support on economic grounds, the minority persisted and created the shop. Today, *Bin*-Café functions as a nodal point for the *Bin-Zib* community and the surrounding neighborhood. The shop serves customers, who may be either *Bin-Zib* residents or non-residents, just like any other neighborhood café. It also provides a venue for social events, from small meetings to seminars and conferences. Some of these events, such as flea markets and festivals, have brought in participation from local residents and shopkeepers in the neighborhood.

Over time, the experiment that began with one apartment has grown into a village with approximately fifty long-term guests residing in eight houses. At present,

Bin-Go, with net assets of $240,000 collected from more than 200 members, supports eight *Bin-Zibs,* a co-op café run by *Bin-Zib* residents, and five communities outside of Seoul with similar if not identical orientations toward sharing the house as a commons. Thus, not only has *Bin-Zib* been able to thrive in the neighborhood, they have also expanded to include networks with communities and movements in other cities and regions without the centralizing effects of an overt political ideology, program, or bureaucratic structure.

In the following section, we explicate the operations of *Bin-Zib* by interposing the autonomist theorization of "the common" with the general theory of "commons" first proposed by Elinor Ostrom.[13]

Bin-Zib: Between "commons" and "the common"

As the editors of this volume identify, the theory of commons suggests three constitutive parts of commons, namely: "common resources, institutions (or *commoning practices*), and the communities (called *commoners*)."[14] While there are similarities, the theory of "commons" needs to be differentiated from the theory of "the common." Roggero points out that commons, always in plural, or what he calls "Polanyian vision" is "usually identified as something existing in nature."[15] The notion of "the common" developed by autonomist Marxists, on the other hand, puts more emphasis on the fact that not only material resources but also ideas, knowledge, affection, and the means of communication can be common goods.[16]

In the following paragraphs, we proceed by looking at *Bin-Zib* first through the lens of "commons," and then explicating it again in terms of the theory of "the common."

We begin our examination of *Bin-Zib* in terms of common resources, the first constitutive part of commons. What kinds of objects qualify as common resources at *Bin-Zib*? Houses or housing space obviously fit the profile, but we must not overlook the co-funded *jeonse* (key money) used to rent these properties. Houses are a resource that the people at *Bin-Zib* draw on in their everyday lives. They are reproduced and managed, thus constituting not just physical structure but also the lived space of the residents' everyday life.[17] The co-funded key money, on the other hand, is not something utilized and/or managed by most of the residents as an everyday resource. However, it is the key money which enables *Bin-Zib* to ensure collectivized living conditions in a monetary economy.

Second, what then are the institutions or practices of commoning at *Bin-Zib?* The most obvious is *Bin-Go*. As we have seen, *Bin-Go* manages the *jeonse* (key money) as a common resource to acquire the housing space as a common resource. Opposing the nature of key money as a kind of rent financialized in the service of rentier capital was a clear intention of the activism-minded founders of *Bin-Go*.[18] Here is an excerpt from their blog:

> If a person shares the 12% profit generated from his/her *jeonse* with all the people in the world, the profit will become virtually zero. The praxis will turn the *jeonse* from capital into the common. *Bin-Go,* thus, aims to share each member's profit with the people of the world by multiplying *Bin-Zib*.[19]

Houses are another institution or practice of commoning at *Bin-Zib*. Here again we refer not to their physical structure but the space of shared residence given within the physical confines. And by referring to houses as institutions, we do not mean in the sense of rational organization as in bureaucracy. Houses at *Bin-Zib* qualify as a commoning institution because they give a boundary to the group of people living together with informal rules and agreements. Residents of a house regularly hold meetings to discuss emergent topics mostly related to the everyday issues of cohabitation. Each house also selects a representative to serve as a committee member of *Bin-Go*.

In understanding houses as commoning institutions/practices, we also need to pay attention to the fact that *Bin-Zib* residents have had to devise spatial living arrangements different from the norms of homes occupied by private individuals or a family. *Bin-Zib* residents made an extra effort to share houses so that there was no private room in *Bin-Zib*. Many postings on their team blog demonstrate that they in fact had the intention to overcome the form of modern housing based on the binary division of private and public space.[20] The concern for maximizing spatial accommodation played only a partial role in creating this condition. In other words, the formation of *Bin-Zib* as an alternative housing movement cannot be separated from the way in which the relations of residents, faced with the emergent circumstances that arise in communal living, made and formed their everyday lived space. Thus, the *Bin-Zib* houses have become a part of everyday community life as commoning institutions/practice in addition to being common resources.

Last but not least, let us examine the notion of community or commoners at *Bin-Zib*. While the residents (the long-term and short-term guests) of *Bin-Zib* seem to fit the profile of commoners, they are anomalous as commoners under the theory of the commons in two respects. First, the commoners of *Bin-Zib* do not have "clear group boundaries."[21] In other words, they come from heterogeneous backgrounds and often leave after a short period of time, effectively making the formation of a bounded collective identity impossible.

Second, more crucially, residents of *Bin-Zib* are not only required to maintain and reproduce the resources for the group, but they are also compelled to expand the common resources for potential, future guests.

> *Bin-Zib* is a house of guests. […] Of course, you can enjoy many things prepared and cultivated by people who arrived earlier. You can enjoy the hospitality given by the people around you. You can also prepare and cultivate something for the people around you as well as the people who will come later. […] This house of guests is an empty place. Since it is empty, anyone can come any time. Regardless of how many people are here, *Bin-Zib* should be vacated for the others to come. Therefore, living in *Bin-Zib* means to expand it.[22]

At *Bin-Zib*, there have always been people who want to come in. As a result, the residents are frequently confronted with a collective existential question, namely "whether to establish a new *Bin-Zib* thereby letting the idea of *Bin-Zib* (empty space for guests) live or shut out the place as well as the idea of *Bin-Zib* entirely."[23] Should they invest a considerable amount of time, money, and effort to open a new *Bin-Zib* for people they do not know? Residents of *Bin-Zib* are in other words asked to break with capitalist relations and instead place themselves in the circle of gift, reproducing the resource becomes possible only if the residents themselves go through the process of becoming common resources of the community.

It is in these instances when multiple parts overlap in which we find the theory of "commons" dovetailing with the theory of "the common" in our examination of *Bin-Zib*. According to Hardt and Negri, the common is "both the form of production and the source of new social relations."[24] Under this rubric, as participants in the common produce new relations, they are in turn formed as new subjectivities of these relations.

Residents of *Bin-Zib* declare that they seek different relations. A statement issued on their website states, "we look for another way to live together […] by opening a house to everyone, by sharing money with others."[25] However, as we have already stated, neither rules nor ideologies are enforced at *Bin-Zib,* and there exists a gamut

Figure 1. On the left, the *Bin-Zib*ites frolic in a paddling pool placed on the rooftop like vacationers at the beach. The parodic picture was used on the cover of their zine *Nonunsaram* (Playing People), available in DIY printed form as well as in digital format (Credits: Nonunsaram). On the right, guests celebrate the six-year anniversary of *Bin-Zib* at *Bin*-Café. Each person holds a small birthday cake with a candle.

of views and sensibilities with regard to commoning. Some even come to *Bin-Zib* simply to save rent. How then do such diverse subjectivities work together to maintain and expand the common? How does such a process of subjectification take place in the everyday life in *Bin-Zib*?

The answer lies in conflict as well as convivial socialization.[26] For the last seven years, the inhabitants of *Bin-Zib* have opened a new empty house (*Bin-Zib*) whenever the existing houses have become too congested. This praxis has been realized more often than not after residents engaged in extensive discussions and sometimes conflicts. The *Bin-Zib*'s website is filled with postings of debates over issues such as spatial arrangement, communal life, management of *Bin-Go,* and last but not least what *Bin-Zib* is or should be. These postings suggest that *Bin-Zib*'s history has been a process of trial and error rather than a teleological program.[27]

Equally significant have been frequent parties and collective events (Figure 1).[28] These convivial occasions have played a crucial role in overcoming such moments of crisis. In addition, what has held sway more often than not has been the recurring awareness and reflection that previous residents' generosity has made *Bin-Zib* available to the conflicted residents in the first place.[29] A meeting transcript reveals one resident posing a poignant question: "are you pleased with what you received? If so, why don't we do the same thing to strangers? We do not want the flow of gift to be stopped by us."[30] Thus, even when conflicts persisted and in some cases plagued the entire community, to the extent that meetings stopped taking place, residents attempted to turn away from the difficulties and hold events of pure conviviality (i.e. drinking parties) to remind themselves of the expanding potentials of shared life. These cycles of sensibilities between collision and fusion have taken place throughout the history of *Bin-Zib*'s constitution as a common.[31]

Commoning at *Bin-Zib* produces a different set of relations through the ongoing process of re-articulation of the meaning of *Bin-Zib*.[32] At *Bin-Zib*, common resources, whether in the form of money or houses, are not resources existing independent of the guests/residents (or commoners), as they are in fact products of the commoners and their social relations. A *Bin-Zib* thus becomes "empty" only to the extent that it becomes open to being shaped and re-shaped by the ways in which the guests/residents enter and make use of it. And only then does *Bin-Zib* become a convivial site of new subjectification (i.e., the common), with each house articulating this phenomenon in its unique way based on how the space is lived by its commoners.

Conclusion

Finding new uses for the city is not only a matter of how we organize and distribute resources, but fundamentally a matter of how we produce ourselves in relation to others. New York-based writer-translator-activist Sabu Kohso asserts:

> Discovering new usages for the city, where a multiplicity of relationships among people is made possible, is the only way to resist the "purgatory of here and now" and forge happiness. Happiness, never to be equated with individualistic pursuit for traces of success, as we have been made so accustomed to, is none other than living with Other(s). This new definition of happiness seems rather simple, but requires a wholly new subjectification.[33]

In this light, *Bin-Zib* is ultimately an attempt to devise a new usage for the city, creating different values and relations to live together with others.[34] It is in this sense that *Bin-Zib*'s attempt to overcome the house-as-private-property, in however a temporally and spatially limited manner, echoes Hardt's discussion of communism as "the autonomous human production of subjectivity, the human production of humanity – a new seeing, a new hearing, a new thinking, a new loving."[35]

Notes

1. We would like to thank the members of Urban Research Group for the insightful comments and critiques made on the earlier version of this paper.
2. This section is based on Didi K. Han's MA thesis, "Communicating Communes; A Case Study of Urban Communing Movement in South Korea (working title)," (Simon Fraser University, forthcoming).
3. The capital region of South Korea consists of Seoul city, Incheon city and Kyunggi do.
4. Donggi Kwak, "The Key Money, Is It Really the Best?" *Oh My News*, September 21, 2010, http://www.ohmynews.com/nws_web/view/at_pg.aspx?CNTN_CD=A0001447915 (accessed May 3, 2014).
5. In the everyday speech of Koreans, the acronym "IMF" primarily indexes the traumatic period of the late 1990s rather than the world financial organization itself.
6. Carlo Vercellone, "The Crisis of the Law of Value and the Becoming-Rent of Profit," *Crisis in the Global Economy: Financial Markets, Social Struggles, and New Political Scenarios,* Andrea Fumagalli and Sandro Mezzadra, eds. (Los Angeles: Semiotext(e) 2010), 85–118; Antonio Negri and Michael Hardt, *Commonwealth* (Cambridge, MA: Belknap Press, 2011), 153–158, 249–260; David Harvey, *Rebel Cities: From the Right to the City to the Urban Revolution* (London/New York: Verso, 2012), 89–113.
7. Nakgu Sohn, *The Real Estate Class Society* (Seoul: Humanitas, 2008), 25.
8. *Jjokbang* (dosshouses) and *gosiwon* typify such urban residential spaces of fragmentation and invisibility in today's South Korea. A *Jjokbang*, approximately 3 square feet, is customarily available for rent without deposit. Usually rooms are not equipped with a bathroom. The residents share a bathroom on their floor. A *gosiwon* was originally a dormitory catering for students preparing for the bar examination or qualification exams for high-ranking offices in the central government.
9. *Jeonse* is a type of housing rental contract that has its roots in the rapid development of industry and urban residence in South Korea. Under a *jeonse* contract, one can rent an apartment by depositing a lump-sum of key money rather than paying a monthly rent. While the key money is returned when the lease expires, the amount of key money required comes to about two-thirds the total cost of the leased property. In lieu of monthly payment, the deposited key money is calculated at 12 percent interest per year. For example, $100,000 in key money functions as $1,000 monthly rent. Key money used to be the predominant way to rent a house or room in South Korea. Kwak states: "while the people who do not own houses deposit their key money that they have laboriously collected, house owners invest that key money into the real estate market and reap huge profits." Donggi Kwak, "The Key Money, Is It Really the Best Choice?"
10. *Bundamgeum* is collected to pay for the monthly interest on the loan, utility bills, and meals. At first, *bundamgeum* was set at "at least two thousand won ($2) per day." Now it is around four or five thousand won ($4–5), depending on the house's condition.
11. The same rate is offered by major banks.
12. Jium, "A Network of Communities for Sharing, Autonomy, and Hospitality," *City and Poverty (Dosiwa Bingon)* 102 (2013): 62–76.
13. Elinor Ostrom, *Governing the Commons: The Evolution of Institutions for Collective Action* (New York: Cambridge University Press, 1990).
14. Introduction of this volume.
15. Gigi Roggero, "Five Theses on the Common," *Rethinking Marxism: A Journal of Economics, Culture & Society* 22, no. 3 (2010): 357–373.

16 Michael Hardt and Antonio Negri, *Commonwealth* (Cambridge, MA: Belknap Press of Harvard University Press, 2009).
17 For the concept of lived space, see Henri Lefebvre, *The Production of Space* (Oxford: Blackwell Publishing, 2007).
18 Vercellone, "The Crisis of the Law of Value and the Becoming-Rent of Profit."
19 Bin-Zib, "*Bin-Zib* and Anti-Capitalism Movement," Team Blog of Guests' House *Bin-Zib*, http://blog.jinbo.net/house/359?commentId=907 (accessed Jun 4 , 2014).
20 Regarding *Bin-Zib*'s spatial arrangement, refer to Han, "Communicating Communes."
21 Ostrom, *Governing the Commons*.
22 Bin-Zib, "Introduction of *Bin-Zib*," Bin-Zib Wiki, http://binzib.net/wiki/index.php/%EB%8C%80%EB%AC%B8 (accessed Dec 1, 2014).
23 Han, "Communicating Communes."
24 Hardt and Negri, *Commonwealth*, 8.
25 Bin-Go, "Statement of Purpose: Why Bin-Go?" Bin-Zib homepage, http://binzib.net/xe/index.php?mid=bingo&category=26078&document_srl=9891 (accessed May 3, 2014).
26 Han, "Communicating Communes."
27 Ibid.
28 Ibid.
29 Ibid.
30 Jigak, "The Duty of a Jangtu (long-term guests)," Bin-Zib Team Blog (blog), October 5, 2009. Accessed Aug. 29, 2014. [http://blog.jinbo.net/house/260]
31 Analysing , Han adopts Rancière's notion of politics as the work of configuring a common place. Ibid.
32 Ibid.
33 Sabu Kohso, *Cities of Death and Streets of Life,* trans., Seoulidarity (Seoul: Galmuri, 2013), 9.
34 Han, "Communicating Communes."
35 Michael Hardt, "The Common in Communism," *Rethinking Marxism: A Journal of Economics, Culture & Society,* 22, no. 3 (2010): 353.

Manuel Lutz

Uncommon Claims to the Commons: Homeless Tent Cities in the US

Introduction

The concept of commons as viewpoint and in praxis – beyond the market and the state – has been discussed on many levels, including material and virtual spatial levels. Building on the work of Elinor Ostrom, authors such as Helfrich, Linebaugh, De Angelis and Stavrides, Harvey, and Marcuse have disputed the alleged tragedy of the commons.[1] These scholars offer sophisticated views about how the commons are organized, detailing their histories and the challenges that accompany the shared ownership of the means of production within capitalism. The aim of this paper is to add an empirical example of the commons from the northern hemisphere, where the urban commons are currently an important political topic. Since the Occupy Wall Street campaign in 2011, there has been much talk about tents as a form of protest and their role in the creation of common space in the urban USA. When the Occupy camps finally closed, most activists returned home, but homeless individuals still had to find a place to survive in the city. In this paper I want to draw attention to these Americans, whose present struggle for tent communities goes back much further than the recent crisis. The focus is on the struggles of these homeless groups, who have actively organized themselves to produce tent cities, establishing them in the midst of revanchist urban policies that criminalize homeless survival.

These tent cities can be described using the concept of commoning – a term rediscovered by the historian Peter Linebaugh, whose writings on the rich histories of past commons provide a powerful reminder as to what the very essence of the commons was and is all about.[2] His books provide valuable stimulus for current debates on the future of the commons. Framing tent cities as commons, this paper responds to De Angelis's argument of the commons fix, which elaborates the recognition that capitalism has always been dependent on modes of reproduction of labor power that operate outside the market, such as unpaid care work.[3] In order to relate the commons fix to the urban, further reference to the literature on urban movements is instructive. Here it is argued that practices and spaces of alternative self-help, creativity, and resistance have been repeatedly co-opted by state and market actors in order to repair and replace the eroding welfare state, as well as to generate new opportunities of capital accumulation in the neoliberal entrepreneurial city.[4] The notion of the commons fix thus implies that, at the present time of crisis, specific forms of commoning are again being co-opted for the restructuring of state and capital.

The structure of this paper is as follows. Firstly, I will identify the key characteristics and qualities of commoning in the tent cities. This is based on Peter Linebaugh's short article "'All for One and One for All!' Some Principles of the Commons."[5] Secondly, I will sketch the terrain of compromise and co-optation which the homeless have to navigate in order to establish and stabilize their tent commons in time and (propertied) space. This section is based on empirical research on tent cities in several cities in the US conducted between 2010 and 2011. I will discuss the struggle for and against co-optation from a Foucault-inspired perspective of governing the poor to examine how commoning in tents is transformed into governing the poor in tents. Thirdly, I will explore the compatibilities and incompatibilities of the commons with capital and the state to show how legalizing tent cities is a textbook example of highly selective neoliberal co-optation. In the conclusion I will underline that, as poverty increases, we have to reckon with more tent cities emerging. For critical researchers and activists faced with the crucial yet perturbing questions of commoning of the poor and poor commons, the binary of either co-optation or emancipation is insufficient. Tent cities represent the ambiguity of the commons in the twenty-first century. As one activist stated, tent cities are "simultaneously the most and the least radical response to a disturbing crisis."[6] More complex and imaginative thoughts are called for on what urban commons could be, for whom, and in which times and places.

Tent commons – Commoning in tents

I propose an interpretation of tent cities as tent commons and commoning in tents. This analysis brings together my own empirical research on several tent cities in the Northwest US with recent ethnographic studies on life in tent cities by Tony Sparks and others.[7] Linebaugh's text offers key descriptions for the commons that capture the qualities of the tent cities,[8] how they emerge and function, and what the homeless are ultimately struggling for when demanding a place for tent cities.

Linebaugh asserts that "commoning is primary to human life."[9] This suggests that the raison d'être and primary driver for encampments to emerge, persist, and evolve into more organized and stabilized tent cities is the basic human survival instinct. The phenomenon of poor people suffering from homelessness collectively organizing makeshift shelters to seek the benefits of community (for security, safety, and human exchange) is nothing new. This phenomenon is not unique to the recent global crisis, which the media have suggested is forcing the middle class into tents. Those expropriated and excluded without the means to acquire a flat or house have always required a place to call home. According to homelessness researcher Peter Rossi, a home is essentially a place to return to for the next night.[10] But the homeless live in a world which is becoming ever more hostile, where there is literally no place for the non-propertied, especially those who cannot or do not want to use the often inadequate and insufficient homeless shelters. They are forced into perpetual mobility, where basic acts of survival are criminalized and their life is reduced to bare existence.

Social ties and communities are forged in tent cities. These communities are based on collective labor to organize shared reproduction and are in contrast to the individualized survival and social exclusion in a society that has learned to either despise the homeless or to look through them as if they were ghosts wandering the streets. As Linebaugh notes, "[h]uman solidarity as expressed in the slogan 'all for one and one for all' is the foundation of commoning […] the activity of commoning is conducted through labor with resources." In addition he states "it is labor which creates something as a resource."[11] Tent cities are "common pool resources" where the homeless create a space they use as their resource through active labor.[12] The commoners appropriate a space, define its perimeters, set up tents, assign a plan of the compound, and organize the basic essentials of life from fire and power to water and food supply to latrines and safety.

Tent city communities can be described as intentional communities. However, their identity politics are less focused on ideological or cultural affinities; they are primarily based on the shared needs and the maintenance of their common shelter resource. Tent city residents are no revolutionaries; most of them simply seek to achieve the basic survival (at a minimum level) which most other Americans take for granted. A recurring statement of interview partners in the camps was, "tent city is family; this is home."[13] To constitute and maintain a community of individuals who at first share nothing more than distress, and to organize a tent commons from loose, non-committal ties spatially manifested in scattered tents is not an easy undertaking; "communal values must be taught, and renewed, continuously."[14] This is demonstrated on a daily basis in the organized encampments, which show a remarkable set of self-government structures. Communities like Dignity Village in Portland, Safe Ground in Sacramento, Nickelsville and Tent City 3 and 4 in Seattle, or Camp Quixote in Olympia, each of which comprises between sixty and a hundred residents, have set up their own rules and codes of conduct to create social order.[15] These rules define the rights and duties of each individual who becomes a resident, ranging from acceptance of basic mutual respect and non-violence, the prohibition of drugs and "stupid stuff," and mandatory security shifts.[16]

The communities mentioned above are governed following the principles of grassroots democracy for collective decision-making, where daily, weekly, or monthly mandatory assemblies are held. These assemblies decide all aspects of community life in consensus or by majority vote. There are leaders called "elders" and an elaborate division of labor with functions such as "head of security," "tent master," "donations master," or "arbitrator." Each of these rotating positions is voted for by the collective. Interview respondents underlined that the potential for "social drama" is huge in the camps, where individuals and couples live together so closely with numbers ranging from twenty to over one hundred. However, "commoning has always been local. It depends on custom, memory, and oral transmission for the maintenance of its norms rather than law, police, and media," and while the camps have written rules, these need to be learned on a daily basis, reinforcing how to become a "good camper."[17] Emphasis is on mutual respect and personal freedom, in contrast to the hierarchical and often demeaning routines of the shelter industry where homeless individuals have to justify themselves on a constant basis.

Even though there is substantial room for consideration ("no one wants to make you homeless again," the head of security in Nickelsville explained), there are sanctions to enforce the social order which usually take the form of bans from the camp (both temporary and permanent). Social tensions and outbursts culminating in sanctions often tear heavily at the social fabric of the camps, but as Linebaugh notes, "commoners are quarrelsome (no doubt), yet the commons is without class struggle."[18] I do not want to romanticize tent cities; they are tough places where living conditions are basic. Tent city residents are also not an avant-garde, eager to overthrow capitalism and the state. Sparks observed, along Linebaugh's lines, that while tent city residents are not outside US society with its regimes and norms of propertied citizenship, they do organize some core social relations differently: access to the tent commons is not determined by property or status, but by need and active participation, which ensure membership.[19] These conditions of access resonate with Linebaugh's core insight that "commoning is exclusive inasmuch as it requires participation. It must be entered into."[20]

It is noteworthy that these communities have managed to sustain and expand their commons for years or even decades. Some communities have been able to integrate constantly fluctuating groups of newcomers, who in turn learn and reproduce the common rules. These makeshift communities not only keep their commons working as place of last resort that is safer than the streets, but also provide a structure for a more self-determined life of empowerment, engagement, and protest. Their practice is banal but also turns the dominant principle of capitalist production of space upside down. In a society in which land is treated as a commodity and where the non-propertied are governed in dehumanizing ways, the practices in the camps illustrate a break in this logic. Tent city activists continue to re-negotiate and politicize their political-economic circumstances and their homelessness management system. When they demand political and legal recognition it is not limited to a place for their own tent city but inevitably extends to opening opportunities for more such tent commons.

Compliant tent cities as a response to the shelter crisis

Tent cities have to be made compatible with the dominant powers in order to be established in space and time. However, because they lack one of the core requirements for surviving well under capitalism – the ownership of private land – they are left with only two options: either to seek informal tolerance, or to protest. The protest camp is a highly effective form of creating political pressure, precisely because it visibly symbolizes the poor not only claiming space, but also taking over a place in the city and in society. Yet, to fulfill this threat means confronting the powers that be. Therefore, even in the case of specifically "protest"-orientated tent cities, the homeless enter the political stage to demand not property per se, but rather to be hosted by either local government or private landowners. Unlike the southern hemisphere, where there still seem to be opportunities to re-negotiate property relations from the bottom up, in the US there is no legal right to housing and only limited legal rights to shelter.[21] Customary rights of the "overnight house,"[22] which were exploited by early American pioneers, were terminated with the end of the frontier era; today, such practice of radical homesteading through squatting is rare in the US.[23] While some groups have tried, and continue trying, to claim commons in public space, opposition is strong. Linebaugh states that the commons is different from "the public."[24] This is certainly true when we think of commons as the exclusive and permanent use of space. Such use has no place in the hegemonic concept of public space. In fact, in order to become recognized, homeless groups and their supporters are committed to dispelling any notion of being squatters or being equated with "radical homesteaders 2.0" taking property. Instead, many homeless groups underline that they only require access to property to enable their commons.

Various groups and organizations coming from different backgrounds have put forward this claim for tent cities, asking local and national government to allow for improved survival through self-help sheltering.[25] What emerged initially in the late 1980s has been fuelled by the most recent financial and housing crisis. In the wake of this crisis, not only homeless activists but also homeless advocacy organizations, concerned service providers, church congregations, and legal advocates (including the UN Rapporteur for the human right to housing) have argued that tent cities are a necessary step in responding to the lack of shelter and housing, and the inhumane and inefficient criminalization of homelessness which violates human rights.[26]

These calls are backed by some organizations that endorse legalizing encampments as an innovative form of problem-oriented policing.[27] Local mayors have also confirmed that the experiment of legalizing homeless camp spaces actually works.[28] Recent studies have shown that legal tent cities provide several benefits for homeless individuals' well-being, countering their legal marginalization and even providing emancipatory aspects.[29] However, in sum, all these voices coalesce in the claim to government that tent commons are not a threat but manageable, and thus a pragmatic way to widen the already strained safety net at times of increased need.

Indeed, self-help sheltering resonates with current post-welfare politics, where neoliberal ideology has breathed new life into the logic that makes the poor responsible for their own survival. The legalized tent cities I examined in my research can be seen as prime examples of such neoliberal, post-welfare governance of the poor: the homeless shelter themselves at little cost to the taxpayer and actively consent to substandard sheltering. By legalizing and regulating homeless camping, different actors and resources from civil society – notably faith-based organizations – are mobilized in new ways to effectively expand sheltering capacities at a time when official emergency shelters are full to capacity (and are often being closed). Simultaneously, the formalization of previously illegal encampments allows for more effective policing of a problematic population that is contained in one place at significantly lower cost than detaining them in jail.[30] Therefore, the tent commons provide a useful fix for multiple crises in an existing homeless management system whose aim is to deal with this potentially troublesome population.

However, the relation of tent cities to the state commons is not quite as harmonious as this analysis may suggest, and in reality proves to be rather more ambiguous. The legalization of tent cities is highly controversial and has been preceded by fierce debates and struggles in the respective cities. A recurring theme in the debates is whether the homeless can, and should, be allowed to self-govern. The case of the homeless camps thus reveals unresolved tensions between (neo)liberal forms of governing the poor through activation for self-sufficiency, and inherited forms of governing the homeless based on discipline, punishment, and containment.[31] The latter are written into prevalent welfare responses which accommodate and assist the homeless. Homelessness researchers remind us that, in general, the homeless are treated as pathologic subjects that by definition are incapable of (proper) self-sufficiency.[32] Shelters and services seek to cure the sinner and the sick or, in today's lingo, rehabilitate the homeless to become "housing ready."[33] This paternalistic subordination means that homeless self-help sheltering is not to be understood as valuable resource but as expression of a deviant or pathologic lifestyle that is to be repressed. Decades of encampment clean-ups and so-called "tough love" interventions to criminalize survival speak volumes about this distinct imperative to govern the homeless.[34]

Managing the co-optation of tent commons

In every city that has legalized a tent city, several discourses have developed to change the status quo of homeless management. Locally, it is argued that governing a tent city is not only a necessary but manageable and adequate form of homeless management that can be co-produced by actors from government, civil society, and the homeless themselves. The following overview offers a glimpse of how homeless commoning has been co-opted in various ways, resulting in a range of legalized tent cities.[35]

In the city of Ontario, California, a tent city was established and managed in a clear authoritarian way. While the homeless were allowed to live in tents, their commoning was tightly regulated. The tent commons here almost entirely served the interests of the state and capital. As a consequence, in 2012, after four years of existence the local government closed their "Temporary Homeless Service Area" (THSA). A year before, the THSA population was cut by half as over 200 residents who were deemed as outside of Ontario were evicted.[36] Many of the remaining residents were then (temporarily) housed in the new sixty-two units of homeless housing, but, a year after the closure, the city estimates again an unmet shelter need for approximately 136 homeless people, indicating that these individuals are forced to survive in the streets and back alleys.[37] Thus, the THSA was not closed because homelessness was ended, or the desire for self-sheltering had ceased, but because the local government had achieved its goals of acquiescing social concerns and political unrest as well as enabling effective policing, containment, and eventually displacing the problematic homeless.

In other places such as Fresno and Ventura, the tent cities that are still legalized exhibit more elements of compromise between homeless commoning and state rationales. In Fresno two "tool shed camps" have been established that allow their residents to practice commoning within confines defined by a supervising non-profit organization that manages the camps. The homeless residents may have a say in and contribute to daily operations, but nothing more. Ultimately, the tool shed commons are low threshold shelters which offer food and shelter with no additional conditions attached. The case of Fresno (Figure 1) highlights the selectivity of co-optation as the legal camps that the city named Village and Community of Hope sit right in the middle of hundreds of still illegal tents and sheds. Here, homeless commoning has been practiced for several decades, but under very precarious conditions and subject to irregular "clean-up" raids.

The broader scope of commoning in tents described earlier can be identified in the tent cities that have been legalized in Seattle and Olympia (Washington State). In the mid-2000s, after homeless organizations fought sustained battles and won legal victories, arrangements were made whereby temporary permits are given to regulate the operation of self-governed homeless encampments. Referring to the

Figure 1. Selective co-optation: Legal "Village of Hope" and adjacent illegal camp "The Hill" in Fresno, California.

constitutional right of free religious expression, the regulatory framework allows tent camps to be hosted by private property owners for three months. Usually these are local church congregations offering their parking lot to Tent City 3 and 4. Here then, control and subordination work more subtly through community control and temporality: in order to be granted a temporary use permit and to be allowed to camp, the commoners have to follow a written code of conduct and have to satisfy their hosts. Being guests at the whim of their hosts effectively reintroduces a range of power inequalities and hierarchical relations, but at the same time the homeless have made the best out of the compromise.[38] First, the code of conduct is co-shaped by the homeless organizations that organize commoning in tents. Secondly, as homeless organizers told me, they do see the benefits of being semi-permanent, as the custodian property ownership prevents the tent commons consolidating where it might become a smallholder's village with all its ensuing problems. The perpetual moves are burdensome but also contribute to community formation and keep alive their political agenda of making the misery of homelessness public through encounters with different communities.

The material set-up also illustrates the differences between commoning that is more externally managed and that which is more self-determined. In Ontario, standardized army-style tents were provided, surrounded by a chain-link fence guarded 24h by private security. Any sense of ownership and opportunities for individual appropriation are minimized, rendering the camp similar to an outdoor shelter-prison. Fresno's prefabricated tool sheds are similarly uniform, with the difference that the residents can use them as their home as long as need be. But the camp

Figure 2. Envisioned trajectory of poor commons from tents to sturdy huts: "Nickelsville" in Seattle, Washington, and "Dignity Village" in Portland, Oregon.

is closed during the day, again reminding the residents as to the imposed character of their commons. In contrast, tent cities such as Seattle's tolerated Nickelsville and Olympia's Camp Quixote have followed the path of Dignity Village in Portland (Figure 2), where residents started to improve their commons by building more permanent and durable dwellings without permits. These little huts are designed and built by the homeless and their supporters according to the users' needs, although they also exhibit elements of compromise. As they are still seeking political acceptance and legal recognition, they are built small enough to be transportable and to avoid building permits. Considerable amounts of energy and organization (including material that campers have bought themselves) are invested in these huts, which become dwelling places for those who built them or who need them most. But the huts are not personal property and remain part of the commons to be used by someone else when vacated.

Re-questioning tent commons as a neoliberal policy fix

While in several cities such as Seattle, Portland, and Fresno existing encampments continue to be legalized, there have been no new examples of legalized tent cities. In various other cities, such as Eugene and Sacramento, discussions continue about whether to legalize new encampments. Since 2010, the number of legal tent cities remains limited, with only nine throughout the country. This number points to limits of the neoliberal policy fix of co-opting tent cities. The constraints go beyond the frequently voiced armada of pragmatic and ideological concerns over the manageability of tent cities, which are perceived as sites of chaos, crime, and insanitary conditions. I would argue that, while the case studies show how tent cities have been co-opted "successfully" in some cities, tent commons continue to exhibit systemic problems that explain the sustained resistance to them. The tent commons potential threats to and incompatibilities with the state are perceived and responded to particularly at the national level; federal bureaucrats and politicians have opposed tent cities to the point where they have intervened directly to discourage local governments in Seattle and Fresno from experimenting further in co-opting tent cities.[39]

The first systemic challenge of co-opting tent cities regards the governing of the homeless. Traditional views and institutionalized patterns of governing the homeless (assistance, disciplining, and rehabilitation) are based on, and reproduce, hierarchical relations with the distribution of services and resources to those not "housing ready" and to assign specific places to them. But where this form of governing denies self-sufficiency per definition, co-optation of tent commons relies on the labor and capacity for self-sufficiency of the homeless (to varying degrees). Thus, the co-opted practices of commoning continue to escape the attempts to control them: active and collective production of a shared space is appropriation and can engender new claim-making politics. Establishing tent cities is often accompanied by a sense of entitlement. With the tent city the homeless claim recognition, respect, and self-determination that oppose subordination and spatial relegation for being homeless. This potential suspension of hierarchical relations makes tent commons less clear and predictable within a homelessness policy system that continues to govern top-down. This challenge became tangible with the major overhaul of US homelessness policies: a system change was introduced in 2001 and officially adopted in 2010 by the US government which set out to end the protracted problem of homelessness by 2020, rather than to merely "manage" it.[40] This ambitious new project to govern the homeless leaves little room (discursively and literally) for homeless who refuse to wait another ten years but demand housing or shelter for tonight.

The second systemic challenge is the governing of homelessness as a way to govern the even greater problem of invisible substandard housing. The separation of homelessness from substandard housing creates a break in the continuum of overpriced, substandard, and precarious housing arrangements, in which millions of poor Americans try to make ends meet to create a home. This break is less tangible for the lived experience of the poorly housed where episodes of homelessness are only one aspect of substandard housing. But defining a population as homeless allows for distinct forms of governing. Those defined as homeless are treated in paternalistic ways because they are perceived as not being self-sufficient (see above), whereas those individuals in substandard housing who are not yet homeless are governed in less invasive ways, in order to achieve more self-sufficiency, which is the basis of the American Dream – a dream that has been significantly damaged by mass foreclosures and the increasing visibility of poverty. While economists and bankers proclaim that the worst of the economic crisis is over and governments try to encourage confidence in "the new normal," mass homelessness remains a highly symbolic manifestation of an ongoing crisis. So far the hegemonic project to "end homelessness" seems to have succeeded; since 2005 the number of officially homeless people has remained stable at approximately 650,000.[41] However, the massive stimulus funds of 2009 that temporarily prevented an increase in homelessness have run out. In this context, any state endorsement of tent cities would be counterproductive: tent cities, whether organized collectively as commons or managed by the state, are highly symbolic and visible manifestations of unresolved housing problems and insufficient welfare state responses. As clear indicator of this attempt to further obscure the crisis, we can see how instead of legal homeless camps quite similar forms of homeless commoning are co-opted indoors: since 2008, more so-called church basement shelters have opened throughout the US. Similar to tent cities, their operation relies on homeless self-help and community, but unlike tent cities they are welcomed by local governments.

Is there a way out? Ambiguous poor commons

To conclude, tent cities as "poor commons" are both providers of a post-welfare fix to sheltering the homeless and a challenge to hierarchical governing of the homeless. Tent cities challenge the paternalistic governance of the homeless which is highly effective in politically neutralizing poverty.[42] But tent commons are not a way out; they do not solve homelessness but manage it differently. What they provide are user-driven forms of improved survival conditions – nothing more, nothing less. Tent cities remind us not only that homelessness persists but also that substantial change, much less a solution, is nowhere in sight.

Homeless activists, advocates, and researchers have pointed out the important role of tent cities as a form of resistance to authoritarian and punitive governing, but they struggle to account for the ambiguity of tent commons where the homeless actually seek co-optation to sustain tent cities for as long as need be.[43] This temporality – where interim, partial solutions become permanent fixes – troubles not only state actors keen on demonstrating that social problems can be solved. In my mind, it is indicative of the unbalanced academic focus on resistance as primary response to punishment; for the last three decades, critical homelessness researchers have rarely addressed the ambiguous debate and praxis of tent commons as means of survival, adaptation, and resistance. The subject has only become of more interest since the media scandalized tent cities as icons of America in crisis.

Don Mitchell argues that, while tent cities offer valuable and important models of alternative social relations and production of space based on needs, solidarity, and humanity, they do not have a place in the city of the future, in which such substandard forms of dwellings are to be overcome.[44] In a similar vein, while recognizing the important survival effects of tent cities, homeless advocates have until today hesitated to launch a larger campaign for homeless camping for fear of compromising the higher goal of good housing for all.

These concerns are not unjustified; however, I contend that there is the need to go beyond the insufficient binaries of either survival and co-optation or system change and autonomy. Tent cities force us to take a realistic look at the needs of the homeless and to adjust our position to these needs when conceptualizing current economic and political perspectives. Whether we interpret tent cities and commoning by the poorest as rearticulated oppression and exploitation or nascent self-determination is unavoidably not only an analytical task but also a normative question, inherently connected to the viewer's political stance.

The discussion of commons opens new terrain for political conversation. However, to move beyond state and market we also need to insert time and space into this discussion and pay close attention to the ambiguity of commons with regards to state and capital. The example of poor commons produced by commoning of the poor shows that additional conceptual tools are required to remain critical of the co-optation of commons. And while capable of discerning co-optation, such a view should also not lose sight of the crucial element of survival and keep open to identify alternative social relations practiced. We need to define criteria and categories for analyzing and evaluating normative processes of social change. Commons are not a silver bullet to dissolve the confines of state and capital.

Finally, the notion of commons cannot be regarded as static, but as dynamic. Critical research is required to identify the interconnectedness and simultaneity of (a) top-down processes to co-opt and instrumentalized commoning and (b) bottom-up processes when commoning means the acquirement of more, albeit partial, rights. For this double perspective, recourse to the emergent literature on the production of urban informalities in the northern hemisphere may be instructive.[45] And yet again, the particular context of poverty within not-quite-yet post-welfare states inevitably provokes the recurring question: are the poor commons/is commoning of the poor the appropriate method for transformation? For the poor and non-propertied especially, commoning remains a constant struggle to achieve what Max Rameau, founder of Take Back the Land, describes as the "twofold goal:"[46] to achieve immediate survival and a better life, while at the same time politicizing the existing conditions, aiming not only for a better but the good life.

Notes

1. Silke Helfrich and Heinrich-Böll-Stiftung, eds., *Commons. Für eine neue Politik jenseits von Markt und Staat* (Bielefeld: transcript, 2012); Peter Linebaugh, *The Magna Carta Manifesto: Liberties and Commons for All* (Berkeley: University of California Press, 2008); An Architektur, ed., "On the Commons: A Public Interview with Massimo De Angelis and Stavros Stavridis" *e-flux* no. 17 (2010); David Harvey, *Rebel Cities: From the Right to the City to the Urban Revolution* (New York: Verso, 2012); Peter Marcuse, "From Justice Planning to Commons Planning," in *Searching for the Just City,* Peter Marcuse et al., eds. (New York: Routledge, 2009), 91–102.
2. Linebaugh *The Magna Carta Manifesto,* Peter Linebaugh, "'All for One and One For All!' Some Principles of the Commons," *CounterPunch* Weekend Edition, January 8–10 (2010).
3. Massimo De Angelis, "Does Capital Need a Commons Fix?" *Ephemera* 13, no. 3 (2013), 603–615.
4. Steven Katz and Margit Mayer, "Gimme Shelter: Self-Help Housing Struggles Within and Against the State in New York City and West Berlin," *International Journal of Urban and Regional Research* 9, no. 1 (1985), 15–46; Justus Uitermark, "The Co-optation of Squatters in Amsterdam and the Emergence of a Movement Meritocracy: A Critical Reply to Pruijt," *International Journal of Urban and Regional Research* 28, no. 3 (2004), 687–698.
5. Linebaugh "All for One and One for All!"
6. Max Rameau, *Take Back the Land – Land, Gentrification and the Umoja Village Shantytown* (Miami: Nia Interactive Press, 2008), 7.
7. Tony Sparks, *As Much Like Home As Possible: Geographies of Homelessness and Citizenship in Seattle's Tent City 3,* dissertation, Seattle: Department of Geography, University of Washington (2008); Tony Sparks "Governing the Homeless in an Age of Compassion: Homelessness, Citizenship, and the 10 Year Plan

to End Homelessness in King County, Washington," *Antipode* 44, no. 4 (2012); Talmadge Wright, *Out of Place: Homeless Mobilizations, Subcities, and Contested Landscapes* (New York: SUNY Press, 1997); National Coalition for the Homeless (NCH), *Tent Cities in America: A Pacific Coast Report* (2010); Abbilyn Miller, *Determining Critical Factors in Community-Level Planning of Homeless Service Projects,* dissertation, Urbana: University of Illinois at Urbana (2012).

8   Linebaugh, "All for One and One for All!"
9   Ibid.
10 Peter Rossi, *Down and Out in America: The Origins of Homelessness* (Chicago: University of Chicago Press, 1990).
11 Linebaugh, "All For One and One For All!"
12 An Architektur, "On the Commons."
13 See also NCH, *Tent Cities in America.*
14 Linebaugh, "All For One and One For All!"
15 NCH, *Tent Cities in America.*
16 Ibid.; Sparks, *As Much Like Home As Possible.*
17 Ibid.; Linebaugh, "All For One and One For All!"
18 Ibid.
19 Sparks, *As Much Like Home As Possible.*
20 Linebaugh, "All For One and One For All!"
21 Kim Hopper, *Reckoning with Homelessness* (New York: Cornell Paperbacks, 2003); UN Special Rapporteur on the Right to Adequate Housing, *Addendum, Mission to the United States of America* (2010).
22 Colin Ward, *Cotters and Squatters: The Hidden History of Housing* (Nottingham: Five Leaves, 2005).
23 Rameau, *Take Back the Land.*
24 Linebaugh, "All for One and One for All!"
25 NCH, *Tent Cities in America.*
26 National Law Center on Homelessness & Poverty (NLCHP), *Tent City Fact Sheet* (2009); UN Special Rapporteur, *Addendum Mission to the USA.*
27 Center for Problem-Oriented Policing (CPOP), *Homeless Encampments. Guide No. 56* (2010).
28 City of Seattle, *Department of Planning Director's Report Relating to Council Bill No. 117288, Regarding Transitional Encampment Amendments* (2010).
29 NCH, *Tent Cities in America;* Miller, *Determining Critical Factors;* Zoe Loftus-Farren, "Tent Cities: An Interim Solution to Homelessness and Affordable Housing Shortages in the United States," *California Law Review* 99 (2011).
30 Chris Herring, "The New Logics of Homeless Seclusion: Homeless Encampments in America's West Coast Cities," *City & Community* 13, no. 4 (2014): 285–309.
31 Hopper, *Reckoning with Homelessness;* Don Mitchell, "Homelessness, American Style," *Urban Geography* 32 (2011).
32 Ibid., Sparks, *As Much Like Home As Possible.*
33 Teresa Gowan, *Hobos, Hustlers, and Backsliders: Homeless in San Francisco* (Minnesota: University of Minnesota Press, 2010).
34 Mitchell, "Homelessness, American Style."
35 See also: NCH, *Tent Cities in America;* Herring, "The New Logics of Homeless Seclusion."
36 NCH, *Tent Cities in America.*
37 City of Ontario, *Policy Plan. Housing Element Technical Report,* draft August 2013.
38 Sparks, *As Much Like Home As Possible.*
39 Lynn Thompson, "As Tent City Struggles, Seattle has no Easy Answers on Homeless" (*Seattle Times*, August 19, 2012).

40 United States Interagency Council on Homelessness (USICH), *Opening Doors – Federal Strategic Plan to Prevent and End Homelessness* (2010).
41 National Alliance to End Homelessness (NAEH), *The State of Homelessness in America 2013* (2013).
42 Peter Marcuse, "Neutralizing Homelessness," *Socialist Review,* 88, no. 1 (1988): 69–97.
43 Wright, *Out of Place;* Don Mitchell, "Tent City: Spaces of Homeless Survival and Organizing in the American City," in *Social Housing – Housing the Social: Art, Property, and Spatial Justice,* A. Phillips and F. Erdemci, eds. (Amsterdam: SKOR and Sternberg Press, 2012), 277–306.
44 Ibid.
45 Nezar AlSayyad and Ananya Roy, eds., *Urban Informality – Transnational Perspectives from the Middle East, Latin America, and South Asia* (Maryland/London: Lexington Books, 2004); Oren Yiftachel, "Critical Theory and 'Gray Space': Mobilization of the Colonized," *City,* 13, no. 2–3 (2009), 240–256.
46 Rameau, *Take Back the Land.*

Institutions

Daniel Opazo Ortiz

Creating and Appropriating Urban Spaces – The Public versus the Commons: Institutions, Traditions, and Struggles in the Production of Commons and Public Spaces in Chile

The commons as social production

Probably the most widely acknowledged approach to the idea of the commons is that of political economy, best represented by the work of Elinor Ostrom and her response to the pessimistic tradition inaugurated by Hardin and his idea of the *tragedy of the commons*. Ostrom's approach focuses mostly on management and polity structures, i.e. institutional design, that allow communities to make use of a natural (common-pool) resource over time and generations while preventing depletion. The concept of self-governance of the commons is built upon empirical research and argues against calls for external intervention, either state or market-oriented.[1]

The discussion about understanding urban space as a commons, however, must delve into a somewhat different and older tradition, namely the constitutional and political tradition that defines the common as both a right and a metaphor of the limits to the power of the sovereign. In this regard, the work of Peter Linebaugh in examining the genealogy of Magna Carta and the link between economic and political organization of life in English history sheds light on the focus our discussion should have. Linebaugh shows how the commons have been the subject of struggles throughout history and even how we can understand the development of capitalism as one strongly based on a continuous process of dispossession, or in a more straightforward manner, "the removal of people from the land or from their means of subsistence."[2]

Although it is possible to say that all commons are socially built, that is to say, transformed into a common-pool resource by the interaction between humans and nature, it is also valid to observe that, to a certain extent, the fact that urban public space is produced instead of being what we could call a given (such as natural resources) makes a big difference, even as obvious as it may seem.[3, 4] This view of the commons as a social product is endorsed by Massimo De Angelis, who stresses that the process of turning commons into rights in the medieval English case didn't have to do with those rights being granted by the sovereign, but instead with him being forced to acknowledge them.[5] De Angelis proposes to understand commons not simply as a resource but rather as a triad:

> First, all commons involve some sort of common pool of resources, understood as non-commodified means of fulfilling people's needs. Second, the commons are necessarily created and sustained by communities. [...] the third and most important element in terms of conceptualizing the commons is the verb "to common" – the social process that creates and reproduces the commons.[6]

The *pobladores* movement as a commoning force against the state

The approach to commons as a verb ("to common" or "commoning") will be useful to situate and analyze our case study. The process of 'governing the commons' in the urban realm and specifically in the case of public space, which is certainly and essentially political, must be perhaps also understood as 'producing the commons.'[7] In this context, the struggles of *pobladores* for the right to the city can be understood as a process of producing new commons (urban space as such) without the participation of the state or even a confrontation with it. The *pobladores* movement can be considered an example of commoning not only because of its practices, but also how its struggles shaped its identity and structure as a collective. Judith Revel and Antonio Negri have stated that what is common to men (and women) is not their origin, 'their soil,' but instead what they build collectively.[8] The common, therefore, is not being but doing and, in that context, the history of struggles for the right to the city by the urban poor in Latin American cities and particularly in Chile can be seen from a new light.

In a very informative book about the history of the *pobladores* movement,[9] we find the following excerpt from a life story by one of the first inhabitants of the *población* San Gregorio, founded in 1959, talking about the process of collaborative self-construction:

> […] the idea was to help each other. It was nice because when we finished our houses we continued working as a whole to pave our sidewalks, build a community room, buy a TV, pay for the funeral of someone whose family didn't have the money […] It was just like that, we helped each other, it was lovely, there was friendship and solidarity.[10]

This is a precise example of what Linebaugh calls commoning: "the practice of commoning can provide mutual aid, neighborliness, fellowship, and family with their obligations of trust and expectations of security."[11] Therefore, the common here, as Revel and Negri would say, is social organization, and the urban space produced in the process of organizing can also be conceptualized as commons.

I will argue that, in terms of the production of space, there is an alternative tradition to the public and private to be found in the organizational forms of the lower classes and specifically of a political subject characteristic to Latin America: the *pobladores* (poorly translated into English as slum dwellers). Furthermore, notwithstanding the absence of a participatory culture within the state,[12] it is possible to assert that the development of institutions responsible for the production of the city and public space throughout the twentieth century is in direct relationship with the struggles led by different social movements, particularly the *pobladores*.

My working hypothesis is that this rich tradition of what we could call 'potential commons' has been historically hindered by the Chilean state, both purposely and as a result of the gaps and voids in its institutional framework, and I intend to show this through the case of Peñalolén Park. This park, built in a private lot previously occupied by an informal settlement for almost seven years, parts of which are still standing, was created by both local and national governments as a strategy to prevent the Toma de Peñalolén from turning into an example for other homeless groups in the country to take private land and later demand the state to purchase it for building homes. The cornerstone for this strategy was to frame using the land for housing as an alleged process of privatization of public space.

The high importance of public space in Chilean society has different explanations: some of them refer to a material reality, namely the lack of green spaces in cities, particularly in poorer districts, while others have to do with Chile's political history. In this last regard, the idea of public space as a 'space for encounter' echoed the policies for reconciliation led by democratic governments after 1990. From a theoretical approach, it is possible to link that use of the concept of public space to the ideas of influential thinkers like Jürgen Habermas and Hannah Arendt, who understand public space as a space for rational dialogue and consensus building. This position has been labelled by Seyla Benhabib as a 'discursive model,' as long as it takes for granted that political subjects have equal conditions to participate of such a space. Chantal Mouffe has also emphasized how both Habermas and Arendt overlook antagonism as a key feature of political public space.[13] More recently, Delgado and Malet have criticized social democratic elites in Europe for using public space as a means to distract and discipline the masses. The authors argue that this conception legally implies state property and full authority over that space, and politically means a sphere of "harmonious and pacific coexistence of heterogeneous society."[14]

Public space, the commons and the Chilean context: Traditions and institutions

Since independence, Chile's republican state has always been ruled by statutory law; the second article of the Chilean Civil Code states that "custom doesn't constitute right, except for those cases where the law complies with it." On the other hand, since the Spanish conquest and during colonial times, urban development based on the checkerboard layout was meant to appropriate land in order to distribute it later to Spanish crown representatives, military authorities, Catholic Church congregations, and soldiers turned into private tenants. Thus, the concept of the commons is not a familiar one within Chilean history. The only references to the contemporary idea of the commons both in the Civil Code and the Constitution speak of "the things that nature has made common for all men." Paraphrasing what Elizabeth Blackmar has stated about the suppression of Indian common property in the US, in Chile the chances are reduced to the binary "simple opposition of public and private."[15]

The existence of a sort of 'third sphere' has only been discussed in the context of the public-private partnership model of urban development, but not necessarily (maybe not at all) in the sense of the commons theory. These discussions (as in the case of the so-called POPS – Privately Owned Public Spaces) and in general, the whole idea of the public and public space, have always been led and defined at the formal level almost solely from the point of view of the ruling elites.

In the Chilean institutional framework, public space is a poorly defined concept. As Sergio León has shown, the Ley General de Urbanismo y Construcciones, LGUC (Planning and Building General Law) and its General Ordinance only state that public spaces are "national goods of public use, destined to leisure and circulation,"[16] basically public roads and urban parks at different scales. In turn, national goods of public use (NGPUs) are defined by the Civil Code in the following manner: "National goods are those which possession belongs to the nation as a whole. If their use also belongs to every member of the nation, as in the case of streets, squares, bridges and roads, the adjacent sea and its beaches, they will be called national goods of public use or public goods." The inclusion of national goods of public use within a larger category is an important issue, because as Elke Schlack has aptly noted, "the law links public space with public property, that is to say, with the control of the state."[17]

Besides this weak legal definition, public spaces in Chile are also affected by its complex structure of administration. The best example are roads: small streets at the neighborhood level are competency of municipalities, urban main streets are under the responsibility of the Ministry of Housing and Urban Planning (MINVU, an acronym for its Spanish name) through one of its branches, while urban highways are developed and administered by the Ministry of Public Works. This same scheme can be found in the process of devising, designing, and administering public spaces, with several agencies involved and without public notion of their competencies and juxtapositions. In the case of Santiago, the problem is aggravated by the fact that there is no city authority but instead thirty-four municipalities that form the metropolitan area. For example, MINVU is responsible for the development of large urban parks, although funding may come from the Regional Government and municipalities may also take part in those initiatives by supplying land.

During the last two decades, democratic governments have developed different programs at the central level to foster the creation of new public spaces or to renovate damaged traditional spaces. Probably the most important among them, in terms of built surface, was the Urban Parks Program, led by MINVU between 1992 and 2002.[18] This program sought to develop recreational parks mostly in disadvantaged zones of the city; after completion, parks were administered by the Parque Metropolitano de Santiago (PMS), an institution originally created to manage the park of the same name at San Cristóbal Hill (the largest urban park in Chile, with a surface of about 700 hectares). However, this model was used only for the seventeen parks built under that program in Santiago and did not turn into a sort of metropolitan public space authority able to manage the over 250 parks in the city; this will later prove an important element in the discussion of our case, as the complexity of administration has seriously influenced the design and development of Peñalolén Park.

Pobladores as a political agent beyond state and market

Notwithstanding this tradition of centralized power within the Chilean republican state, during the second half of the twentieth century, several social movements linked to the struggles for the right to housing, and, from a more contemporary view, the right to the city, attempted to produce their own living space through *tomas* (literally takings) of former farming lands or derelict lots in order to build informal settlements which then, in time, evolved into definitive neighborhoods. It is possible to identify a historical and social tradition in the phenomenon of the *tomas*, where the *pobladores* developed a particular identity related to class consciousness and political struggle, and where the built environment was the result of a participatory, community endeavor.

Several scholars, among them sociologists and historians, have stated that it is necessary to go beyond modern social categories in order to understand the *pobladores* as a political subject in Latin American history. Mario Garcés has insisted on the idea that the *pobladores* movement differs from the traditional conception of working class, precisely in that the former do not relate to industrial work as in the case of 'classic' Marxist theory and leftist thought. Moreover, Garcés states that the working class: "was always only a fraction of the popular class and that a huge number of poor men and women never achieved the worker condition," remaining in a category that he defines as "sub-proletariat"; however, both women working as laundresses or domestic maids and men working in temporary jobs or as independent artisans "were key protagonists of the *pobladores* movement."[19]

Most historical studies about the *pobladores* movement focus on the period between 1957 and 1970, beginning with the founding of Población La Victoria, the first massive and successful *toma* from the second half of the twentieth century,[20] and ending with the inauguration of Salvador Allende as president. During that period, the housing problem in Santiago became critical due to the continuous migration from smaller cities throughout the country and the lack of public institutional policies adequately addressing the issue. Most *tomas* followed the same pattern: people who lived along the banks of rivers and canals, many of whom were registered in the public social housing programs and tired of waiting for the possibility of acquiring a house, then organized to occupy nearby land in order to build houses themselves. This land usually met two criteria: it belonged to the state (mostly to CORVI, the State Housing Corporation, whose financial and organizational capacities were insufficient to meet the goals of public policy) and it was located in the city outskirts.

Even though the first examples of *poblaciones* created out of occupied land dated back to the 1930s, as in the case of the famous Población La Legua (1931), as already mentioned, during the 1950s the housing problem and the population's discontent became critical, not only due to a population increase but also due to the expectations created by the government of President Carlos Ibáñez del Campo (1952–1958), a former dictator from the 1920s revamped as a populist politician. Ibáñez had won the elections with a great majority and during the first years of his mandate he introduced major changes to public administration, based on concepts like 'coordination,' 'rationalization,' and proposing 'plans' for 'integral solutions'[21] that aimed, in the case of housing, to end the shanty towns by building a large number of units. However, these announcements and plans did not work as planned, mainly due to lack of coordination between government and industry, with the former failing to provide announced incentives for the construction industry, but also certainly due to the inability of the government to bolster the aforementioned new institutions. Near the end of the decade, the economic crisis related to the low price of copper led to a decrease in public investment and consequently to the failure of the housing plans.

In 1957, the 'success' of La Victoria as a *toma* created a new mentality among the urban poor, namely the certainty that, in light of the shortcomings of the state, it was up to them to satisfy their need and fulfill their right to housing. Although the following governments between 1958 and 1970 acted with more efficacy and diligence with regard to the housing problem, the number of *tomas* and the *pobladores* movement as a whole continued to grow, taking the form of a political subject (for example, their organizations evolved both in form and content, from the National Front for Housing to the National Federation of *Pobladores*). In terms of urban development, *tomas* and *poblaciones* were part of the sprawl model of urbanization that characterizes Santiago, which has been mostly driven by speculation and links between public policies and the private surpluses of land commerce.

One of the foundations of the conservative and neoliberal revolution forcibly imposed during the last forty years in Chile was the dismantling of social organizations, especially those related to the working class. This process first took the form of straightforward repression in the seventies and eighties during the dictatorship. During that time *pobladores* were politically very active, not only in the resistance within established *poblaciones* but also in creating new *tomas* (then known as camps) in the early eighties;[22] some of these were evicted, however some developed into more formal settlements. In many aspects, this policy on civil organization was given continuity by democratic governments after 1990, when the violent repression successfully evolved into a strategy of transforming individuals from a social subject into a client of public policies. In terms of urban space, the 1990s were marked by the development of public-private partnerships to build motorways and the construction of new parks (the already mentioned Urban Parks Program) as a means to pursue social equality, but also as tools for granting social peace without necessarily involving communities (for instance, the *pobladores*) in the process of production of such infrastructures. The other key element of the decade in terms of production of space was the massive construction of social housing, based on the still current model where the state allegedly plays only a subsidiary role and the private sector builds housing units for people already registered through public procedures. This scheme worked to alleviate the huge deficit in terms of numbers and it was labelled as a non-traditional export by the Chilean government.

However, this model produced serious social segregation and degradation given the state criterion of buying the cheapest possible land, which meant locating housing in former farming land without urban infrastructure and repeating the pattern of the *tomas* of the 1950s and 1960s. In this context, the *pobladores* behind the Toma de Peñalolén managed to identify location as a central argument of their struggle, acting directly against the 'public' rationale and recovering the tradition of ground-up processes of production of urban space.

Peñalolén Park: A failed possibility for a new commons?

The discussion about the use of the commons as a concept to analyze public space in the Chilean political context can be further explained through the example of the Toma de Peñalolén and its subsequent transformation into Peñalolén Park, a sports and recreation area currently under construction in the eastern part of Santiago. To a certain extent, this case is exemplary of the complex institutional arrangement underlying the production of public space in Chile, due to the way social movements, central and local governments interact within the restrictions and agendas of the political and legal framework. It is also an interesting example of how the *pobladores* movement can be seen as a driving force behind the possibility of creating new commons in Chile and therefore as a threat to the dominant public-private model of production of space.

The Toma de Peñalolén was a land taking that began in April 1999, occupying a large private lot (approximately twenty-three hectares) that belonged to Miguel Nasur, a somewhat polemic businessman linked with football and public transportation. Although there were almost 140 families living in the lot before that year, the land taking was notorious for its massive scale and almost perfect coordination: in a single morning, 500 families, most of them coming from other historical neighborhoods (*poblaciones*) in the same municipality, entered the lot and installed their tents, then their shacks. Within less than a year, there were around 1,800 families living in the *toma,* giving the taking its 'definitive' shape. Less than fifty percent of these people were former Peñalolén residents. During its first year, the *toma* developed into an ordered settlement, with an inner street network; later on, the municipality provided provisional sewerage via a government-funded project, while it also regularly paid for electricity bills. With the aid of organized groups from older *tomas* in the area, the dwellers rapidly established their claim in the public opinion, namely: to obtain housing subsidies from the government in order to remain in the lot instead of moving to 'normal' social housing located in the outskirts of Santiago.

The incumbent mayor at the time, Carlos Alarcón (center-right wing) did not take action against the occupation (in fact, there were rumors from early 1999 that the taking could take place, but the municipality didn't actively try to prevent it); on the contrary, he kept himself at a distance, trying to gain the *pobladores'* support by providing certain municipal services like trash collection or water supply. However, this strategy did not work as he had hoped and in the 2000 elections he was replaced by Claudio Orrego, a Christian Democrat and a former Minister of Housing and Urban Planning, who was a member of the coalition in power and therefore attempted to address the political problem posed by the *toma* by involving the central government in its solution.

Since taking office, Mayor Orrego has adopted a twofold position towards the *toma:* while he favored the idea that its inhabitants should get definitive housing in Peñalolén, avoiding expulsion, he rejected their claim to remain in the lot. During his first term (2000–2004), the public discussions about the *toma* were actually centered on the negotiation between the *pobladores* and the central government about the purchase of the land in order to build social housing in it; with this in mind,

Figure 1. Mosaic developed by Peñalolén community organizations depicting their visions for the park, 2009.

Orrego named staff close to him to form a 'political committee' in order to channel the demands by the *pobladores,* contain them and try to convince them that they were not to remain in the lot but would have to leave for housing somewhere else in Santiago. By this time, the landowner had changed his strategy in court from trying to get the *pobladores* evicted to forcing the state to buy the land at a 'market price.'

When running for his second term, Orrego devised the idea of a large public park for Peñalolén, although the location he first proposed during the campaign was the Quebrada de Macul, a mountainside ravine that in 1993 had been the scene of a great flood that killed thirty-four people and left more than 32,000 homeless.[23] Only afterwards, in early 2005, did the mayor publicly address the project for a new park on the land occupied by the *toma,* coining the idea of a 'Chilean Central Park'[24] that would play the role for the disadvantaged in Chile that the famous New York park played for immigrants (Figure 1).

The proposal of a park can be read as a strategic political decision regarding the conflict posed by the *toma*: by proposing the development of a public space, politicians, with help from corporate media, reframed the focus of the conflict, transforming the *pobladores*' struggle for the right to the city and housing into an organized pressure group with a sort of 'privatizing agenda.' With such a move, local authorities gave the central government the chance to maintain the status quo in their housing-related land policy, namely buying the cheapest land possible, while closing the door to other initiatives claiming centrality and integration.

The association between local and central government proved effective in every scale of comparison when the Ministry of Housing and Urban Planning made a change in the Metropolitan Zoning and Land Use Plan of Santiago in order to transform the use of the private lot from residential to green area, thus significantly reducing the price of the land. The owner had to politically negotiate with the government and the purchase of the lot was set at a low price, which however was still five times the price MINVU would have paid for land earmarked for social housing.

This operation marked a watershed in the process of contested production of space, because the land occupied by the *toma* entered the status of 'national good' and therefore became state property; however, as has been explained, that does not necessarily mean that this good became open to public use. The proposal by central and local government in order to build a park in the lot became a sort of indisputable argument within the struggle for the right to the city (in this case, centrality), considering that it posed the prestige of a public space for everybody against the 'private interests' of the *pobladores*.

Thus, the latter were in a way dispossessed of the 'national good' they had helped to create in the first place through their organization and struggle. Besides acquiring the land legally, the state appropriated it symbolically, denying to a certain extent the possibility of imagining urban space from a different perspective than the binary (and misguiding) opposition between private and public (meaning state property). Later, and maybe mirroring the problems and mistakes of the public institutions of the 1950s, the park went through different projects and directions, transforming from a community park (the prestigious promise of democratic public space) to a sports facilities park, largely controlled by the central government and designed to host part of the 2014 South American Games (Figure 2). But that's a different story to tell.

Conclusions

In a historical moment where the Chilean elites congratulated themselves on the success of the so-called 'transition to democracy' and an economic model that portrayed mass production of state-financed housing as one of this process's highest achievements, the *Toma de Peñalolén* implied a harsh refutation to these discourses and set the state and corporate machineries into motion in order to prevent this ex-

Figure 2. View of the velodrome built in Peñalolén Park for the 2014 South American Games, 2014.

periment of creating a 'new commons' from becoming a wider and deeper movement to imitate historical precedents.

When trying to define what the concept of the commons applied to public spaces would mean in the Chilean context, it is important to review history in order to understand the weak role and position that 'civil society' has endured throughout history within a context heavily marked by the existence of a highly centralized, presidential state with authoritarian tendencies. On the other hand, the growing influence of corporate power in the decision-making process regarding urban development, especially since the 1980s, defines a context where the commons approach necessarily implies a counter-cultural stance or even a radical political position.

Is it possible to define urban public space in the Chilean context as a commons? Probably this is not an accurate question, in the light of the cases analyzed here; maybe the proper question should be: how can we foster the idea of the commons as a collective endeavor and a culture of collaboration in the process of rethinking institutions and processes of production of public space in Chile? History generously provides us with examples; the current challenges are to develop methodological tools and imagine new political arrangements to change the *state* of things.

Notes

1. Elinor Ostrom, *Governing the Commons. The Evolution of Institutions for Collective Action* (New York: Cambridge University Press, 1990).
2. Peter Linebaugh, *The Magna Carta Manifesto. Liberties and Commons for All* (Los Angeles: University of California Press, 2008), 49.
3. Elinor Ostrom, "Collective Action and the Evolution of Social Norms," *The Journal of Economic Perspectives* 14, no. 3 (2000): 137–158.
4. Henri Lefebvre, *The Production of Space* (Oxford: Blackwell, 1991).
5. An Architektur, "On the Commons: A Public Interview with Massimo De Angelis and Stavros Stavrides," *e-flux journal,* no. 17 (2010).
6. Ibid.
7. Edella Schlager, "Common-Pool Resource Theory," in *Environmental Governance Reconsidered: Challenges, Choices and Opportunities,* Robert F. Durant, Daniel J. Fiorino and Rosemary O'Leary, eds. (Cambridge: MIT Press, 2004), 145–175.
8. Antonio Negri and Judith Revel, "Inventing the Common," *generation-online.org,* May 13, 2008, http://www.generation-online.org/p/fp_revel5.htm (accessed September 4, 2013).
9. Mario Garcés, *Tomando su sitio. El movimiento de pobladores de Santiago, 1957–1970* (Santiago: LOM Ediciones, 2002).
10. Ibid.
11. Linebaugh, *The Magna Carta Manifesto,* 59.
12. Olga Segovia, ed., *Espacios públicos y construcción social. Hacia un ejercicio de ciudadanía,* (Santiago: Ediciones SUR, 2007).
13. Daniel Opazo, *Espacio transitorio. Producción, prácticas y representaciones del espacio público político en Santiago de Chile 1983–2008* (Doctoral dissertation, Pontificia Universidad Católica de Chile, 2010).
14. Manuel Delgado and Daniel Malet, "El espacio público como ideología," *Diputació de Barcelona,* 2007, http://www.diba.cat/documents/523487/523545/participacio-dretshumans-fitxers-altres_recursos-2forum-article_delgado-pdf.pdf (accessed May 22, 2014).
15. Elizabeth Blackmar, "Appropriating 'the Commons': The Tragedy of Property Rights Discourse," in *The Politics of Public Space,* Setha Low and Neil Smith, eds. (New York: Routledge, 2006), 49–80.
16. Sergio León, "Conceptos sobre espacio público, gestión de proyectos y lógica social: reflexiones sobre la experiencia chilena," *EURE* 24, no. 71 (1998): 27–36.
17. Elke Schlack, "Espacio público," *ARQ* 65 (2007): 25–27.
18. Opazo, *Espacio transitorio,* 106.
19. Garcés, *Tomando su sitio.*
20. Matías Ocaranza, "Renovación sin gentrificación. Proyecto de vivienda social y propuesta de metodología participativa para el mejoramiento urbano en la Población La Victoria," (Dipl. Arch. thesis, Universidad de Chile, 2010).
21. Garcés, *Tomando su sitio.*
22. SUR, "Tomas de terreno," *Hechos Urbanos* no. 18 (1983): 1.
23. Luigi Brignardello, interview with author, August 7, 2013.
24. El Mercurio, "Proponen creación de parque en terreno de toma de Peñalolén," *El Mercurio,* May 15, 2005.

Ignacio Castillo Ulloa

Acting in Reality within the Cranny of the Real: Towards an Alternative Agency of Urban Commons

Introduction: The question of the agency of the (urban) commons

The question of the agency of the commons is a question of 'who' is to deal with such a task and 'how'. The commons, though defined in manifold ways in the literature, seems to be constituted essentially of three elements:[1] (1) one or multiple resource(s); (2) people making use of such resource(s) (the 'commoners') that ensure the commons' production and reproduction; and (3) the processes of negotiation, decision-making and action-taking (i.e., the practices of 'commoning') which determine 'how' resources are to be utilized, i.e., "the rules of appropriation."[2] The agency of the commons, on such account, relates closely to this latter characteristic of the commons — which does not mean that it averts its other two co-constitutive aspects — and has traditionally oscillated between two poles: strong state intervention and privatization.[3] In either scenario, the management of the commons has to do with the level of access to it in order to ensure an 'adequate' use. To put it differently: the question of the agency of the commons is, ironically, a question of its *enclosure*.

This chapter explores the agency of urban commons and focuses on more 'traditional' commons, namely public spaces and goods, that is, "those shared resources that a community builds and maintains (libraries, parks, streets)."[4] To that end, the chapter deals with the interplay between state and civil society in terms of the urban commons enclosure dialectic and how "it produces specific materialities, spatialities, and subjectivities."[5] Moreover, the notion of urban planning and, particularly, its master plans, is thought to be the mechanism utilized by the state, par excellence, to control the access to the aforementioned 'traditional' urban commons. More specifically, a language of planning expertise circumscribes the urban commons enclosure dynamic by determining, through master plans, the principles of exclusion/inclusion. As a result, the "governmentality"[6] (the rationalities and mentalities driving the 'will' of the state) is able to not only deploy, but also spatialize power. Here the Lacanian difference between 'reality' and 'the Real' is encountered, given that the former "is the social reality of actual people in interaction and in the productive process," while the latter "is the inexorable, 'abstract', spectral logic"[7] of the master plan commands which takes place in socio-spatial reality. The state is then able to advance its ideological project since "the ultimate experience of the Real is not that of 'reality' which shatters illusions, but that of an 'illusion' which 'irrationally' persists against the pressure of reality, which does not give way to 'reality'."[8]

The chapter begins with a brief overview on the Foucauldian conceptualization of power to see how rationalities (i.e., the general justifications to govern certain spaces in a specific manner) and technologies (i.e., the means whereby rationalities are implemented) come together to produce the 'spatialization of governmentality.' The discussion about power closes with a reflection on its paradoxical nature, that is to say, the everlasting 'loose end' of power that allows resistance to emerge. Such contradiction may well allow the alteration of domineering relationships between state and civil society and possibilities to bridge and rearrange the discursive rift between reality and the Real. For such a proposal to crystallize, both the notion of autonomy – spatial as well as political – and the performance of "spatial practice"[9] are required, for they orchestrate the action within the crannies of official planning devices (i.e., in the 'interstices of the Real') and facilitate the advancement of different discourses, and thus of rationalities. Consequently, new relationships between knowledge, social practices, forms of subjectivity and power, which bring the 'reality' to the fore, are likely to flourish.

These assumptions are, subsequently, elaborated in the case of Paso Ancho, an urban community[10] in southern San José, Costa Rica, where autonomous political organization and action of its dwellers triggered a process of self-steered participation aimed at improving social and spatial conditions. Spearheading the strategy and course of action was, first, demand for and, next, taking over and redefining public goods and public spaces which were thenceforward to be turned into urban commons. This process was tension- and conflict-ridden, after all "commoners are diverse among themselves, and do not necessarily know in advance how to agree upon or achieve shared goals."[11] However, it was possible, despite this hurdle, to make room for an alternative 'radical commoning' – that is "the social practices and traditions that enable people to discover, innovate and negotiate new ways of doing things for themselves."[12]

The chapter concludes that both autonomous organization and spatial practice not only forge a wider public sphere, where (urban) commons functions as the substance that either connects or separates people, but may also underpin an alternative agency of urban commons through which a different future can be envisaged and engendered. In consequence, substantial socio-spatial change (grounded on needs, wants, worries, etc. of people) is brought about, 'reality' is altered and premises of 'the Real' defied. This, additionally, is seemingly more plausible at the local level, where individuals, through daily activities and struggles, collectively constitute the social fabric of cities and simultaneously create a common framework within which they all can live.

The paradox of power

Power is an unremitting topic throughout the extensive work of Michel Foucault. In his 1976 lecture, *Meshes of Power,* the key to grasp the complexity of power is pinpointed as going beyond its conceptualization as negative, repressive and – which is largely related to "government as sovereign" – to move on to "the technologies of power," i.e., the means whereby power is employed and closer to government as the "conduct of conducts." Such conceptual change requires, Foucault explains, drawing on Marx, the acknowledgment of not one, but several heterogeneous powers. They are, furthermore, to be understood in their "historical and geographical specificity" for they are "procedures that have been invented, perfected and which are endlessly developed. There exists [therefore] a veritable technology of power or, better, powers, which have their own history."[13] Foucault thus identifies a clear shift of emphasis from government as a "simple retention of territorial control to a more nuanced notion of government over a 'complex' of men and things constituted as population."[14] Within such transition, from 'territory' to 'population,' Foucault notes how power evolved to give way to "bio-power" (aimed at securing control at the individual scale of the body as well as of the society as a whole) that, by means of the "governmentality" (the technological framework of government that establishes the limits of action and behavior of individuals and social groups), creates spatial arrangements able to render societies governable – in other words, the 'spatialization of governmentality.'

The spatialization of governmentality

An era of a "bio-power" emerged with the perfection of the disciplinary powers over the body ("anatomo-politics") and over the population ("bio-politics"), which altered the relation of power to the subject and "brought life and its mechanisms into the realm of explicit calculations and made knowledge-power an agent of the transformation of human life."[15] This bio-power creates a variation of government, which, for Foucault, can be synthesized as "the conduct of conducts"[16] entailing a comprehensive power aimed at fashioning the behavior of others as well as of the self.[17] Government is thus the kind of power through which "human beings are made subjects"[18] and with the ability, somewhat deliberately, to alter certain behavioral aspects in order to reach certain goals.[19]

Foucault coined the neologism "governmentality"[20] to refer to the set of aspirations, rationalities, and mentalities that, entangled with both "anatomo-politics" and "bio-politics," try to impose a particular conduct on the subjects. The governmentality, moreover, is supported by the "production of truth,"[21] that is, all those "regimes of truth," embodied by the "ways of speaking the truth, persons authorized to speak truths, ways of enacting truths […] invention and assemblage of particular apparatuses and devices for exercising power and intervening upon certain problems."[22] Governmentality therefore evidences the asymmetrical opportunities that different political actors have to enter the deliberative arena, which, in consequence, leads to disenfranchised groups of societies ending up being subjected to dominant discourses propelled by more powerful and resourceful actors.[23] Governmentality allows understanding the way decision-making processes are mediated and manipulated even before any consensus is sought, rendering decisions heterodirected rather than autonomous.[24]

Ultimately, the rationalities and mentalities of the government are crystallized in and through space. The deployment of power, accordingly, far from being the mere coercion of statecraft practitioners over "undifferentiated blocks of subjects fixed in absolute spaces,"[25] is asserted by a "series of overlapping and discontinuous spatialities of power."[26] Space, thus, plays a central role in the application of power and in the materialization of governmentality, not only because space, as Foucault observes, "is fundamental in any form of communal life; space is fundamental in any exercise of power,"[27] but also because spatial rationalities emerge bringing to the fore causal qualities of space that are an integrative part of the operational dimension of government.[28] Consequently, in order to delve into the histories of spaces and powers shaping them, one has to look into the interrelation between power and government and the implementation of tactics and strategies meant to produce space according to particular ends. Governmentality is, all in all, "indelibly spatial, both in terms of spaces it seeks to create and in the causal logics that imbue such attempts with their rationality."[29]

The power paradox: Counteraction in the 'loose ends' of (spatialized) power

Foucault's analysis of power has been sometimes regarded as defeatist, for (state/market) power is seen as omnipresent and there is a lack of precise foundational grounds to take political stand and further counteractions.[30] There are, nevertheless, some 'hints' underlying Foucault's work as to how power relations could actually be readjusted. In *Society Must Be Defended*,[31] Foucault, while addressing and deconstructing power in the various ways that it transverses 'real' societies, highlights the role of knowledge and discourse, predicating that it is at the 'local' that knowledges and discourses are subjugated to and occluded by hegemonic forces; but, at the same time, stating that "it is through the challenge of these counter ['conquered'] knowledges and their local settings that alternatives can emerge."[32] In addition, there seems to be a rather puzzling outcome of the interaction between (the exercise of both) power and resistance: the persistent aspiration of power to preempt defiance results in a surfeit that cannot be restrained. In other words, "power itself generates resistance to itself, the excess it can never control, and the reactions [...] to its subjection to disciplinary norms are unpredictable."[33]

This 'fissure' that is opened up, and that may well let the counter local knowledges and discourses arise, carries also a 'spatial echo.' The 'spatialization of the governmentality,' for instance, through urban planning tools, fosters spatial arrangements capable of averting the organization of popular formations, i.e., those individual and collective social spaces from which resistance may spring. Nevertheless, space, as Doreen Massey sustains, is never finished, there are always loose ends that, in turn, generate opportunities for change to happen.[34] Such change can stem from the reconfiguration of space via the liberation of local knowledges and discourses, because,

> no matter how terrifying a given system may be, there always remain the possibilities of resistance, disobedience, and oppositional group-

ings [...] Liberty is a *practice* [...] The liberty of men is never assured by institutions and laws that are intended to guarantee them. That is why almost all of these laws and institutions are capable of being turned around. Not because they are ambiguous, but simply because "liberty" is what must be exercised.[35]

It is therefore by exercising liberty that governmentality, spatially projected onto societies via urban planning instruments and safeguarded by institutional frameworks, can actually be overcome. As argued by Foucault, liberty is not essentially something guaranteed from 'above' by formal institutions – it is not about having the 'legal right' to be free. In fact, the performance of liberty is, sometimes, to antagonize the very institutional structure that sets social and spatial rules of behavior and discipline for a given society. The catch, though, is that liberty is not performed in just one ubiquitous way. As is here sustained, liberty, in order to fight back against the spatialization of governmentality, should result from the strategic combination of autonomy and spatial practice, so that suppressed local knowledges and rationalities, first enter and, then become a substantial part of the deliberative political arena.

The paradox of power, all things considered, can be summarized as follows: despite any attempt to tame space and people, there is a continuous chance for contestation, given that the fantasy of absolute order and control is never fully realized – neither in social nor in spatial terms. A possibility of counteraction in the 'loose ends' of spatialized power is next explored building on the case of Paso Ancho to see how the complementarity of autonomy and spatial practice might infuse local discourses and knowledges with enough political import to 'turn around' master plan schemes and advance an alternative, locally and collectively conceived, socio-spatial reality, in which dynamics of inclusion/exclusion of urban commons, rather than be a domain of governmentality, are handled by people themselves.

Paso Ancho: Acting in reality within the cranny of the Real

Urban planning, its master plans and its languages and knowledges of 'truth' usually appear to be an undisputable totalizing force. There is, nonetheless, the possibility to invert the interrelation between 'the dystopian Real' (imbued with the unalterable logic of master plans) and 'utopian reality' (produced by people in close contact throughout the productive process), because of the inherent contradictory nature of power and the potential a 'spatially practiced autonomy' holds. It is, in other words, plausible to act, spatially and autonomously, not only *in* but also *from* reality within the cranny – produced by the power paradox – of the Real.

Advancing 'utopian reality' against an ambiguous 'dystopian Real'

Urban planning in Costa Rica has a marked state-led tradition. Master plans have been carried out, though not all that successfully implemented, to control urban development at different geographical scales:[36] *Plan Nacional de Desarrollo Urbano* (PNDU, nationwide), *Plan GAM 83* (a regional plan conceived for the *Gran* Área *Metropolitana,* the country's largest urban agglomeration), and the *Planes Reguladores* (local plans that each municipality is supposed to have and apply).[37] Additionally, citizen participation is granted within a highly statutory planning framework, at least theoretically, as a requisite to produce and supervise the execution of the master plans. In practice, however, citizen participation is, if anything, tokenistic.[38] As a result, the technical-scientific jargon of official planning practitioners secures the governmentality and underplays any 'uprising' of local knowledges and discourses.

Paso Ancho is an urban community located south of the *Gran* Área *Metropolitana* that has undergone the somewhat fuzzy effects of the *Plan GAM 83*, which have been echoed by the various versions of the *Plan Regulador* of the municipality of San José, the local government. The *Plan GAM 83* was put together to envisage a well-ordered urban region; that is, it propelled 'order and control' as the governmentality's "master signifier," i.e., an encompassing idea that functions as a nodal point within a larger net of supporting signifiers and, though tending to be fixed, "their descriptive features will be fundamentally unstable and open to all kinds of hegemonic rearticulations."[39] Based on classical modern planning principles, the master plan contained a zoning scheme in which diverse activities were clearly and spatially demarcated and linked to each other by transport networks, conceived around privately owned vehicles. The resulting zones (residential, industrial, leisure, etc.) were to fit inside an 'urban growth containment ring' according to accurate demographic and construction density indicators – as though the birth rate of the population could actually stick to them and existing buildings, all of a sudden, be wiped out. Out of these 'bio-political guidelines,' the zoning proposal, and the complex connection between political (electoral support) and economic (land market speculation) interests, a center-periphery dynamic progressively created a spatial hierarchy, largely reflected in the access to, and quality of, public goods and public spaces, giving, in the course of time, rise to an "urbanization of injustice."[40]

Along with nearby urban communities, Paso Ancho was, in the midst of an adamant urban chaos, progressively relegated to the 'excluded periphery' and experienced the scarcity of public goods and public spaces as compared with other more 'privileged' districts of the canton of San José. Yet, this cluster of disenfranchised urban communities became known, rather pejoratively, as *Barrios del Sur* (southern neighborhoods), due partly to the ferocious struggles and claims people from these barrios – as well as from other divested metropolitan areas – advanced to fight back the asymmetries of the urban expansion within the GAM, and which revolve around better access to public services (electricity, water, transportation, housing, and the like) and public goods (roads, parks, etc.).[41] Although there were a couple of victories here and there, communities as 'political spaces' became increasingly dominated by both the central state and traditional political parties, which sensibly limited the potential to orchestrate citizen mobilizations and further a more just urban development.[42]

Be that as it may, a 'utopian reality' (the alternative vision of the future that 'ordinary' people sought to create based on a critical analysis of their present conditions and overriding taken-for-granted norms) challenged the ambiguous 'dystopia of the Real' that the governmentality impelled, socially and spatially, through the master plans, both the *Plan GAM 83* and the *Plan Regulador*. This was even possible in spite of the governmentality's internal contradiction: though the illusion of an 'order' was not entirely, as foreseen, achieved, political, social, and spatial control was, to a certain extent, obtained. These mobilizations, moreover, can be seen, following Manuel Castells, as "urban social movements"[43] combining "struggles for improved collective consumption with struggles for community culture as well as for political self-determination,"[44] a particularity that, in time, turned out to be determinant for rekindling activism in Paso Ancho.

Going deeper into the cranny: The revival of citizen mobilization and self-organization in Paso Ancho

While this wave of mobilizations, which dates back to 1980s and the beginning of 1990s, was contained, it also left a sort of 'organizational sediment' within the social fabric of Paso Ancho that could profit, once more, from the incompleteness of the spatialization of governmentality – i.e., the 'spatial cracks' that the *Plan GAM 83* and the *Plan Regulador* ironically could not help producing. In 2008, under the umbrella of the *Comité Patriótico*[45] (patriotic committee), a group of community-based organizations triggered a process to alter and directly influence their living environment socially and spatially. To that end, a local development agenda was elaborated drawing on needs, wants, desires, priorities, worries, etc. that people themselves stipulated.

Deliberation to come up with this development agenda, far from being easy and smooth, was permeated with tensions and conflicts, which were internally addressed and overcome. Once collective agreement was acquired, a campaign was launched to stress the eroded quality of public infrastructure (e.g., sidewalks, roads, street lighting) and public services (e.g., solid waste management). Through canvassing, distribution of leaflets, workshops, and gatherings, a significant number of people[46] were engaged and a protest was conducted to demand the construction of a pedestrian bridge, given the increasing number of accidents that were happening at different points along freeway 39 – known as the *Circunvalación* – as residents of Paso Ancho and neighboring communities tried to cross from one side to another. The pedestrian bridge, furthermore, was regarded as the greatest infrastructural dearth and its construction had been pursued, for over two decades, by more 'traditional' means such as lobbying and garnering letters 'promising' a prompt solution – thus the need for more 'radical' and 'aggressive' measures.[47] Despite the fact that the bridge was not immediately built, by exercising civil disobedience to demand solutions, people in Paso Ancho became aware, on the one hand, of their "political opportunity structure" (i.e., "when ordinary people amass their resources to overcome their disorganization and gain the knowledge of where and how to use their resources")[48] and, on the other hand, of the importance to revitalize the "communitarian politics" for advancing new claims,[49] since linkages with people are easier to establish, ideas are better conveyed, broader support may be attained and, eventually, a political space can be (re)opened.

'Radical commoning': Turning public goods and public spaces into urban commons

Given that residents in Paso Ancho were able to level their 'daily personal rhythms' and interests with those of the community and, alongside, gain emotional security

to join the mobilization, new strategies to carry on the local development agenda could be outlined and executed. Thus, the *República de Haití* elementary school, the *Emma Gamboa* public library, and an abandoned public park were targeted to frame upcoming actions.

The elementary school was used to create the *Escuela Popular Pablo Presbere*. This initiative consisted, in the first place, of providing students with non-traditional and progressive pedagogical methods. Afterwards, it became an 'open social forum,' where ideas, comments, preoccupations, proposals, etc., regarding not only the education system, but also other dimensions of the community, could be expressed, discussed and, if possible, executed. The public library was equipped with texts about the history, traditions, data, etc. of Paso Ancho and was occasionally employed as a venue for the sessions of the *Escuela Popular Pablo Presbere* as well as plays organized by an amateur theater group. The so-called *Parque de los Héroes* (park of the heroes), an abandoned public space located next to the public library, was cleaned and made available to the public. The process of renewal involved the active input of dwellers to bring about physical improvements (painting a mural, mowing the lawn, repairing benches, etc.) and establish opening hours, secure free access and disambiguate 'proper' uses.[10] The park was also, less frequently, a site where get-togethers to tackle issues of the local development agenda took place.

The gradual, dynamic and autonomous reappropriation and redefinition of these public goods and public space, are, indeed, spatial practice, because "the spatial practice of a society secretes that society's space; it propounds and presupposes it, in a dialectical interaction; it produces it slowly and surely as it masters and appropriates it."[51] Residents of Paso Ancho were, in effect, able to 'decipher' and 'secrete' their own space in close affinity with "people's perception of the world, of their world, particularly in its everyday ordinariness."[52] The ability, moreover, to go beyond citizen participation mechanisms sanctioned by authorities and invent new self-steered spaces of substantial deliberation, facilitated the 'insurrection' of 'subjugated local knowledges' and action 'within the cranny,' since the irruption of the governmentality was kept to a considerable limit. Also, discourses were able to place as 'master signifier' the expression of a local identity in terms of the rich past, the present culture, and the potential future of Paso Ancho. A clearer message was then being delivered, in contrast to abstract notions like 'quality of life,' which are all too often encountered in master plans and outspokenly put forward by official planning practitioners.

Equally, the Paso Ancho 'spatially practiced autonomy' may be seen as 'radical commoning,' the process through which the vigorous political action of citizens turns public goods and public spaces, conventionally under state power and public administration, into urban commons. Therefore, the minute the social force of Paso Ancho influenced the education system directly, and people gathered in the public park, the public library, the elementary school, or any corner in the barrio for that matter, to share their political views and demands, a radical socio-spatial practice of commoning was, in effect, being performed. In other words, an alternative agency of urban commons was, autonomously and radically from the bottom up, being prompted and so new commons created or existing ones taken over and redefined, for the divergent gap between 'insurrectional' local (entwined with 'reality') and 'unobjectionable' technical-scientific (entangled in 'the Real') knowledges was progressively bridged. This was possible because urban commons, after all, are "not to be construed [...] as a particular kind of thing, asset or even social process, but as an unstable and malleable social relation between a particular self-defined social group and those aspects of its actually existing or yet-to-be-created social and/or physical environment deemed crucial to its life and livelihood."[53]

What happens when the cranny shrinks?

Because of the alternative agency of urban commons performed in Paso Ancho, "unscripted [political] spaces,"[54] where freedom of speech can be exercised, were gained and, in parallel, the community, as a whole, became a "liminal space; that is, space at the limits of control, limits that permit the appearance of things, acts, and persons unforeseen, yet focused and sited."[55] This, similarly, reveals the key role public space plays in enabling different means of citizen participation in political decision-making, which, in turn, is vital for the "generativity of the commons to manifest itself, [for] it needs the 'open spaces' for bottom-up initiatives to occur in interaction with the resources at hand. In this way, citizenship and governance are blended and reconstituted."[56]

Radical, alternative and autonomous as commoning in Paso Ancho was, it did not go unnoticed by the local government authorities, and the leverage of the municipality to disrupt actions became a burden quite hard to circumvent. Oddly enough, the aid of the local government was actually first sought in regard to some specific initiatives (e.g., a solid waste management program, the recovery of the park, amid others). Meetings were held, certain assistance (e.g., facilitation of equipment) was granted and middle- and long-term promises were made; but, in the end, it became clear that local officials were only paying lip service. Afterwards, the unorthodox uses (i.e., theater plays, assemblies of the *Escuela Popular Pablo Presbere* or gatherings to discuss specific ideas/initiatives) of the public library as well as of the elementary school were called into question by municipal authorities contending that they did not conform to established house rules and they were thus no longer allowed. According to two interviewed Paso Ancho activists, the theater plays were forbidden due to their alleged 'improper' political content, i.e., ideological censorship. The municipality, building on stilted arguments and jargon, claimed that the public library was not meant to be used for activities from which profit was generated (alluding to the symbolic donations people made after every theatrical or other cultural performance). Similarly, assemblies were subtly suppressed by drastically changing the opening hours and days of the public library and keeping the access to the elementary school to a minimum (the building was shut down during weekdays once the school hours were over and throughout the whole weekend no entrance was permitted).

In addition, people's engagement and enthusiasm was sensibly, though not entirely, worn out due to the reactivation of clientelistic tactics and strategies such as promising improvements in infrastructure (e.g., sidewalks, streets, sewage systems, etc.), construction of long-needed amenities (e.g., public plazas or parks, basketball courts, communities centers, etc.), social housing bonds, and others of that ilk. This deeply rooted tradition of clientelism is aimed at disseminating a 'why bother?' culture and passivity among citizens, drawing on a "patronage system in which the municipality both identifies and fulfils the 'real' necessities of the communities under its jurisdiction seeking to ensure electoral support and thus deploy political control."[37] In consequence, the status quo could be restored as the municipality positioned itself as the single responsible party for local development issues.[38]

Little by little, the mobilization and self-organization in Paso Ancho did lose momentum, but it did not cease to exist. Nowadays, the situation seems to be, so to speak, on 'stand by.'[39] Activists from the different organizations involved, and in particular from the *Comité Patriótico,* still meet every now and then to come up with ideas and proposals to surmount the social and spatial control that the municipality exerts and, in so doing, reach out for empowerment, triggering again "a process of conquering *autonomy* and overcoming *heteronomy*."⁶⁰ The 'cranny,' accordingly, remains open due to a synergic combination of factors: the autonomy and independence that the mobilization has had at all times (avoiding, for instance, attempts at co-optation and further developing the ability of people to do things themselves); the level of compromise exhibited not only by activists but also, and perhaps more importantly, by 'the commoners'; the strong feeling of attachment to the place of residence (i.e., a place-based identity)⁶¹ that underpins the 'communitarian (spatial) politics'; and the acquirement and utilization of a series of skills (teamwork, articulation of ideas, deliberation, etc.) which, eventually, led to a certain degree of "conscientization," that is to say, the capacity "to perceive the social, political and economic contradictions and to take action against the oppressive elements of reality."⁶²

People in Paso Ancho, by acting *in reality* within the cranny of *the Real*, though they have not transformed society anew, have indeed, building on Manuel Castells' basic goals of urban social movements, transformed 'urban meanings' due to: first, the rearrangement of the community around its *use* value (against the logic of *exchange* value); second, the search for a cultural identity as well as the creation of autonomous local cultures (i.e., direct and close interaction between 'commoners' to generate a socially defined 'communal' meaning); and, third, "the urban self-management in contradiction to the centralized state and a subordinate and undifferentiated territorial administration."⁶³ These three elements composed the forefront of the 'radical commoning' in Paso Ancho and furthered the imagination and crystallization of a different future.

Conclusion: Imagining a different future in present tense

> Without commons, there's no room for people to maneuver, there's no space for change, and no space for life. The future is literally born out of commons.⁶⁴

Paul Valéry's famous and shrewd statement, "the future, like everything else, is no longer quite what it used to be,"⁶⁵ connects well with Neal Gorenflo's assertion of just how critical 'conquering' public goods and public space and turning them into urban commons is for advancing change and, in the long run, make a different future possible. Urban commons, as the case of Paso Ancho shows, underpin individual and collective life; they allow communities to establish linkages with the places they inhabit, forge endogenous identities and develop social ties of reciprocal solidarity. That being so, urban commons are essential to open paths so that socio-spatial reality can be imagined and materialized as *"the process of achieving more social justice through changes both in social relations (institutions, laws and norms) and in spatiality (from the spatial structures in a material sense to the territoriality and the images of places)."*[66]

At least ideally, such a process entails deliberative and inclusive democratic practices. It is, for this reason, not surprising that struggles are quite likely to arise around the agency of urban commons, because "questions of the commons are contradictory and therefore always contested [and] behind these contestations lie conflicting social interests."[67] Though people in Paso Ancho were able to work out, to a considerable extent, divergences of interests and opinions among themselves, they could not all that successfully deal with the bigotry of the local government. Thus, the incisive and precise deployment of power by the municipality – negating concrete petitions, reducing support to a minimum, and purposely creating tensions about the use of reappropriated urban commons – did demand more devious responses. Above all, the radical and autonomous seeding of new kinds of urban commons enterprises almost inevitably alters the status quo and defies power relations, since they "must often work within the existing system of law and policy, which risks co-optation of the commons and the domestication of its innovations. Despite this real danger, commons initiatives need not lose their transformative, catalytic potential simply because they work 'within the system'."[68]

It is, indeed, viable to work 'within the system' for the system, or better said, the Real inherently produces it owns spatial crannies from which people can perform a fundamentally different agency of urban commons. There, accordingly, exists the perennial possibility for counteraction, for the insurrection of local knowledges and languages, for imagining an alternative future in the present tense. Tales, like the one of Paso Ancho, attest to the fact that radical emancipatory outbursts are not, de facto, to be read along a past-present continuum; they instead constitute "fragments of a utopian future that lies dormant in the present as hidden potential" and can only be decoded from an "engaged position."[69] In the same vein, people in Paso Ancho conflated a 'historical moment' (i.e., the critical analysis and challenge of the present as in how it came to be what it is) with a 'political moment' (i.e., the envisioning and proclaiming of other versions of what is yet to be). This breakthrough is what allows us to fully and appropriately grasp the far-reaching input of an alternative agency of urban commons in which the future is, effectively, no longer what it used to be – meant, evidently, in a regressive sense – but what we all wholeheartedly and progressively would want it to be.

Notes

1. See the editors' introduction for a more detailed discussion about the commons and its three basic features in light of the "urban."
2. Andreas Exner and Brigitte Kratzwald, *Solidarische Ökonomie & Commons* (Vienna: Mandelbaum, 2012), 23.
3. David Harvey, "The Future of the Commons," *Radical History Review,* 2011, no. 109: 101; David Harvey, *Rebel Cities: From the Right to the City to the Urban Revolution* (London: Verso, 2012), 68.
4. David Bollier, "The Commons: A Neglected Sector of Wealth-Creation," in *Genes, Bytes and Emissions: To Whom does the World Belong?,* Silke Helfrich, ed. (Berlin: Heinrich Böll Stiftung, 2009), 1.
5. Alex Jeffrey et al., "Rethinking Enclosure: Space, Subjectivity and the Commons," *Antipode* 44, no. 4 (2012): 1249.
6. Michel Foucault, "Governmentality," trans. Rosi Braidotti, *I&C,* 1979, no. 6. Rpt, in *The Foucault Effect: Studies in Governmentality,* Graham Burchell, Colin Gordon and Peter Miller, eds. (Chicago: University of Chicago Press, 1991).
7. Slavoj Žižek, *The Year of Dreaming Dangerously* (London: Verso, 2012), 102.
8. Slavoj Žižek, *Did Somebody Say Totalitarianism?: Five Interventions in the (Mis)use of a Notion* (London: Verso, 2001), 166.
9. Henri Lefebvre, *The Production of Space,* trans. Donald Nicholson-Smith (Oxford: Blackwell, 1991 [1974]).
10. Community is hereafter understood as a "set of commoners who share [...] resources and who define for themselves the rules according to which they are accessed and used" (Massimo De Angelis and Stavros Stavrides, "On the Commons: A Public Interview with Massimo De Angelis and Stavros Stavrides," *e-flux Journal* 6, no. 17 [2010]: 2).
11. David Bollier and Silke Helfrich, "The Commons as a Transformative Vision," *Shareable: Sharing by Design Blog,* October 31, 2012, http://www.shareable.net/blog/the-commons-as-a-transformative-vision (accessed December 15, 2014).
12. Ibid.
13. Michel Foucault, "The Meshes of Power," trans. Gerald Moore, in *Space, Knowledge and Power: Foucault and Geography,* Jeremy Crampton and Stuart Elden, eds. (Hampshire: Ashgate, 2007), 156/158.
14. Stuart Elden and Jeremy Crampton, "Introduction Space, Knowledge and Power: Foucault and Geography," in *Space, Knowledge and Power: Foucault and Geography,* Jeremy Crampton and Stuart Elden, eds. (Hampshire: Ashgate, 2007), 7.
15. Michel Foucault, *The Will to Knowledge: The History of Sexuality Volume 1,* trans. Robert Hurley (New York: Random House, 1978 [1976]), 143.
16. Michel Foucault, "Afterword: The Subject and Power," trans. Leslie Sawyer, in *Michel Foucault: Beyond Structuralism and Hermeneutics,* Hubert Dreyfus and Paul Rabinow, eds. (Chicago: University of Chicago Press, 1983), 220–221.
17. Margo Huxley, "Geographies of Governmentality," in *Space, Knowledge and Power: Foucault and Geography,* Jeremy Crampton and Stuart Elden, eds. (Hampshire: Ashgate, 2007), 187.

18 Foucault, "Afterword: The Subject and Power," 221.
19 Mitchell Dean, *Governmentality: Power and Rule in Modern Society* (London: Sage, 1999), 10.
20 Foucault, "Governmentality."
21 Ibid., 79.
22 Nikolas Rose, *Powers of Freedom: Reframing Political Thought* (Cambridge: Cambridge University Press), 19.
23 Álvaro Sevilla, "Urbanismo, Biopolítica, Gubernamentalidad: Vida y Espacio en la Renovación de los Estudios Urbanos," *Boletín CF+S,* 2010, no. 44: 44.
24 Álvaro Sevilla, "Missing Biopolitics: Governance vs. Governmentality in the Management of Neighborhood Movement in Madrid" (paper presented at the International Conference City Futures '09, Madrid, June 4–6, 2009), 1–2.
25 Mathew Coleman and John Agnew, "The Problem with *Empire*," in *Space, Knowledge and Power: Foucault and Geography,* Jeremy Crampton and Stuart Elden, eds. (Hampshire: Ashgate, 2007), 321.
26 Elden and Crampton, "Introduction," *Space, Knowledge and Power,* 12.
27 Michel Foucault, "Space, Knowledge and Power," trans. Christian Hubert, in *The Foucault Reader,* Paul Rabinow, ed. (New York: Pantheon Books, 1984), 252.
28 Huxley, "Geographies of Governmentality," 194.
29 Ibid., 199.
30 Elden and Crampton, "Introduction," *Space, Knowledge and Power,* 9.
31 Michel Foucault, *"Society Must Be Defended": Lectures at the Collège de France 1975–1976,* trans. David Macey (New York: Picador, 2003).
32 Elden and Crampton, "Introduction," *Space, Knowledge and Power,* 12.
33 Slavoj Žižek, *The Year of Dreaming Dangerously,* 106.
34 Doreen Massey, *For Space* (London: Sage, 2005).
35 Foucault, *Space, Knowledge and Power,* 245, italics in the original.
36 The political and administrative division of Costa Rica is as follows: provinces, cantons, and districts. Given the uncertainty as to the authority responsible for the regional scale, the implementation of the *Plan GAM 83* experienced diverse setbacks.
37 Some municipalities do not have a *Plan Regulador* at all, or the plan has only a partial territorial coverage. In either case, the 'planning voids' are filled with the normative body conceived for regions or the country as a whole.
38 Ignacio Castillo Ulloa, "Unravelling Spaces of Representation through Insurgent Planning Actions," in *Cities to be Tamed? Spatial Investigations Across the Urban South,* Francesco Chiodelli et al. eds. (Newcastle: Cambridge Scholars Publishing, 2013), 269.
39 Ernesto Laclau, Preface to *The Sublime Object of Ideology,* Slavoj Žižek, trans. Jon Barnes (London: Verso, 1989), xiv.
40 Andy Merrifield and Erik Swyngedouw, eds. *The Urbanization of Injustice* (New York: New York University Press, 1997).
41 Patricia Alvarenga, *De Vecinos a Ciudadanos: Movimientos Comunales y Luchas Sociales en la Historia Contemporánea Costarricense* (San José: Editorial UCR and Editorial UNA, 2005); José Valverde and María Trejos, "Diez Años de Luchas Urbanas en Costa Rica (1982–1992)," *Revista de Ciencias Sociales UCR,* 1993, no. 61.
42 Jorge Mora, *Juntas Progresistas: Organización Comunal Autonoma Costarricense 1921–1980* (San José: Fundación Friedrich Ebert, 1991); José Valverde et al., "Movimientos Sociales Populares y Democracia," in *Costa Rica: La Democracia Inconclusa,* ed. Manuel Rojas (San José: DEI/ISS-UCR, 1989); Alvarenga, *De Vecinos a Ciudadanos.*

43 Manuel Castells, *The City and the Grassroots: A Cross-Cultural Theory of Urban Social Movements* (London and Victoria: Edward Arnold, 1983).

44 Margit Mayer, "Manuel Castells' *The City and the Grassroots*," *International Journal of Urban and Regional Research* 30, no. 1 (2006): 202.

45 The patriotic committee of Paso Ancho was part of a larger network that spread throughout the country to oppose the endorsement of the United States-Dominican Republic-Central America Free Trade Agreement (CAFTA-DR). After a referendum was held to decide for or against the CAFTA-DR, some committees were dismantled, whereas others, as in the case of Paso Ancho, joined forces with existing local citizen organizations and focused on issues affecting the community.

46 The first of a series of meetings registered approximately fifty people, in its majority elderly women of a markedly popular class composition (Jeremy Rayner, "Vecinos, Ciudadanos y Patriotas: Los Comités Patrióticos y el Espacio-temporalidad de Oposición al Neoliberalismo en Costa Rica," *Revista de Ciencias Sociales UCR* 121, no. 3 [2008]: 80).

47 Jeremy Rayner, "Vecinos, Ciudadanos y Patriotas," 80.

48 Sidney Tarrow, "National Politics and Collective Action: Recent Theory and Research in Western Europe and the United States," *Annual Review of Sociology* 14 (1988): 429.

49 Rayner, "Vecinos, Ciudadanos y Patriotas."

50 During an interview with a Paso Ancho activist, it was underscored that, rather than banning possible "misuses" of the park (for instance, drinking alcohol) and their associated groups of users (which, in reality, was deemed not realistic), these uses and groups were taken into account and incorporated in order to prevent future conflicts. Up to now, said the interviewee, there has not been any significant problem.

51 Lefebvre, *The Production of Space*, 38.

52 Andy Merrifield, *Henri Lefebvre: A Critical Introduction* (New York: Routledge), 110.

53 Harvey, *Rebel Cities*, 73.

54 Richard Sennett, "The Occupy Movements Have Dramatised the Questions about Public Space: Who Owns It? And Who Can Use It?," *LSE British Politics and Policy Blog*, October 10, 2012, http://blogs.lse.ac.uk/politicsandpolicy/archives/27607 (accessed December 15, 2014).

55 Richard Sennett, "The Open City," *Towards an Urban Age*, 2006: 9–11. Rpt. in *Culture: City*, Wilfred Wang, ed. (Berlin: Akademie der Künste, 2013), 53.

56 David Bollier and Silke Helfrich, "The Commons as a Transformative Vision."

57 Castillo Ulloa, "Unravelling Spaces of Representation through Insurgent Planning Actions," 273.

58 At the local-neighborhood level, clientelism is enacted via the *Asociaciones de Desarrollo*, official community-based organizations whose mandate is directing local development.

59 As of July 2012 it was decided, after various meetings, to join struggles unfolding regarding the national health care and the education system. The presidential elections of 2014 have also provoked changes of scope for next steps to be taken. Just as it was possible to draw attention to local matters after the referendum, national circumstances seem to be gaining importance again.

60 Marcelo Lopes de Souza, "*Together* with the State, *Despite* the State, *Against* the State: Social Movements as 'Critical Urban Planning' Agents," *City* 10, no. 3 (2006): 329, italics in the original.

61 There exists a "general" place-based identity in Paso Ancho, which, in a highly complex way, derives from the diverse identities of smaller barrios located within Paso Ancho. During meetings, it was often the case that people would further "micro problems" taking place in their own barrios or even in the very street that they live (Jeremy Rayner, "Vecinos, Ciudadanos y Patriotas," 80).

62 Paulo Freire, *Pedagogy of the Oppressed*, trans. Myra Bergman Ramos (Harmondsworth: Penguin Books, 1970), 15.

63 Castells, *The City and the Grassroots*, 319–320.

64 Neal Gorenflo, "Introduction in 'Chris Carlsson Interviewed David Harvey on Rebel Cities'," *Shareable: Sharing by Design Blog,* September 5, 2012, http://www.shareable.net/blog/interviewed-david-harvey-on-rebel-cities (accessed December 15, 2014).
65 Charles Doyle et al., eds. *The Dictionary of Modern Proverbs* (New Haven: Yale University Press, 2012), 90.
66 Marcelo Lopes de Souza, "Urban Development on the Basis of Autonomy: A Politico–Philosophical and Ethical Framework for Urban Planning and Management," *Ethics, Place and Environment* 3, no. 2 (2000): 187, italics in the original.
67 Harvey, "The Future of the Commons," 102.
68 David Bollier and Silke Helfrich, "The Commons as a Transformative Vision."
69 Žižek, *The Year of Dreaming Dangerously,* 128/129.

Agnes Katharina Müller

From Urban Commons to Urban Planning – or Vice Versa? "Planning" the Contested Gleisdreieck Territory

Introduction

"Berlin is poor but sexy"[1] is one of the most repeated quotations from former Berlin mayor Klaus Wowereit. Since 2003, this phrase has become not only a label for Berlin but also for its urban policies. Berlin supports the growth of its tourism sector and the flourishing media industries with a keen eye towards becoming a serious player in the competition of international "creative cities[2]" and touristic capitals. In turn it has lately sold many of its empty plots and decayed abandoned buildings to private investors in order to fill its empty coffers and pay its tremendous debts.[3] By auctioning its property, Berlin has not considered the consequences future private developments may have on the city. As a result, the center is now filled with luxury homes, hotels, and office buildings, and the city has, to a certain extent, lost control over its own urban development in recent years. Unsurprisingly, concerned citizens, already gathered in different activists groups,[4] have initiated several protest campaigns against the urban development policies of Berlin's local government, and taken an ongoing collective stand against the clearance sale of their city. We can observe similar urban protests worldwide. The reasons and tactics differ: some are frightened to lose housing or a public space and organize campaigns such as protest camps, demonstrations, or online petitions. These collective actions show citizens' desire to keep, defend, or create a common commodity in an urban setting. Especially among academics, these movements are often related to so-called "urban commons."

Commons is, according to Michael Hardt, "an act of making and reclaiming that which we manage collectively."[5] Thus urban commons is a collective activity in an urban environment. Furthermore, urban commons can also embody a civic platform[6] to discuss urban needs and problems and a place/space to autonomously and democratically develop concepts beyond state and market tutelage. Referring to the introduction of this book, we conceive that three elements constitute commons: common pool resources, a community, and institutions or regulations created by the activities of the commoners.[7] As we already stated in the introduction, urban commons face other problems than the rural commons[8] did and do. The situation in cities is in constant societal transformation. In Western cities, for example, values and conditions in urban family and work life are changing, and time is a precious commodity: men and women claim equal rights in career and family issues, and work is no longer merely a money-making job, but a form of self-identification.[9] This situation demands more flexibility and mobility in daily life. Therefore, current urban commons need to be flexible and an open community for changing commoners,[10] be able to react to changing urban politics and summarize differing concerns of commoners.

Urban politics, of course, encounter the same transformation of society and subsequent new urban requirements (e.g. the need for more kindergartens and more apartments close to work, different use of public space, etc.). Consequently, city governments that look after a more equitable urban development have to change objectives and methods of urban planning processes as well.

In this essay I attempt to analyze the role urban commons could play in urban planning processes. By using the development of Gleisdreieck Park in Berlin as a case study, I argue that urban commons are able to pull down official planning processes and become an active counterpart to state and market actors on an urban platform. On the other hand they could also be capable of becoming 'bottom-up' initiators for and within urban participatory planning processes. Governments often do not perceive the strong collective power urban commons are able to develop, yet it is this collective power that makes both alternatives feasible. However, it is important to make the various potentials of urban commons visible in order to facilitate "collective action."[11] Enabling urban commons in planning procedures goes beyond the usual involvement of the general public. Therefore it is necessary to scrutinize the characteristics of the different roles urban commons might have within planning procedures.

In the first part of this article I discuss the meaning of "urban planning," the outcome of public participation, and how urban commons get connected. Secondly, I tell the story of Gleisdreieck Park to show the different forms of political involvement urban commons could have. In the third section, I link this history to the definition of urban commons. In part four, I analyze the role(s) urban commons might have in the planning processes, and finally I conclude by offering a few general thoughts about urban commons in urban development processes.

Participatory planning and urban commoning

Urban planning has been explained as the "design and regulation of the uses of space that focus on the physical form, economic functions, and social impacts of the urban environment and on the location of different activities within it. Because urban planning draws upon engineering, architectural, and social and political concerns, it is variously a technical profession, an endeavor involving political will and public participation, and an academic discipline."[12] This definition implies that urban planning is a political tool[13] as well as a technical profession, which should aim to ensure an equitable and sustainable urban development.[14] It also integrates a notion of *public participation,* which was (and still is) not always an obvious part of urban planning.

Until the 1970s, urban planning in Western societies was mostly a top-down approach, which means that politicians, architects, and investors shaped the structure of the city without direct participation of the inhabitants.[15] During the 1960s and 1970s, city dwellers started to reject this tutelage. In Berlin protesters expressed opposition mainly against huge urban planning schemes that aimed to remove traditional tenement houses in order to build modernist social housing and massive traffic infrastructures.[16] Resident protests against these schemes triggered local government to implement differing forms of "public participation" in further urban planning processes. Today, "public participation" can be conducted on several levels, starting with informing, consulting, involving, collaborating, and finally even empowering the citizens.[17] Interest in the different methods of public participation in planning processes is increasing among professionals, particularly academics. Hitherto, historians, geographers, sociologists, and urbanists have done broad research on participatory planning.[18] Concurrently, various scholars have discovered the urban commons within the debate of urban transformation and governance.

Radywyl and Biggs, for instance, focus on public spaces within the urban commons debate. They describe how the appropriation of public spaces can generate urban commons and state, "tactical urbanism offers a mechanism for instigating more targeted disruptions within urban systems. It represents particular value as a short-term process for instigating long-term change and which mitigates political or financial risks while engaging the public at a normative, values-based level by making the value of public space as a common asset visible and explicit."[19] Meanwhile Sheila R. Foster focuses on methods of legally managing urban common resources, and demands a third category called "collective action" as an alternative to governmental management.[20] Parker and Johansson also worry about the challenges of cross-sector collaborations between government and commoners. One difficulty they identify is the different understandings of a resource which create complicated interrelations between groups in and related to urban commons: "development of collaborative governance of shared resources in the urban setting might therefore hinge on finding low-cost and effective means to mediate between groups with different understandings of what constitutes a resource."[21]

The authors mentioned above agree that city governments should change their perception of urban commons and accept and deepen its enabling. However, the methods of achieving this are not always evident. The story of the Gleisdreieck Park shows the different conflicts urban commons might face within urban development politics, but it also offers a new approach for how to perceive and include urban commons in official planning procedures.

The story of Gleisdreieck Park[22]

> Without the engagement of citizens and initiatives, Gleisdreieck Park would have never existed. If the politicians had had their way, there would have been a highway, a bus terminal, the unfinished construction of a Ferris wheel and many more construction sites. Only due to the commitment of hundreds of citizens during almost four decades was such a scenario circumvented.[23]

In 1974, a group of residents tried to prevent the Berlin local government from demolishing a playground on the "Schöneberger Insel"[24] and building a highway in its place. At the same time this group was searching for an alternative site for a new playground. Surveying the surrounding area, they found an attractive wilderness: the approximately 63 hectare (156 acre) Gleisdreieck territory.

In industrial times, the area consisted of many railway and subway tracks, train stations, and industries. During World War II, many tracks and industrial buildings were destroyed. In the post-war era, the area remained vacant; after the Berlin Wall was constructed, the subway could no longer cross the nearby border at Potsdamer Platz, instead stopping at Gleisdreieck station.[25] Additionally, the territory became a political vacuum as ownership was complicated and ambiguous. Officially, the

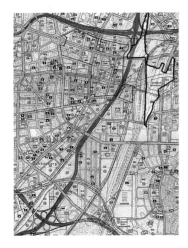 

Figure 1. "Westtangente" (extract of Zoning Plan from 1965), "Grüntangente" (alternative plan of the citizens' initiative Westtangente). Today's park area is indicated in both figures.

former German Reich still owned the area and therefore the Allies were now in charge. Geographically, Gleisdreieck territory belonged to the Western part of the city and the administration of the Western Railway assets was trustee of large parts of the area. On the other hand, the train company of East Berlin *(Ostdeutsche Reichsbahn)* had the authority to use the railroad properties on the territory. As a consequence, the vegetation in the abandoned zone had a chance to grow uncontrolled over the former industrial facilities and railway tracks.

Nevertheless the Western city government planned a highway called "Westtangente" on the site (Figure 1). This scheme was part of the previously described large-scale modernist infrastructure ideas. In 1974, motivated by the successful protests against the "Osttangente"[26] in Kreuzberg, the residents formed a local citizens' initiative.[27] Their slogan was: "Grüntangente statt Westtangente" ("Green tangent instead of West tangent"). At that point they changed to a grander plan rather than only rescuing a playground: they aimed to stop the highway plans and envisioned an alternative design not only for the territory of the Gleisdreieck but beyond. The activists imagined a green landscape which connected the northern parts of the city (Tegeler Forst) over the central Tiergarten park to the Gleisdreieck territory at the southern end of the city.

Four years later, the initiative officially litigated against the Berlin government's highway plans, which would have destroyed the extraordinary wilderness that by now had grown untouched for over twenty years and included rare plants imported by former international trains.[28] The activists provided an alternative plan with the "green" solution for the area instead (Figure 1). However, it took ten more years until the highway was finally taken off the zoning plan because of the continuing protests.

In 1988, West Berlin planned to host the 1995 National Garden Exhibition on the contested area.[29] Three years later, in 1998, it organized a design competition to develop a park of about 60 hectares (148 acres). However, the intervening fall of the Berlin Wall in November 1989 changed the political situation within the city drastically. The design and construction of the nearby Potsdamer Platz to reunify the city became more urgent and politically relevant.

At last, in 1992, Berlin canceled its plans to host the garden exhibition at Gleisdreieck. The territory was needed to build a construction logistics center[30] to develop the nearby Potsdamer/Leipziger Platz. This plan again provoked (unsuccessful) protests among the activists, although the Berlin Senate promised to build a park on the territory after the logistic center was no longer needed. The future park was now designated as a compensation area[31] for the huge constructions at Potsdamer Platz, and would be financed with the money of its main investors.[32]

In 1995 the local initiatives (by then called "Interessengemeinschaft Gleisdreieck"), together with environmental organizations, started to litigate against the construction schemes of the Potsdamer and Leipziger Platz, reasoning that there were not enough ecological compensation areas planned on the Gleisdreieck territory.[33] These official attempts were accompanied by various informal protest actions which continued until 1998, when the case was finally dismissed.

One year before, in 1997, the Berlin Senate urban planning department published a new concept for how to develop the Gleisdreieck territory, designating a park and various construction sites. Although at that point the opportunity for public participation had already been provided, the local districts and citizens were not yet engaged. As a consequence, different neighborhood associations organized a "planning workshop" to garner the ideas and desires of the citizens.

Nevertheless, only a few months later, a private automobile investor got permission to build a parking garage[34] for 1,500 cars next to the Gleisdreieck station, and the highway was again on the political agenda. Furthermore, the Berlin government changed the zoning plan to create more available construction sites, against public objection. The senate department for economics even suggested a huge amusement park on the site. These developments necessitated bringing the power of the various initiatives into focus, and in 1999 the "Aktionsgemeinschaft (AG) Gleisdreieck Park," consisting of several local initiatives,[35] was founded to fight for a common park on the territory.

From that moment onwards, a long and heated debate and many complex negotiations commenced among the different actors in the fight over the territory: the Berlin government, the owner of the territory (the real estate company of the German national train company, represented by EIM, later called VIVICO),[36] and the activists together with the interested public.

In 2001 the AG Gleisdreieck organized a circulating exposition about the history and different development possibilities of the area to inform the wider public about the ongoing process. Even VIVICO used the opportunity to display its plans. Three years later the AG Gleisdreieck, together with other initiatives, founded a cooperative and considered renting all designated green areas to be able to start (and secure) the park development.[37] At the same time, Berlin's mayor Wowereit dreamed of a giant Ferris wheel as a touristic attraction on the site.[38]

Finally, after a long struggle, the local government of Berlin, the administrative district of Friedrichshain-Kreuzberg, and the owner VIVICO signed an urban design contract in 2005. Their compromise included the definition of ownership, function, and zoning of the park, and construction areas – which were much larger than the activists wanted them to be. At the end of the same year the government staged an open landscape competition for the public park, which was won by the urban planners and landscape architects Atelier Loidl the next year. From this date onwards, a very intense participatory planning procedure started, beginning with a citizen survey, an online dialogue, various events and on-site activities organized by two communication offices specializing in planning discourses.

Up to 2006, the initiatives kept on with their struggle to prevent the devastation of the area by organizing different activities on the site; these included public promenades through the space, a self-made playground, and urban gardening. Within a year – against the strong objections of the activists and neighborhood residents – construction of the park started with the felling of numerous trees and the replacement of the contaminated soil.[39] When the actual planning procedure started at the beginning of 2007, a working group (PAG, Projektbegleitende Arbeitsgruppe) was established. This group consisted of the landscape architects Atelier Loidl, the project management company Grün Berlin GmbH,[40] the representatives of the senate administration of city and environment, the district offices, and the AG Gleisdreieck,

Figure 2. Actual park design, Gleisdreieck Park 2014.

who all worked together on the development of the park. In these meetings the residents presented their own design visions of the park, which were quite distinct from the ideas of the architects, the senate, and Grün Berlin GmbH. Whereas the residents desired to keep as much of the wilderness, meadows, ruins and overgrown railroad tracks as possible, the architects had planned a visual axis, low maintenance lawn, and playgrounds and community gardens along only the borders of the park.[41] One of many other issues was the future of the allotment gardens dating from the nineteenth century at the eastern part of the territory, where the landscape architects had designed new sports fields instead. However, in 2009, it was finally decided that the allotment gardens could stay and the planned sports fields were realized on the Tempelhofer Feld and on the territory of the hardware store at "Yorckdreieck."

Finally, the eastern part of the park was completed and opened in 2011, followed by the western part in 2013 and the last part (called Flaschenhals – which was realized without any public participation) in 2014 (see Figure 2).

Although the planning history of the park is over now, the initiative remains alive and meets regularly, as the park development was only one element of a grander planning scenario. And official public participation continues: in November 2014, residents, park users, and interested parties were, for the first time, able to elect a group of ten civic representatives. These have the assignment to decide, together with other designated actors from different private and governmental interest groups, about any emerging subject concerning the park in the present and future. The private representatives came, for instance, from the allotment gardens, the beach volleyball court owners, and the hardware store Hellweg, while the government was represented by the self-governmental institutions of nearby neighborhoods, the senate, the districts of Friedrichhain-Kreuzberg and Schöneberg, and Grün Berlin GmbH.[42]

The Gleisdreieck territory struggle seen through the lens of urban commoning

The story of Gleisdreieck Park shows the influence residents finally had in this specific urban-planning process. Although these inhabitants were not able to realize all their goals, they were able to terminate and alter some of the schemes imposed by the city government. The modus operandi of the activists in the process of protests and negotiations could be understood as a form of commoning, the citizens' initiatives as the community, the contested territory as the common resource, and finally the Gleisdreieck Park in total as a commons.

Common resource – the Gleisdreieck territory: Although the area was neither property of the residents nor an official public space, it was an "abandoned illegal zone"[43] which was appropriated creatively by the nearby residents and used as a recreation area. Many people considered both the emerged wild nature and the historical tracks and buildings precious and felt a responsibility to preserve them. Over time, the area, and thus the resource, changed: a lot of the wild nature and some historical structures were demolished. For a few years the area was not accessible because of the logistics center. Later the area grew smaller as parts of it were occupied by the construction of a parking garage and apartment buildings. However, today the common resource once more exists, now in the form of a large public park, including various playgrounds, a skater park, the remaining historical buildings, and wild nature. Further integrated into the park are the beach volleyball courts, which started as an interim usage, and the allotment gardens, which today include a public café and various scheduled events. Even the architects, who initially did not want to keep the original allotment gardens, had to admit that it adds an unusual, but very pleasant quality to the park.[44]

Community – the activist groups and residents: First the community consisted of a small group of residents fighting against the highway. Over time the community grew. The commoners were families, nature lovers, historians, allotment gardeners, and sportsmen; they all represented different interests. They started in individual initiatives, finally joining to bring their collective power together at the moment the liberal-conservative party of Germany (CDU) put the highway on the political agenda again. The AG Gleisdreieck was founded consisting of the IG Gleisdreieck, Kreuzberger Horn e.V., Anwohnerinitiative Flaschenhals, BI-Westtangente, Bürgerinitiative B 101, the neighborhood association Tiergarten Süd, the cyclist association Grüne Radler, and the NGO Friends of the Earth Germany (BUND). However, despite emerging from distinct backgrounds, they had the common goal to preserve the area and stop any plan threatening their common resource, e.g. the highway or an amusement park with a touristic Ferris wheel. By defining the common enemies (government and investors), the group created a common identity as well.

Institutions – urban political activism: The commoning process can be considered to have started as early as the formation of the first initiative, "Bürgerinitiative Westtangente." This group gave the activists a kind of 'official' status. They defined the common resource they fought for and developed a strategy for the struggle. The initiative began to meet regularly to organize protests and to litigate officially against the highway. As time went by, further plans by the Senate threatened their resource, which the enlarged group had already started to use for urban gardening and other activities. Since the beginning of the official Gleisdreieck planning process, the initiative (by then regrouped as) AG Gleisdreieck Park took as active a role in the development and design of the park as possible. Following the completion of the park, the initiative and residents have continued to take care of the resource. Representatives are elected to negotiate all issues concerning the park, such as maintenance, security, ecological and financial questions, etc. with other official interest groups.

Furthermore, this identified commons is located in an urban setting (in the center of Berlin) and was (and somehow still is) dealing with urban problems such as the need for open public space for city dwellers, the threat of environmental pollution, imposition of prestigious schemes by the government, investor interests, complicated planning procedures, etc. Furthermore, the adjacent districts of Kreuzberg (on the eastern side of the Gleisdreieck) and Schöneberg (on the western side) brought very different histories and demographics together; Kreuzberg has enjoyed a very lively activist scene[45] since the 1970s, and the part of Schöneberg closest to the park has a long tradition of prostitution[46] and criminality.

Therefore the urban commons "Gleisdreieck Park" and its struggle can be seen as a civic platform where very different interest groups were confronted and had to communicate collectively. On the one hand they discussed within the community, yet on the other hand they collaborated directly with opposing actors such as the government, investors, and planners.

The urban commons' role in official planning procedures

Looking at the struggle of Gleisdreieck Park, the role of urban commons in urban planning processes could be analyzed in two ways: commoning as a tool to obstruct 'top-down' planning processes or commoning as the foundation of public participation in official planning procedures.

Hindering top-down planning: The Gleisdreieck commoners successfully stopped the huge infrastructural and touristic visions of the Berlin local government. They were able to preserve at least a part of the piece of land which they had declared as their common resource. The commoners used two methods to reach this result. First, they made the public aware of the unused territory by organizing interim usages (for example, urban gardening, playgrounds) and explaining its potentials (extraordinary nature, fresh-air corridor for nearby neighborhoods, historical landmarks, space for experiments/creativity) in public events or through expositions. By doing so, they gained the interest and support of a wider public. Second, they used their collective power to litigate officially against the project and never stopped protesting for their resource.

Enabling participatory processes: A participatory approach for the landscape project was obligatory; this was stated in the announcement of the Gleisdreieck design competition in 2005.[47] After the long history of protests, the government had realized that this time it was necessary to integrate the public voice from the beginning and it started a new form of public participation (the previously described PAG). Apparently the participatory planning was an exhausting experience.[48] All participants, the residents, the planners and the client (the government) had conflicting aims. The final result can therefore only be seen as a compromise, but one which still seemed to be very successful at the end: today a public park exists that is open to everyone, offers many different kinds of leisure and recreation possibilities, preserves parts of wild nature and buildings, and provides a permanent home for the allotment gardens. However, the size of the park is much smaller than the citizens wanted and only a small amount of wilderness has been saved. The investors built luxury apartments on larger areas than they agreed upon and the park became a prestigious urban design project[49] which attracts not only Berlin residents but also tourists.[50]

Both cases illustrate that, from 1972 up to the present, hardly any planning process by the senate or the investors involving Gleisdreieck Park was accomplished without conflict or discussion with the commoners. Of course, the general situation changed over time. Whereas at the beginning the protests and alternative ideas by the residents were not acknowledged at all, at the end of the development process the commoners became an active yet unequal part of the planning process.

This example demonstrates that commoning within urban development issues is a form of political action. *Urban* commons cannot exist completely autonomously, but rather are partially dependent on state and market systems. However, the collective power of urban commons can influence the dialogue between the different interest groups and actors and initiate changes in political decision-making processes.

Gleisdreieck Park – a model for urban participatory planning?[51]

The story of Gleisdreieck Park seen as an urban commons reveals several interesting thoughts concerning urban planning culture:
1) Urban commons can be regarded as an indicator showing the actual necessities of certain groups of city dwellers (for example, space for common activities, retreating from the city etc.).
2) Governments and urban planners often perceive urban commons as a threat or disturbing opponents because their goals might seem too contrary. However it could be an advantage to understand them as serious partners in urban development processes and offer them the possibility to take part legally in their planning, since it is then more likely that civil protests will not spoil the process. Additionally, more ideas and expertise could be gathered freely, as the participation of the commoners is not motivated by profit and happens on a voluntary basis.

3) In contrast, urban commoners should not forget that their engagement in urban development could lead to unintended consequences as well. The 'rescued' or achieved resources in some cases (e.g. in the present example) increase the popularity of the surrounding neighborhoods. Rising rents, leading to the feared 'gentrification' of the area, are the consequence. The common and free resource is then turned into additional capital for investors.[52]
4) In order to achieve a long-lasting successful urban development, it seems to be advisable not only to 'inform' and 'consult' the public, but to consider all levels of public participation including 'involving,' 'collaborating,' and 'empowering.'[53] Whenever residents are fully integrated in planning processes, the level of identification and responsibility with the object/resource increases. So people are more likely to continue to take care of their resource/neighborhood/park even after the completion of the planning process. For example, in the case of Gleisdreieck, citizens have elected civil representatives who take part in the future decisions about the park (e.g. how to deal with vandalism, security, renovation of old park furnishing, etc.).
5) Referring to the 'collaborating' and 'empowering' level of public participation, urban commons could be more adequate partners than the 'general public.' Urban commons have already developed common visions and requirements and could be able to bring the necessary collective power along to take an active political role.

Certainly clients (city or investors) and urban planners (governmental or private) have to be interested in the necessities of and collaboration with citizens (and vice versa). A neutral moderation among different interest groups to achieve fair and equal negotiations for everyone is necessary. In the case of Gleisdreieck, it cannot be said that the activists felt they were always treated as equal dialogue partners, especially as the citizens were only asked to take part in the development of certain parts of the territory (although they fought initially to take part in the planning of all of it), and many of their objections were not accepted. Therefore, both in practice and academia, a lot of effort is still necessary to make the understanding of urban commons fertile for urban planning processes.

Notes

1. Klaus Wowereit, "Lassen Sie uns über Geld reden…," interviewed by Gerda Frey and Anja Zwittlinger-Fritz, *Focus Money,* November 6, 2003.
2. The academic debate on creative cities is controversial and was initiated by authors such as Richard Florida (*The Rise of the Creative Class* and *Cities and the Creative Class*, etc.) and Charles Landry (*The Creative City*).
3. Cf. Statistisches Bundesamt, *Schulden der öffentlichen Haushalte am 30. 9. 2014 – Vorläufiges Ergebnis*, https://www.destatis.de/DE/ZahlenFakten/GesellschaftStaat/OeffentlicheFinanzenSteuern/Oeffentliche-Finanzen/Schulden/Tabellen/Schulden_VJ.html (accessed January 23, 2015).
4. For instance the initiative *Media Spree Versenken!* is fighting against the huge investor project "Mediaspree," and neoliberal urban development politics in general. The initiative *Stadt Neudenken* is fighting against the real estate politics of the city of Berlin and for sustainable and social urban development.
5. Michael Hardt, "The Right to the Common," conference organized by Bildungswerk Berlin der Heinrich-Böll-Stiftung, Berlin, June 2013, in Francesca Ferguson, "Make_shift City: Renegotiating the Urban Commons," in *Make_shift City: Renegotiating the Urban Commons,* Francesca Ferguson and Christina Gaugliz, eds. (Berlin: Jovis Verlag, 2014), 14.
6. Ferguson, "Make_shift City: Renegotiating the Urban Commons," 14.
7. See writings of authors such as Andreas Exner and Brigitte Kratzwald, Silke Helfrich, David Harvey, Massimo De Angelis, and Elinor Ostrom.
8. See contribution by Brigitte Kratzwald in this volume.
9. Cornelia Koppetsch, *Das Ethos der Kreativen: eine Studie zum Wandel von Arbeit und Identität am Beispiel der Werbeberufe* (Konstanz: UVK Verlagsgesellschaft, 2006).
10. Elinor Ostrom, on the other hand, demands defined group boundaries in order to achieve successful commons. See Elinor Ostrom, *Governing the Commons: The Evolution of Institutions for Collective Action* (New York: Cambridge University Press, 1990).
11. Sheila Foster, "Collective Action and the Urban Commons," *Notre Dame Law Review* 87, no. 1 (2011): 63.
12. *Encyclopaedia Britannica*, "Urban Planning," http://www.britannica.com/EBchecked/topic/619445/urban-planning (accessed December 3, 2014).
13. Every government has its own urban planning department. Its urban planners are able to make unilateral decisions concerning urban development, for instance with regard to the creation or change of zoning plans; these plans determine, for example, whether residential or business districts, buildings or parks will be built at a certain location. Investigations and final project realizations are often outsourced to independent and specialized offices. The awarding of projects to offices for larger projects usually follows a public design competition.
14. Wikipedia, *Stadtplanung*, de.wikipedia.org/wiki/Stadtplanung (accessed January 15, 2015).
15. Peter Hall, *Cities of Tomorrow: An Intellectual History of Urban Planning and Design in the Twentieth Century* (Oxford, UK / Malden, MA: Blackwell Publishers, 2002).
16. Tobias Morawski, *Reclaim Your City: urbane Protestbewegungen am Beispiel Berlins* (Berlin: Assoziation A, 2014).
17. See different levels of public participation: International Association for Public Participation, IAP2 spectrum, 2007; Ariane Bischoff, Klaus Selle, and Heidi Sinning, *Informieren, Beteiligen, Kooperieren: Kommunikation in Planungsprozessen; eine Übersicht zu Formen, Verfahren, Methoden und Techniken* (Dortmund: Dortmunder Vertrieb für Bau- und Planungsliteratur, 2005).

18 Rainer B. Jogschies, *Bürgerbeteiligung an der Stadtplanung: Unters. zur Bürgerinitiativen-Bewegung u. d. Legitimationskrise d. Parlamentarismus aus forschungsmethod. Sicht* (Frankfurt am Main: Lang, 1984); Marcus B. Lane, "Public Participation in Planning: An Intellectual History," *Australian Geographer* 36, no. 3 (November 2005): 283–99; Judith Eleanor Innes and David E. Booher, *Planning with Complexity: An Introduction to Collaborative Rationality for Public Policy* (Abingdon, Oxon/New York: Routledge, 2010); Daren C. Brabham, "Crowdsourcing the Public Participation Process for Planning Projects," *Planning Theory*, August 2009.
19 Natalia Radywyl and Che Biggs, "Reclaiming the Commons for Urban Transformation," *Journal of Cleaner Production* 50 (2013).
20 Sheila Foster, "Collective Action and the Urban Commons."
21 Peter Parker and Magnus Johansson, "Challenges and Potentials in Collaborative Management of Urban Commons," in *Multi-Faceted Nature of Collaboration in the Contemporary World*, Tamara Besednjak Valic, Dolores Modic, and Urša Lamut, eds. (London: Vega Press, 2012), 92–113.
22 The following chapter is based on information from http://www.berlin-gleisdreieck.de/ and http://gleisdreieck-blog.de/. Besides a huge collection of contemporary commentary on the transformation of the Gleisdreieck, both websites provide information about the history of the development, including plans, official meeting protocols, etc. Other important sources were numerous newspaper articles and the following publication: Senatsverwaltung für Stadt und Umwelt (ed.), *Der Park am Gleisdreieck. Idee, Geschichte, Entwicklung und Umsetzung* (Berlin: Medialis Offsetdruck GmbH, 2013).
23 Statement of a Berlin citizen (translation by the author); see poster on the exhibition "Gleisdeieck – vier Jahrzehnte Bürgerengagement" by the initiative Gleisdreieck from 2011: http://gleisdreieck-blog.de/wordpress/wp-content/uploads/2011/Gleisdreieck-4-Jahrzehnte-Buergerengagement.pdf (accessed November 18, 2015).
24 This was a famous working-class neighborhood in Berlin, also called "red island" because of the politically left-oriented population.
25 Markus Jurziczek von Lisone, "U-Bahn Berlin, Hochbahnstation Gleisdreieck," *Berliner Verkehrsseiten*, April, 2010, http://www.berliner-verkehrsseiten.de/u-bahn/Strecken/Gleisdreieck/Gleisdreieck_1945/gleisdreieck_1945.html (accessed January 6, 2015).
26 The Eastern highway that was also part of the urban renewal plans.
27 It was called "Bürgerinitiative Westtangente," more information is available at http://www.bi-westtangente.de/context.php?action=chronik (accessed January 6, 2015).
28 "Hier wird Troja begreiflich. Der Untergang der West-Berliner Technik-Landschaft 'Gleisdreieck'," *Spiegel*, November 2, 1981.
29 The "Bundesgartenschau" is a biennial exhibition of garden design which is often utilized to develop certain areas into parks. As an urban development tool, it is sometimes also criticized, as the landscape design often destroys existing nature, requires a huge infrastructure for the visitors, and is fee-based.
30 A logistics center is a place where materials and construction vehicles are coordinated. In the case of the gigantic construction site at Potsdamer Platz, all construction logistics were organized at this center, and it offered the only connection to the construction site. This avoided heavy construction vehicle traffic within the city center and, in consequence, Potsdamer Platz became an international example of an outstanding efficient and ecological logistic project; cf. http://www.stadtentwicklung.berlin.de/planen/staedtebau-projekte/leipziger_platz/de/planungen/planungsgrundl/baulogistik/index.shtml (accessed January 19, 2015); "Faszinierend wie unauffällig das alles von statten geht," *Welt*, November 2, 2000.
31 The creation of ecological compensation areas is determined by German law, and forms one important instrument of nature protection.

32   Deutsche Bahn AG, debis, Sony/Tishman, Speyer, ABB, Land Berlin.
33   The government had included a park of only 16 ha (39 acres) as a compensation area, although at least 33 ha (81 acres) were demanded by environmental experts.
34   Today the parking garage is slated to be replaced by apartments, as it was not used sufficiently.
35   See the initiatives listed in the next section.
36   In 2001, the state-owned train real estate company EIM (Eisenbahn Immobilien Management) was changed into the VIVICO Real Estate GmbH so that it could be privatized. Instead of privatizing the company, however, it was finally sold to CA Immo, an Austrian real estate company, in 2011.
37   Karin Schmidl, "Genossenschaft fürs Gleisdreieck", *Berliner Zeitung*, May 25, 2004, http://www.berliner-zeitung.de/archiv/buerger-wollen-ihren-park-genossenschaft-fuers-gleisdreieck,10810590,10179332.html (accessed January 27, 2015); Sascha Tegtmeier, "Neues Kapital für ein grünes Gleisdreieck", *taz, die tageszeitung,* May 25, 2004, http://www.taz.de/1/archiv/?id=archivseite&dig=2004/05/25/a0287 (accessed January 27, 2015).
38   Cay Dobberke, "Wowereit dreht am Riesenrad Senat soll das Projekt am Gleisdreieck unterstützen," *Der Tagesspiegel,* October 29, 2004, http://www.tagesspiegel.de/berlin/wowereit-dreht-am-riesenrad-senat-soll-das-projekt-am-gleisdreieck-unterstuetzen/558402.html (accessed January 12, 2015).
39   Christoph Villinger, "Dreieck mit tausend Konflikten," *taz, die tageszeitung,* January 15, 2008, http://www.taz.de/Stadtplanung/!10992/ (accessed November 18, 2014).
40   Grün Berlin GmbH is "the service company of the Berlin region for all open space development projects." Further description about Grün Berlin is available at http://www.gruen-berlin.de/about-us/ (accessed January 22, 2015).
41   Uwe Rada, "Die Mauer im Park," *taz, die tageszeitung,* January 21, 2009, http://www.taz.de/!29034/ (accessed November 18, 2014).
42   Cf. announcement of the elections, "Wahlen zum Nutzer_innenbeirat für Gleisdreieck- und Flaschenhalspark," *gleisdreieck-blog.de,* October 19, 2014, http://gleisdreieck-blog.de/2014/10/19/wahlen-zum-nutzerbeirat-fuer-gleisdreieck-und-flaschenhalspark/ (accessed December 19, 2014).
43   Access to the territory was officially prohibited until 2005.
44   Felix Schwarz, "So einen Park bauen zu dürfen ist Wahnsinn," interviewed by Plutonia Plarre, *taz, die tageszeitung*, Oktober 28, 2014, http://www.taz.de/1/archiv/digitaz/artikel/?ressort=bt&dig=2014%2F10%2F28%2Fa0148&cHash=3409ba7c9c6ae16b4632bb5bb6c10b54 (accessed November 15, 2014).
45   Martin Düspohl and Bezirksmuseum, *Kleine Kreuzberg-Geschichte* (Berlin: Berlin-Story-Verl., 2009).
46   Christiane Howe, "Nachbarschaften und Straßenprostitution. Konfliktlinien und Lösungsansätze im Raum rund um die Kurfürstenstraße in Berlin," November, 2011, https://www.tu-berlin.de/fileadmin/f27/PDFs/Forschung/Nachbarschaften_und_Strassen-Prostitution_Bericht.pdf (accessed January 26, 2015).
47   Cf. Senatsverwaltung für Stadtentwicklung und Umwelt, "Auslobung," http://www.stadtentwicklung.berlin.de/aktuell/wettbewerbe/ergebnisse/2006/gleisdreieck/auslobung.shtml (accessed January 22, 2015).
48   Schwarz, "So einen Park bauen zu dürfen ist Wahnsinn"; cf. planning meeting reports http://www.berlin-gleisdreieck.de/Seiten/aktuelles/Park_Planung.htm (accessed January 20, 2015).
49   The project won several design awards, for instance: "Sonderpreis/ Auszeichnung Deutscher Städtebaupreis 2014."
50   Kalle Harberg, "Park am Gleisdreieck. Alles im grünen Bereich," *Der Tagesspiegel,* June 22, 2013, http://www.tagesspiegel.de/berlin/park-am-gleisdreieck-alles-im-gruenen-bereich/8390510.html (accessed November 18, 2014).

51 A group of students of the TU Berlin analyzed the first steps of the participatory process of Gleisdreieck Park, see Sebastian Holtkamp, *Projekt Gleisdreieck zwischen Nutzen und Planen* (Berlin: Univ.-Verl. der TU, Univ.-Bibliothek, 2007), http://d-nb.info/987851098/34.
52 See contribution by Brigitte Kratzwald in this volume.
53 International Association for Public Participation, IAP2 spectrum, 2007.

Melissa García Lamarca

Insurgent Acts of Being-in-Common and Housing in Spain: Making Urban Commons?

Introduction

In the second decade of the twenty-first century, it is clear that the urban is no longer merely a site of contentious politics, but one of its primary stakes.[1] Indeed, the urban has (re)emerged across the world as ground zero for insurgent struggles over democracy, capitalism, and urban space itself. Shaped by context-specific social, political, and economic factors, those engaged in occupying public spaces seek to universalize principles of equality and demand their voices be heard at the same level as those that constitute the order that maintains the status quo.[2] At the same time, these oppositional movements face a pressing need to develop long-term im/material infrastructures towards building real and lasting alternatives.[3]

These struggles, furthermore, rub uneasily against the dynamics of urbanization, embedded in a system with a perpetual need to find profitable terrains for economic surplus production, appropriation, and absorption.[4] The capitalist mode of production is rooted in the commons that necessarily become part of the urban through the production of space in the city. Urban real estate thus acts as a key mechanism through which the common wealth of the metropolis is privatized,[5] feeding an economic sector founded on credit and rent that facilitates a fundamental redistribution of value. In such a context, what possibilities do insurgent[6] acts of being-in-common have to make urban commons as emancipatory configurations, as processes towards offering a real and durable alternative?

This chapter unfolds three paths to address this question, developed in three sections. Towards defining the urban commons, the first section unpacks "the commons" and "the common" as socio-historically produced configurations, highlighting how both are material and immaterial as well as natural and historical, with both emancipatory and repressive potential. The second section unravels how urban real estate encloses commons at multiple scales, while the third and final section explores how emancipatory urban political activities, specifically acts of being-in-common, relate to making urban commons. These last two sections are grounded in the Spanish urban political economic context of the country's 1997–2007 speculative real-estate boom and the forms of being-in-common of Spain's most extensive housing rights movement, the Platform for Mortgage Affected People (PAH), respectively. The conclusion reflects on the question driving this paper, namely, the potential of acts of being-in-common in building emancipatory urban commons.

Urban commons: Conceptualizing the commons and the common

Early modern European social theorists conceived of "the commons" as the bounty of nature available to humanity, such as air, water, and land, elements often posed in religious terms as the inheritance of humanity as a whole.[7] Garrett Hardin's *Tragedy of the Commons* (1968) was crucial in popularizing, and grossly oversimplifying, the idea of the commons through a neo-Malthusian approach; his influence has endured in creating a false dichotomy between public and private property forms as the only solutions. While the extensive work of Elinor Ostrom and her colleagues[8] has disrupted some of Hardin's thinking through attempts to empirically understand how complex systems of collective management operate, they tend to focus on the internal dynamics of so-called 'natural' commons while neither contextualizing nor questioning the larger political economic structures (e.g. the dynamics of capital accumulation and expansion) of which they are a part.

This raises a larger point regarding much of this 'natural resource' commons literature based on Ostrom and her colleagues' work: it is either conservative or apolitical, neither addressing nor questioning the socio-natural relations of capitalism underlying property relations and the organization of social life, and operates uncritically within liberal-democratic capitalist frameworks. Capitalist development is compatible with many common property systems of resource management,[9] just as the common, discussed below, is an integral part of the capitalist mode of production. Yet if one seeks to ascertain how commons can contribute to a more emancipatory political configuration, it is critical to embed explorations of commons in their historical and current political economic dynamics.

Furthermore, references to the commons as resources, or 'natural' resources, reflects a utilitarian and static conceptualization that sweeps their political and socio-natural reality under the table.[10] This emerges in much of the writing around the 'new commons,'[11] where the urban commons, defined flatly as collectively shared urban resources, is a growing field. Urban studies and planning[12] and legal studies[13] are just two fields where these (largely depoliticized) explorations are emerging. Conceptualizing the commons instead as an activity – as relational, not static – is fundamental to unpack the dynamic relationships in society that are inseparable from relations to our environment.[14]

The common, intimately connected to the commons, refers to language, affect, knowledge, creativity, and thought; in other words, "immaterial" dynamics collectively shared through networks of social relations. A shifting importance from the commons to the common has been increasingly recognized. Agamben[15] highlights how capitalism has been directed not only towards expropriating productive activity but also to the alienation of the very linguistic and communicative nature of humans. Hardt and Negri discuss how the figure of immaterial labor-power occupies an increasingly central position in capitalist production, where the common is the basis of economic production both as a productive force and as the form in which wealth is produced.[16] Much of this writing on the common focuses on how the neoliberal assault is subsuming people into the equation through its seizure of knowledge, language, and affect, among others,[17] in what Jodi Dean[18] defines as communicative capitalism.

The common plays a key role in one of the contradictions of capitalism identified by Marx, namely between productive *forces* and the social *relations* of production, which generates crises and conflicts that provide potential openings for a transition to socialism. The common, and the commons, are thus clearly embedded in the forces of production through socio-historical processes, and indeed the common is generated through labor's inherently collective process such as pooling resources and the social cooperation of labor.[19] Hardt and Negri[20] envision that the contradiction Marx invokes between the *social* nature of capitalist production and the *private* character of capitalist accumulation will result in capitalism sowing the seeds of its own downfall.

While the common is, without a doubt, transforming capitalism in new and unforeseen ways, I posit that it is fundamental to understand how such processes feed into and interact with social struggles over access to, control over, and enclosures of the commons. Following Dean,[21] I believe that the commons must be conceived as equally material and immaterial, as well as relational and historical. The commons are often considered only in material terms, characterized by scarcity, but they also have an important immaterial component in their relational meaning that emerges through affect, knowledge, and language. As long as such elements are contextualized in the commons, such thinking can open up ways of instituting politically being-in-common and making commons beyond debates around property regimes and institutional formations. Similarly, while the common is infinite and characterized by surplus, it is embedded within and constitutive of material production and, especially, relationships. So while the common plays a fundamental role in the new frontier of capitalism, the material basis that enables the production of the common is deeply intertwined in the commons.

I thus conceptualize urban commons as a dynamic social relationship that is configured and reconfigured through time and struggle, through socio-historical relations and urban socio-spatial practices; they are a contested, collective material and immaterial terrain. As these dynamics have both repressive and emancipatory potential, politicizing commons is fundamental in order to question how and who creates what kinds of commons. Towards this end, employing the enclosure-commons dialectic can be used to think through processes of exclusion and alterity,[22] as explored in the following section in the case of Spain.

Enclosing commons: Spain's urban political economic condition

The enclosure of the commons has become the modus operandi of neoliberal urbanism today, a process aimed at finding new outlets for capital accumulation through controlling the use and exchange value of urban space or shutting down access to any urban space or sociality that creates non-commodified means of reproduction and a challenge to capitalist social relations.[23] Enclosure speaks not only to original accumulation[24] or the resurgence of statist violence, but also to a messy, practical, and highly conflicted claiming of the commons.[25] It forcibly incorporates dynamics that were outside capital accumulation into capitalist production and circulation,[26] as capital acts as a life-colonizing force seeking endless growth and self-reproduction.[27]

Urban real estate acts as a key mechanism through which the common wealth of the metropolis is privatized.[28] This process occurred both at the scale of the urban and at the scale of the body in Spain's third real-estate cycle (Figure 1) from 1997 to 2007, the most extensive and profitable boom in the country's history. In terms

Figure 1. Spanish real-estate cycles, 1970–2011.

of the first scale, the construction of housing was embedded in a process where the expanding built environment transformed 'public' wealth and wealth held socially in common into private property. During this period, the compound annual growth rate in nominal house prices was over 10 percent[29] and the total housing stock increased by over 6 million units.[30] With almost 900,000 housing starts in 2006 alone – exceeding those of France, Germany and Italy combined[31] – the country's built area expanded by almost a quarter of total built area during the boom.[32] In 2006, Spain held the dubious position as the European leader in its use of cement, and stood fifth globally.

While the construction sector has traditionally held a central role in the process of capital accumulation in Spain,[33] the built environment extended far further and deeper than it had previously, both mediated and compounded by the liberalization of housing, mortgage, and land markets, as well as various phases of EU integration.[34] By 2008, Spain ranked next to the United States in the league of countries with the largest net import of capital, with most private foreign investment fuelling the real-estate sector.[35]

The political and ideological project of homeownership, on the other hand, has a long history as a vaccine against social instability during Spain's dictatorship.[36] This project has shifted strategy since democracy was introduced but has by and large continued, with almost 85 percent of Spanish households becoming homeowners by 2007, one of the highest rates in Europe. Despite real average wages falling 10 percent during the boom,[37] over 820,000 mortgages were signed each year as people repeatedly heard from real-estate agents, developers, builders, financial

169

entities, public administrations, and news media alike that "the price of housing never falls" or "housing is a safe investment."[38]

This process of enclosure also occurred at the scale of the body in urban space, as people were a fundamental piece of the puzzle furthering the enclosure of the commons and urban capital accumulation. The enormous increase in the 'wealth' of Spanish households – from 480 percent of Gross Domestic Investment (GDI) in 1995 to 800 percent in 2006, of which 540 percent corresponded to property wealth[39] – occurred at the expense of massive indebtedness, as total outstanding residential loans increased over fourfold from 155 billion euros in 1999 to 647 billion euros in 2007.[40] Mortgages tied an ever-greater portion of the population into homeownership, plugging them into the financial sector's rent extraction mechanisms.[41] In this way, mortgages can be conceived as another strategy by capital to act as a life-colonizing force. They aid in the enclosure of commons into private property, providing an income stream to financial institutions as land and housing titles are given to 'homeowners' as claims on their future labor.

Between 1997 and 2006, household indebtedness increased from 55 percent to 130 percent of disposable income,[42] placing Spain first worldwide for the highest percentage of long-term household mortgage debt with respect to disposable income.[43] This expanding enclosure of the commons, in its extreme, can also be thought of as a process of proletarianization of those who are thereby excluded from their own substance,[44] in other words, as the dynamic creation of a social group (homeowners) through the way in which capitalism produces, uses up, and discards those it needs.[45] This is particularly true as Spain's Mortgage Act obliges those who default on their mortgage payments to continue paying if, once foreclosed and evicted, the bank's confiscation and sale of their house does not cover all outstanding costs.[46]

Since the bust of Spain's boom in 2007, such dynamics have become piercingly acute; unemployment has skyrocketed to over 25 percent and housing has become a massive point of contention as people are increasingly unable to meet their mortgage payments. More than half a million foreclosures and 250,000 evictions have occurred between 2008 and 2013 according to Spain's justice department, leaving hundreds of thousands with no place to live and a debt to pay for life. At the same time, at least 3.5 million units of housing are empty and banks have been bailed out with tens of billions of euros of public funds. Working- and middle-class people are bearing the brunt of austerity, debt, foreclosures, and evictions in Spain, dynamics that have instigated and fed into a politics of forms and insurgent acts of being-in-common through housing rights platforms, amid countless other mobilizations, in cities across the country. The final section of this paper provides some preliminary thoughts on how such forms and acts relate to the (emancipatory) making of urban commons.

Making urban commons? Forms and insurgent acts of being-in-common

Considering the dominant tendencies of capitalist urbanization illustrated by the Spanish case and echoed in dozens of others across the world, the construction of being-in-common is intimately related to struggles over urban commons. Resisting enclosures of the commons is not new;[47] indeed, enclosures happen all the time, as does constant commoning.[48] Following Harvey, commoning is understood here as a social practice that establishes a dynamic, collective, and non-commodified social relationship between a self-defined social group and aspects of the existing or to-be-created social and/or physical environment that is crucial to its life and livelihood.[49]

Being-in-common is a subjectivity produced from a reconfiguration of the field of experience[50] when engaged in collective struggles over modes of urbanization and urban life. It is the substance and the essence of the political, aligned with De Angelis's depiction of forces that reclaim life from the privatizing and alienating dynamics of capital accumulation to rearrange social relations according to their own terms.[51] It also sides with Jodi Dean's concept of the "people as the rest of us"[52] – the 99 percent – as well as with Jacques Rancière's notion of "the part of no part." This idea designates the *interruption* of a given order by those who have no part in it, illustrating exactly this gap between the existing order and other possible futures.[53]

Those who constitute housing rights platforms in Spain were people who allegedly 'had a part,' who obtained the credential of 'first-class citizens' through being property owners,[54] but are now the part with no part as they have been foreclosed, evicted, and often indebted for life. The Platform for Mortgage Affected People (PAH), the most active housing rights movement in the country, was founded in Barcelona in 2009 for the right to housing and has since mushroomed to over 200 branches across Spain. Their three basic, non-negotiable demands include the cancellation of mortgage debt upon handover of the property to the bank *(dation in payment)*, an immediate stop to all evictions where it is the family home and sole property, and the creation of a public park of social housing from empty houses held by financial institutions.

The PAH's method of organization is rooted in various forms of being-in-common, grounded first and foremost in weekly assemblies where people who can no longer pay their mortgage and/or are facing eviction and other solidarity activists come together to coordinate actions and carry out collective advising for mortgage-affected families. Assemblies are fundamental spaces where collective knowledge on how to stall or counteract foreclosure and eviction processes is shared and expanded, and where individuals' fear and shame are shed; it is a place of collective support and support of the collective. Aside from coordinating broader campaigns and actions, here people organize to accompany people seeking mortgage debt forgiveness on visits to their bank branch to demand a response from the director, or to occupy the bank if negotiations are stalled, to mobilize to stop an eviction by placing their bodies in front of the entrance so that the police and the judicial committee carrying out the eviction order cannot enter, or to support empty bank-owned flat occupations for mortgaged/evicted families with no housing alternative, among many other strategies. Commoning is ever-present through the PAH's ways of speaking and acting, where a collective – and conflictive – struggle and response is built from individually experienced housing problems.

On the one hand, the PAH fights for and demands that the state fulfill its role as a universal provider of welfare, in particular housing, to all of Spain's residents. But since the state has been too slow or unable/unwilling to provide political and practical solutions, the PAH acts through a collective, horizontal, non-violent, assembly-based, and non-party affiliated process, creating a dynamic and non-commodified social relationship between the group and its social and/or physical environment. They generate tools and knowledge based on experience and actions that are shared with everyone, not only homeowners facing mortgage or eviction problems.[55]

In response to urgent needs, the PAH reclaims the material and symbolic use value of the city, appropriating conceived space and time[56] to simultaneously challenge the hegemony and to rupture the consensus that such spaces hold. Some of these insurgent acts of being-in-common include blocking evictions of mortgaged households and occupying empty bank-owned buildings for mortgaged evicted families. The former involves dozens upon dozens of bodies physically blocking the entrance to properties as eviction orders are being delivered, a tactic first used in November 2009 in Catalonia. Since this time over 1,130 evictions have been blocked across Spain, and banks have been forced to negotiate social rent (30 percent of a family's income). Building occupations target those vacant dwellings owned by banks that were bailed out by public purses. PAH members have recuperated over thirty buildings across the country, most concentrated in the Barcelona Metropolitan Region and in Madrid, rehousing over 1,150 people. Once occupied, the PAH enters into negotiations with the bank that owns the building for occupying families to pay a social rent.

The relation of such actions to making urban commons as emancipatory configurations is by no means stable, but is rather undergoing constant temporal and spatial change. For example, the im/material combination of bodies, the gathering of support, solidarity, and affect when the PAH acts in common to block evictions can be understood as a process of commoning. Yet what happens to these im/material dynamics once the eviction is blocked? How is the collective and non-commodified relationship between the social and physical environment sustained, for example through assembly spaces and further collective actions? Commoning can be seen in a more sustained fashion in the PAH's collective recuperation of housing, through the relationships built between the occupying group and their social and physical environment as they dwell together and organize themselves. The PAH's occupation manual[57] advises building recuperators to hold regular collective meetings, to legitimize the social value of the occupation by distributing information sheets and talking to neighbors, and to create a neighborhood association for the building to normalize their status, for example. While these give some sense of the urban commons being created, and how they might traverse outside the building, it remains to be seen how and if they can be sustained towards a long-term enactment of realizing other possible futures that transform the existing order.

Closing thoughts

Regarding thinking through the role of forms and insurgent acts of being-in-common in making emancipatory urban commons, this paper began by theoretically unpacking the commons and the common, defining the urban commons as social relationship continuously (re)configured through socio-historical relations and socio-spatial practices, a contested, conflictive im/material terrain with both emancipatory and repressive potential. The case of Spain was used to illustrate how the enclosure of commons through urban real-estate development during the 1997–2007 boom was deeply intertwined with the rent extraction processes embedded in urbanization, and how this operated at the urban scale with the building boom and at the scale of the body through the provision of mortgages. Countering capital as a life-colonizing force, the life-reclaiming forces that emerge through being-in-common were explored theoretically and through the actions of the Platform for Mortgage Affected People (PAH) in Spain, thinking through the connections that some of their forms and acts of being-in-common rupturing the current order might have to making urban commons.

Critically thinking through urban commons opens up a possibility to rethink neoliberalized urban political economic and ecological orders, opening another window to assess who participates in and who benefits from how built environments are produced and reproduced. Due to the emancipatory and repressive potential of urban commons, their creation in itself does not necessarily lead to a real or durable alternative to capitalism and/or the dominant 'police' order. While they offer valuable potential to think through other configurations that are inherently contested and problematic, this exploration, grounded in the urban struggles over housing in Spain, illustrated the importance of understanding the spatial and temporal dimensions of urban commons, highlighting the need to unpack them through a sustained experience that, in this case, is still in the making. Actions of politically being-in-common might only create dynamic, temporally limited urban commons that enact equality for those who have no part, although – depending on their spatial extension, reception and impact – in the long term they could have a profound impact on capitalist social relations and the production of urban space. Nonetheless, sustaining these insurgent activities remains one of the central components of an emancipatory politics, for those who do not form part of the system – the 99 percent – to be-in-common and enact equality on their (our) own terms.

Notes

1. Neil Brenner, "Theses on Urbanization," *Public Culture* 25, no. 1 (2013): 89.
2. Erik Swyngedouw, "'Every Revolution has its Square': Politicizing the Post-Political City," in *Urban Constellations*, Matthew Gandy, ed. (Berlin: Jovis, 2011), 22–25.
3. Jeff Shantz, *Commonist Tendencies: Mutual Aid Beyond Communism* (Brooklyn, NY: Punctum Books, 2013), 1.
4. David Harvey, *The Urbanization of Capital* (Oxford: Basil Blackwell, 1985).
5. Michael Hardt and Antonio Negri, *Commonwealth* (Cambridge, MA: Harvard University Press, 2009), 154.
6. Insurgency is understood here as: "a provocation, a forceful intervention that aims not to constitute a singular new order from whole cloth but to radically destabilize authorized forms of power, knowledge and organization and, in so doing, to create the space necessary for new acts of constitution" (*Insurgent Encounters: Transnational Activism, Ethnography, and the Political,* Jeffrey Juris and Alexander Khasnabish (London/Durham: Duke University Press, 2013), 7).
7. Ibid., viii.
8. For example see Elinor Ostrom, *Governing the Commons: The Evolution of Institutions for Collective Action* (Cambridge, UK: University of Cambridge, 1990); Elinor Ostrom, "Coping with Tragedies of the Commons," *Annual Review of Political Science* 2 (1999): 493–535; Thomas Dietz, Elinor Ostrom and Paul C. Stern, "The Struggle to Govern the Commons," *Science* 302 (2003): 1907–1912.
9. George Caffentzis, "A Tale of Two Conferences: Globalization, the Crisis of Neoliberalism and the Question of the Commons," *the Commoner,* December, 2010, http://www.commoner.org.uk/wp-content/uploads/2010/12/caffentzis_a-tale-of-two-conferences.pdf (accessed August 20, 2013).
10. It is important to recognize that "resources can be defined only in relationship to the mode of production which seeks to make use of them and which simultaneously 'produces' them through both the physical and mental activity of the users" (David Harvey as cited in Erik Swyngedouw, "The City as a Hybrid: On Nature, Society and Cyborg Urbanization," *Capitalism, Nature, Socialism* 7, no. 2 (1996): 65).
11. See for example Frank van Laerhoven and Elinor Ostrom, "Traditions and Trends in the Study of the Commons," *International Journal of the Commons* 1, no. 1 (2007): 3–28.
12. For example Shin Lee and Chris Webster, "Enclosure of the Urban Commons," *Geojournal* 66, no. 1/2 (2006): 27–42; Ian McShane, "Trojan Horse or Adaptive Institutions? Some Reflections on Urban Commons in Australia," *Urban Policy and Research* 28, no. 1 (2010): 101–116; Jeremy Németh, "Controlling the Commons: How Public Is Public Space?" *Urban Affairs Review* 48, no. 6 (2012): 811–835.
13. For example Sheila R. Foster, "Collective Action and the Urban Commons," *Notre Dame Law Review* 87, no. 1 (2011): 57–134; Nicole Stelle Garnett, "Managing the Urban Commons," *University of Pennsylvania Law Review* 160 (2012): 1995–2027.
14. Peter Linebaugh, *The Magna Carta Manifesto: Liberties and Commons for All* (Berkeley: University of California Press, 2008), 279. From here onward, the commons is understood as a dynamic social relation configured and reconfigured through socio-historical relations and socio-spatial practices, a contested, collective terrain that is under constant transformation, holding both emancipatory and repressive potential.
15. Giorgio Agamben, *The Coming Community* (Minneapolis: University of Minnesota Press, 1993), 79.
16. Hardt and Negri, *Commonwealth,* 280.
17. See Michael Hardt, "The Common in Communism," in *The Idea of Communism,* Costas Douzinas and Slavoj Žižek, eds. (London: Verso, 2010), 134.

18   Jodi Dean, *The Communist Horizon* (London: Verso, 2012), 124.
19   Massimo De Angelis, "The Tragedy of the Capitalist Commons," *Turbulence*, http://turbulence.org.uk/turbulence-5/capitalist commons/ (accessed September 19, 2014).
20   Hardt and Negri, *Commonwealth*, 288.
21   Dean, *The Communist Horizon*, 135.
22   Alex Jeffrey, Colin McFarlane, and Alex Vasudevan, "Rethinking Enclosure: Space, Subjectivity and the Commons," *Antipode* 44, no. 4 (2012): 1247.
23   Stuart Hodkinson, "The New Urban Enclosures," *City: Analysis of Urban Trends, Culture, Theory, Policy, Action* 16, no. 5 (2012): 515.
24   Karl Marx, *Capital: A Critique of Political Economy, Volume I*, 1867 (New York: Penguin Books, 1982), 873.
25   Alex Vasudevan, Colin McFarlane, and Alex Jeffrey, "Spaces of Enclosure," *Geoforum* 39, no. 5 (2008): 1642.
26   Isaac Kamola and Eli Meyerhoff, "Creating Commons: Divided Governance, Participatory Management, and Struggles Against Enclosure in the University," *Polygraph* 21 (2009): 6.
27   Massimo De Angelis, *The Beginning of History: Value Struggles and Global Capital* (London/Ann Arbor: Pluto Press, 2007), 6.
28   Michael Hardt and Antonio Negri, *Commonwealth*, 156.
29   European Mortgage Federation, *2010 EMF Study on the Cost of Housing in Europe* (Brussels, 2010), 11.
30   European Mortgage Federation, *Hypostat 2010: A Review of Europe's Mortgage and Housing Markets* (Brussels, 2011), 73.
31   Isidro López and Emmanuel Rodríguez, "The Spanish Model," *New Left Review* 69 (2011): 20.
32   José Manual Naredo, Óscar Carpintero, and Carmen Marcos, *Patrimonio inmobiliario y balance nacional de la economía española (1995–2007)* (Madrid: Fundación de las Cajas de Ahorros, 2008), 57.
33   Daniel Coq-Huelva, "Urbanisation and Financialisation in the Context of a Rescaling State: The Case of Spain," *Antipode* 45, no. 5 (2013): 1220.
34   See for example Isidro López and Emmanuel Rodríguez, ibid.; María-Teresa Sánchez Martínez, "The Spanish Financial System: Facing up to the Real Estate Crisis and Credit Crunch," *European Journal of Housing Policy* 8, no. 2 (2008): 181–196; and Josep Roca Cladera and Malcolm C. Burns, "The Liberalization of the Land Market in Spain: The 1998 Reform of Urban Planning Legislation," *European Planning Studies* 8, no. 5 (2000): 547–564.
35   Marisol García, "The Breakdown of the Spanish Urban Growth Model: Social and Territorial Effects of the Global Crisis," *International Journal of Urban and Regional Research* 34, no. 4 (2010): 969.
36   As illustrated by the first Minister of Housing in his inaugural 1957 speech: "we want a country of homeowners, not proletarians" – see José Manuel Naredo, "El modelo inmobiliario español y sus consecuencias," *Boletín CF+ S* 44 (2010): 18.
37   López and Rodríguez, "The Spanish Model," 12.
38   Ada Colau and Adrià Alemany, *Vidas hipotecadas: De la burbuja inmobiliaria al derecho a la vivienda* (Barcelona: Cuadrilátero de Libros, 2012), 29.
39   Sánchez Martínez, "The Spanish Financial System: Facing up to the Real Estate Crisis and Credit Crunch," 189.
40   European Mortgage Federation, *Hypostat 2010: A Review of Europe's Mortgage and Housing Markets*, 81.
41   Isidro López and Emmanuel Rodríguez, *Fin de ciclo: financiarización, territorio y sociedad de propietarios en la onda larga del capitalismo hispano (1959–2010)* (Madrid: Traficantes de Sueños, 2010).
42   Albert Puig Gómez, "El modelo productivo español en el período expansivo de 1997–2007: insostenibilidad y ausencia de politicas de cambio," *Revista de Economía Crítica* 12 (2011): 69.
43   Naredo et al., *Patrimonio inmobiliario y balance nacional de la economía española (1995–2007)*, 151.

44 Slajov Žižek, "How to Begin From the Beginning," in *The Idea of Communism*, Costas Douzinas and Slavoj Žižek, eds. (London: Verso, 2010): 220.
45 Jodi Dean, *The Communist Horizon*, 75.
46 Jesús Castillo, "Current Reform of Spain's Mortgage Law," *Natixis special report* 47 (2013): 3.
47 Peter Linebaugh, "Enclosures from the Bottom Up," *Radical History Review* 108 (2010): 11–27.
48 An Architektur, "On the Commons: A Public Interview with Massimo De Angelis and Stavros Stavrides," *e-flux* June–August (2010): 1–17.
49 David Harvey, *Rebel Cities: From the Right to the City to the Urban Revolution* (London: Verso, 2012), 73.
50 Jacques Rancière, *Disagreement: Politics and Philosophy* (Minneapolis: University of Minnesota Press, 1999), 36.
51 De Angelis, *The Beginning of History*, 6.
52 Dean, *The Communist Horizon*, 69.
53 Rancière, *Disagreement*, 11–12.
54 Colau and Alemany, *Vidas hipotecadas*, 74.
55 These collective tools are available at http://afectadosporlahipoteca.com/documentos-utiles/.
56 Henri Lefebvre, *The Production of Space* [1974] (Oxford: Blackwell, 1991).
57 See La Plataforma de Afectados por la Hipoteca, *Manual de Obra Social*, available at http://afectadosporlahipoteca.com/wp-content/uploads/2013/07/MANUAL-OBRA-SOCIAL-WEB-ALTA.pdf.

Resources

Ivo Balmer, Tobias Bernet

Housing as a Common Resource? Decommodification and Self-Organization in Housing – Examples from Germany and Switzerland

1 Introduction

Housing is something intimate. One could say that our homes represent a 'third skin' after clothing. Like clothes, shelter is regarded as a basic human need. Since this does not automatically translate into universal access in a less-than-perfect world, the provision of such basic goods is a fundamental political issue. A wide range of answers to the housing question have been developed in different times and places depending on the economic conditions and political hegemony. Both the market and the state have been hailed as the primary provider of housing and, even though the 'third sector' has mostly played a rather marginal role, there are noteworthy traditions of philanthropic and especially of self-help (cooperative) initiatives in housing.

The latter are certainly worth discussion in the context of the current 'rediscovery' of the commons, as is the field of public housing. In this chapter, we will attempt to sketch a typology of housing tenure and provision from a 'commons perspective,' examining to what extent housing can be seen as a common resource within different institutional arrangements. We will do this by analyzing a number of contemporary examples from Germany and Switzerland, two countries that are known as 'tenants' nations' by virtue of having some of the lowest rates of owner-occupied homes among industrialized countries,[1] and which thus represent a specific arena of marked contestations within the housing sector. Our analysis will follow the "analytical triad" that the editors of this volume put forth in defining the commons,[2] following Exner and Kratzwald,[3] Helfrich and Haas,[4] and De Angelis and Stravrides,[5] among others, namely that:

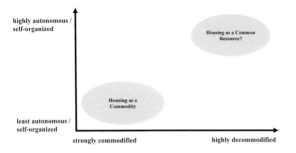

Figure 1. Decommodification and self-organization: Two criteria to assess arrangements of housing Provision.

a) Housing is a basic urban *resource,* similar to infrastructure[6] or land (but unlike the latter it is an 'artificial' resource,[7] and thus costly).
b) Different *actors* play different roles in any arrangement of housing provision. We may broadly speak of 'owners' and 'users' (e.g. tenants), but, following Peter Marcuse,[8] we might be better off analyzing the specific 'incidents of ownership,' i.e. the rights, powers, privileges, and immunities which individuals, groups or organizations hold with regard to a dwelling.[9]
c) This 'bundle of rights' perspective points to the importance of *institutions* that regulate the allocation of housing. These mainly encompass 1) property rights, and 2) public policies, i.e. legislative and financial interventions on behalf of the (welfare) state.[10]

Analyzing specific cases according to this 'commons triad,' we will consider two major points in order to assess the 'commons character,' or lack thereof, of any given mode of housing provision, as illustrated in Figure 1.

First, we examine the extent to which housing is *decommodified* through a specific arrangement, i.e. how sustainably it is withdrawn from the sphere of profit-oriented, speculative real-estate markets. According to Andrej Holm, "decommodification, i.e. the withdrawal of housing provision from the market sphere, can be understood as the aim and the benchmark of housing policies and regulations."[11] Hence, we focus on the relation between housing as a resource and the institutional framework (property rights or policies) that might prevent this resource from being treated as a commodity. In a commons-based arrangement, housing would have to correspond to De Angelis' description of "some sort of common pool of resources, understood as non-commodified means of fulfilling people's needs."[12]

Second, to bring into focus the relevant actors, we consider the level of *autonomy* or *self-organization* that the inhabitants enjoy, individually or collectively, as the users of the resource that their homes constitute. This means determining which opportunities they have to influence decisions concerning their homes, i.e. whether they fit De Angelis's definition of commoners "who share […] resources and who define for themselves the rules through which they are accessed and used."[13]

In the next section (2) we will offer a brief outline of the specific qualities of housing as a unique type of good and its role in the capitalist economy. Following this, we will describe and analyze different legal and economic arrangements from both the public and the cooperative sector in relation to the two criteria just described with regard to public policies (3) and property rights (4). Our 'two-axis' approach aims to contribute to an understanding of "what a particular form of tenure really means."[14] In the conclusion (5) we will reflect on the paths that commoning efforts in the housing sector can take in the complex contemporary 'late liberal' situation, in which neither the state nor the market are fully capable of offering satisfactory solutions for a just and sustainable provision of basic urban resources, yet in which both must inevitably be taken into account – and actively engaged – in the course of any struggle for the commons.

We will argue that, although demands for public policy interventions in the housing sector are still necessary and justified, one should take into account the fact that these types of welfare provisions have proven vulnerable to swift enclosure, i.e. privatization. In this light, creative 'hacks' of property rights may be the more promising path towards institutional arrangements that provide housing as a kind of common resource: "If […] the components can be reduced to some basic enough common denominators […] one should, procedurally, be able to rebuild quite different systems with different arrangements of the pieces."[15]

2 Housing as a unique kind of good and as a commodity

In order to grasp what is at stake in the field of housing provision, it is crucial to consider a number of qualities that make housing a unique kind of good. First and foremost, housing is, as already mentioned, an absolutely essential, *necessary* good. Not having a home is considered to be a severe impediment to a dignified human existence. Consequently, housing is considered a basic human right according to

Owner-occupied Hosing	Rental Housing
– ouright	**Commercially Rented**
– mortgaged	– from small / privrae landlords
	– from large / corporate landlords
	Non-Profit Housing ("Social Rented")
	– public housing (government-owned)
	– privately owned social hosuing (government-subsidized)
	– cooperative housing (government-subsidized on some cases
	– "philanthropc" non-profit housing (provided by charitable foundations, religious organizations etc.; government-subsidized in some cases)

Figure 2. Types of housing tenure and provision.

article 25 of the Universal Declaration of Human Rights. Secondly, housing is, in the vast majority of cases, the most immobile and, thirdly, the most durable of goods in modern capitalist economies. And, mainly because this durability makes it expensive to produce, it is, fourthly, also the most economically significant good in the life of most people, in that they spend more on it than on any other class of goods, be it via rent or via mortgages.[16]

This differentiation between renters and mortgage debtors points to what could be listed as the fifth particularity of housing: its institutional diversity, following Figure 2. "[W]hatever the constitutions of western countries might say [...], in general the populations of these countries do not have practical rights to housing by virtue of citizenship."[17] In spite of its necessity, housing thus appears in various 'institutional guises' in the reality of contemporary capitalism.[18] The same material object – a house (or an apartment) – can take on different legal and economic forms. It can be a state-provided benefit or, as we will attempt to show, something like a common good, however it is currently more often treated like a commodity.

The 'normal,' i.e. prevalent, type of housing tenure in the majority of industrialized countries is the owner-occupied home.[19] By virtue of its 'personalization,' it might seem like a relatively strongly decommodified form of housing if one applies the well-known definition of Esping-Andersen,[20] which posits that decommodification of a good or benefit means that one does not need to generate income in order to acquire, access, or maintain it. Yet perceiving decommodification as a measure of withdrawal of a good from market mechanisms, and in light of real-estate bubbles like the one in the United States that partly triggered the ongoing global

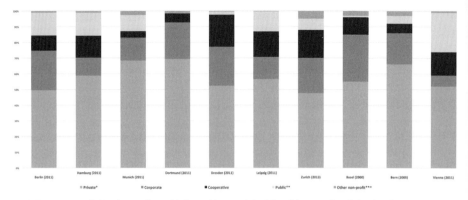

* Owner-occupied and rented out, ** Owned by municipal, Land/cantonal or federal authorities, *** Charitable foundations, religious organizations etc.

Figure 3. Types of housing tenure and provision in selected German and Swiss cities (and Vienna, Austria), in percentages.²²

economic crisis, it is evident that owner-occupied housing is indeed utterly commodified nowadays, constituting an indebtedness-ridden mass market. Yet the position of the indebted homeowner is a very solitary one. In accordance with the phantasm of *homo oeconomicus,* to default on a mortgage seems like a personal failure, rather than the consequence of specific political and economic conditions beyond the individual debtor's control.²¹ It may be that the discrepancy between the needs of everyday life and the basic tendency of a capitalist economy is more obvious for tenants whose monthly payments not only cover maintenance and administration, but are, in most cases, also expected to yield a profit for the landlord. For-profit rental units, which, together with owner-occupied homes, make up the "commercial" housing sector, are the most common type of housing tenure in many urban areas. An illustration of the distribution of the various housing forms in the cases discussed can be found in Figure 3.

The treatment of homes as an 'ordinary' commodity has often been questioned. As exemplified by recent tenants' struggles and 'right to the city' movements in various German cities, which have succeeded in extending beyond the usual leftist suspects, rising rents, and forced evictions, i.e. the tangible facets of gentrification continue to be capable of raising disquiet at a very basic level.²³ Housing issues thus constitute an arena for passionate contestations of the status quo.

3 Decommodifying housing through public policies

The insistence on housing's special status as a basic necessity, as articulated by social movements throughout the twentieth century, has brought forth institutions that provide housing which is, to some degree or another, decommodified. Examples can be found in many urban areas in the two countries this chapter focuses on. As with other necessary social goods, the state – in the case of housing often in the form of local governments – has mostly been seen as the foremost agent of such decommodification measures. These can take a variety of forms whose characteristics we want to explore in the following sections. We will first focus on public policies, such as subsidy schemes or zoning, and then turn to property-rights-related instruments.

3.1 Demand-side subsidies

The least 'invasive' instruments in governments' surgical kits regarding housing provision are demand-side subsidies, which give people below a certain income-level money with which to pay their rent. In both Germany and Switzerland, these kinds of benefits are part of the standard ('income maintenance') welfare payment systems, and are regulated at the national level. In both cases, beneficiaries receive a separate payment for housing costs corresponding to their actual rent (whereas the basic monthly benefit for all other living costs is fixed).[24] These welfare payments thus do not form part of any explicit housing regulation, even though they influence the residential sector in major ways. Many landlords who offer inexpensive housing, for instance, cater directly to welfare recipients, demanding the highest possible rent that welfare agencies will allow per square meter or per apartment, thus securing a steady source of revenue. At the same time, as recent studies have shown,[25] demand-side subsidies tend to turn many centrally located districts into 'forbidden cities' for the welfare-dependent. The 'subject-based-support' approach thus fails to counter (and in part supports) the spatial segregation of different social groups which itself ultimately threatens the distinct qualities of 'the urban' that lie in "social differentiation without exclusion."[26] Demand-side subsidies attempt to remedy an individual disadvantage without addressing the underlying question of how the allocation of a necessary good through market mechanisms can ever work for those lacking sufficient 'purchasing power.' Therefore, they certainly don't encourage arrangements that would provide housing as a common resource. And since the affected tenants are only regarded as market players, the issue of strengthening their autonomy and self-organization does not even come into view.

3.2 Supply-side subsidies

It thus seems evident that governments should consider intervening on the supply side of housing provision as well. Although housing has been called a "wobbly pillar" of the welfare state (compared with the classic trinity of health care, education, and income maintenance),[27] there have indeed been major public efforts to provide decent and affordable housing for both the working and the middle classes, especially during the inter-war and the post-war periods.[28] In the command economies of state socialist regimes such as the German Democratic Republic, the state directed virtually the entire housing and construction sector in a centralist, top-down manner. In the post-war heydays of expanding welfare states, this was to some extent paralleled by Western governments' housing programs. In the aftermath of World War II, West Germany funded the construction of 3.3 million homes in just a decade.[29] *Objektförderung,* the subsidizing not of individuals' housing costs, but of "objects," i.e. buildings, can work in different ways. In both Germany and Switzerland, construction of affordable housing was mainly subsidized through low-interest loans as well as non-repayable *("à fonds perdu")* contributions from government agencies at the local, *Länder*/Canton, and, in some instances, national level. In return, the owners of the newly constructed homes were obligated to subtract the subsidy from their "cost rent" (*Kostenmiete* – rent covering the costs of the capital taken up for the investment and running costs, including maintenance, but not yielding an additional profit), thus passing it on to the tenants. The make-up of rent prices is illustrated in Figure 4.

One core element of the (West) German social housing system *(sozialer Wohnungsbau)* that continued throughout the second half of the twentieth century was that subsidies were generally paid regardless of a building's ownership. Publicly owned corporations and cooperatives (see below) benefited from this system, yet so did private (individual or corporate) owners who were left to do with their property as they pleased once the contractually agreed subsidy period was over. This system of

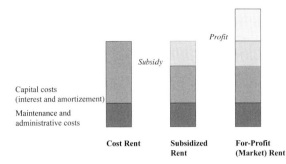

Figure 4. Composition of rent prices.

"social housing as temporary occupation"[30] was, after numerous cutbacks starting in the 1980s, de facto ended on the federal level in 2001[31] and continues only in heavily downsized forms in the *Länder*. It came to be regarded as notoriously prone to inefficiency and downright corruption, since it contained no real incentives to keep production and administration costs low. It yielded absurd arrangements in some cases, notably in (West) Berlin, where the rents in some (formerly) subsidized estates are now above average while private or corporate owners and banks have been making handsome profits.[32] Considering that the subsidized units are destined from the outset to revert into regular, commercially rented homes in this type of arrangement, it offers at best a temporary barrier to the commodification of housing (while breeding its own brand of speculation). And as it supports housing providers regardless of their general purpose and organizational set-up (profit-oriented and hierarchical as well as non-profit and participatory entities), it entails no particular promotion of inhabitants' self-organization either.

3.3 Zoning

Apart from implementing (demand- or supply-side) 'market intervention' policies, governments can also facilitate the provision of affordable housing through their administrative powers. Recent amendments to a number of local zoning laws in Switzerland present one interesting example in this regard.[33] Thanks to regulation similar to what is known in the United States as "inclusionary zoning," municipalities can proscribe a percentage of 'affordable' housing (in the 'cost rent' sense described above) for all new or redeveloped residential buildings within areas whose land-use designations are changed, allowing for higher building density. Although housing affected by such regulation might be in the possession of owners who pursue a strongly profit-oriented strategy elsewhere (as with the 'non-affordable' part of the development in question), this form of development is decommodified to some extent in the sense that the specific 'incident of ownership' that gives the owner the right to ask for payments for its use by others is restricted – as long as this zoning law is in place. Examples of such projects show that real-estate developers tend to strike a deal with non-profit organizations that acquire part of the lot through leasehold *(Baurecht)* and take over construction and management of the "affordable" part of the development. Since these are often cooperatives organized on a membership-basis (see below), this type of zoning may indirectly foster dwellers' self-organization.

4 Decommodifying housing through property rights

While the policies described so far may influence the provision of affordable housing to a notable degree, they can be changed, watered down, or abandoned. Arrangements primarily regulated through government policies are subject to the political *zeitgeist*. In contrast, property rights in a narrower sense are consistently respected in capitalist democracies, regardless of current political majorities. Instruments that are directly linked to the property rights system might thus be capable of decommodifying housing in a more sustainable way and guaranteeing dwellers' self-organization in the long run.

4.1 Public housing

Public housing in a strict sense, being the property of municipalities themselves, continues to play a significant role in many German and Swiss cities, as elsewhere, with local authorities being in possession of up to 15 percent of the total housing stock (please see Figure 3).[34] In the current German discourse, it is often favorably compared by those who advocate decommodification of housing stocks to the *Objektförderung* model described above. (Neo-)liberals, on the other hand, often criticize governments' direct involvement in a sector that can be a highly profitable part of the capitalist economy.

Yet ideally, well-built and well-managed rental housing is financially self-supporting, i.e. the revenue generated through rents should cover the costs of the capital used to pay for its construction (and, if applicable, for land purchase), as well as administrative and maintenance costs. Public housing thus need not cost a municipality anything per se and might, in the long run, become a valuable asset. Publicly owned homes produced in this manner count as 'affordable housing' in the sense that they are rented out at cost rent (see above). Due to production costs, however, they are usually not particularly inexpensive for decades after construction. This segment of public housing can thus be regarded as targeting a 'broad segment' of the population, including the middle classes. Only some municipalities, usually ones with a strong social democratic tradition, adhere to this 'broad' public housing approach, but this includes some of the major cities in German-speaking Europe.

A well-thought-out public housing system which goes beyond this residual supply to cater to broader parts of the population, rather than only those in the direst need of support, can be said to provide housing in a manner that exhibits a considerable degree of decommodification. Yet this is only the case as long as the local government provides the necessary organizational means and refrains from cashing in on its public housing stock by selling it to either the inhabitants (as in the UK case of the Thatcher government's "right to buy" scheme), thus turning public dwellings into owner-occupied ones, which are theoretically resalable and thus commodified property, or even directly to corporate investors. We have lumped public housing in with those institutions that are linked to the property rights system, yet because this one very powerful incident of ownership – the right to sell – lies with (local) governments, it is, in fact, subject to similar threats of enclosure as dwellings within the mainly policy-influenced arrangements described earlier. In other words, just because city-owned homes are not destined to be *automatically* converted into for-profit rentals (as in the case of the German subsidy scheme described above), they can still be privatized by a decision of the local legislative body, which is exactly what happened in the past few decades to hundreds of thousands of apartments in German cities.[35] Furthermore, regarding the second axis in our model, the question of self-organization, public housing cannot be assessed too positively, as the welfare traditions it represents are closely connected to notions of control and surveillance. In this light, it is not surprising that "many urban movements today have lost confidence" not only "in the market as the optimal (and equitable) provider" but also "in [...] the state as a trustworthy steward for collective consumption," as noted in the introduction to this volume. This points to the importance of non-state actors with respect to our topic.

4.2 Self-organization in housing: The cooperative/third sector

Although many types of providers of "third way" housing exist (e.g. charitable foundations, religious communities), cooperatives are the most important ones in German-speaking Europe. A cooperative (*Genossenschaft* in German), broadly understood, is an association of people with the purpose of governing a certain set of economic affairs collectively. This often entails access to and use of a shared resource. The cooperative model can thus be said to represent a classical institutional form to organize what we call the commons. A housing cooperative's members are commoners in that they are usually both the tenants and, collectively, the owners of the real estate. Furthermore, although membership is based on subscription for shares, the general assemblies of German and Swiss housing cooperatives usually operate on a one-person-one-vote basis, regardless of the value of each member's holdings.

Thus, other than in the housing provision arrangements discussed previously, (democratic) self-organization can be said to constitute a core element of the cooperative model. And since cooperatives' members obviously have no incentive to extract profits from themselves, it seems plausible that they manage their housing stock as a "non-commodified means of fulfilling people's needs."[36] Yet depending on a cooperative's members' interests, they might, for instance, choose to sell a portion of the housing stock on the open market. The adherence of cooperatives to the purpose of sustained decommodification of their housing stocks depends, to some extent, on regulation prescribed from outside. This can, for example, come in the form of membership in an umbrella organization that oversees the observance of such basic rules. In Switzerland, there are two national associations of housing cooperatives,[37] both of which ask their member organizations to comply with the principles laid down in the "Charter of Non-Profit Housing Providers"[38] which declares, among other things, that they are to provide affordable housing which remains withdrawn from speculation, that they use the cost rent model, and that they forgo profit-seeking. The relevance of this charter lies in the fact that adherence to it is widely used as a criterion for access to loans and other kinds of support from local and cantonal governments. It is also a requirement for receiving low-interest loans from two bank-like institutions supported by the Swiss Confederation that cater exclusively to cooperatives and other non-profit housing organizations.[39] The legal concept of *Gemeinnützigkeit* (non-profit status; literally "the quality of operating in favor of the common good") was, in contrast, never paramount in the German system of *Objektförderung,* and the tax benefits connected to this status within the housing sector were abolished in 1989.[40]

Recognizing only non-profit organizations as eligible for public support, the Swiss system of *Trägerförderung* ("financial support for providers") has clearly proven more up to the task of permanently decommodifying certain housing stocks.[41] While only a marginal influence in most rural and suburban areas, *Trägerförderung* has been influential in creating a significant portion of non-profit housing in some cities. The most notable example is Zurich, Switzerland's largest city, where cooperative housing amounts to about 18 percent of the total stock, in addition to about 7 percent public housing, thus placing the total share of the *"gemeinnützige"* sector at a quarter (see Figure 3). In 2011, voters approved a referendum obliging the city government to raise this percentage to a third by 2050. Apartments whose construction is directly subsidized by municipal (often supplemented by cantonal) funds, and which are therefore allocated on a needs basis, only make up a small part of cooperative estates. The city government's arguably most important instrument in supporting cooperatives is not a financial policy, but relates, again, to the property rights system. Through leasehold contracts (*Baurechtsverträge*), cooperatives can acquire city-owned land for very long periods, usually sixty years, for an annual rent. This title allows them to construct housing on these lots and to use them as collateral when raising the necessary capital for the project. The municipality, on the other hand, can facilitate the construction of affordable, non-profit housing without spending money of its own and without giving away public property irretrievably.

4.3 Commoning by "hacking" the law?

Leasehold agreements are part of the property rights system and can govern the relation between any landowner and leaser, but they are by no means specifically designed to support cooperative housing. Zoning laws (which fall within the domain of public policies) are also not intended to require a percentage of affordable housing, as described above; their main purpose is rather to determine the permissible *physical* design of buildings – height, density etc. – in a given area. In order to achieve a measure of decommodification for certain housing stocks, these legal instruments were thus used in different ways than originally intended in the cases we have examined. This could be described as "hacking" the law[42] – a concept that might become clearer once we introduce its arguably most accomplished application in the cooperative sector.

Many cooperatives in Germany and Switzerland became estranged from their social movement roots after World War II. Their way of managing property hardly differed from the commercial real-estate business, and their members were less keen on actively participating in the democratic structures of self-organization that were theoretically still in place. This stagnation was criticized by a new, post-1968 generation of housing activists with ties to various tenants' struggles and protests against inconsiderate urban renewal projects; here squatting became one of the main protest methods.[43] New organizational structures and legal models have since emerged among groups of squatters and former tenants that managed to become the lawful owners of their houses. The prime example is the *Mietshäuser Syndikat,* a network of collectively owned houses founded in 1992 which today comprises more than eighty individual housing initiatives all over Germany. It is technically *not* a cooperative as specified by German law, but a sort of elaborately checked and balanced federation of limited liability companies (*Gesellschaften mit beschränkter Haftung,* GmbH). An association of the inhabitants of each house within the network holds half of the shares in the company in possession of the respective building. The other half is held by the *Syndikat,* enabling it to prevent the house from ever being resold, even if its inhabitants wanted to cash in on it.[44] The idea behind this veto function is to preserve the houses as strictly decommodified common resources, regardless of the current users' intentions. This organizational model, we argue, is an excellent example of a clever "hack" of property rights, i.e. of "components [...] reduced [...] to rebuild quite different systems with different arrangements of the

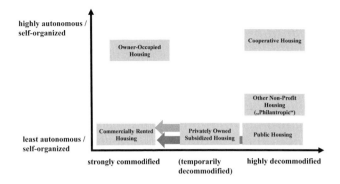

Figure 5. Types of housing tenure and provision – decommodification and self-organization.

pieces,"[45] turning the "arch-capitalist"[46] corporate structure of a GmbH into a vehicle for strictly non-profit projects. Considering this emphasis of access and use-value as well as the high degree of autonomy that the individual inhabitants' groups enjoy within the network, the houses belonging to the *Syndikat* can thus be said to more clearly constitute a common resource than traditional cooperative housing.

5 Conclusion

In order to highlight the defining characteristics of the various types of housing tenure described in this chapter, we suggest, as mentioned, arranging them along two axes, one marking a commodification-decommodification scale, the other denoting the extent of self-organization. As we have seen, public housing may, for instance, be quite strongly decommodified, but it usually offers little room for tenants' self-organization, embodying instead hierarchical and centralist principles. As an owner-occupier, on the other hand, one might find a home to feel relatively independent in, but only as long as one can afford to pay the mortgage (Figure 5).

As we have attempted to show, and as Figure 5 illustrates, the crucial issue regarding the decommodification of housing stocks is the permanency of the measures taken: public policies can restrict certain incidents of ownership that enable the use of housing as a commodity, yet often only temporarily – be it because a subsidy scheme is set up to function in this way to begin with, as in the West German *sozialer Wohnungsbau,* or because of a policy change, typically privatization (cf. the arrows in figure 5). Only if the most powerful incidents of ownership lie with organizations that are perpetually bound, by internal and/or external regulation, to adhere to a non-profit strategy, can a housing stock be regarded as sustainably decommodified.

This diagram is obviously a simplification of the actual institutional diversity in this field, but it can help us reflect on the paths that commoning efforts can take nowadays.[47] Cooperative organizations that correspond to commons principles as neatly as the *Mietshäuser Syndikat* are currently a niche phenomenon. Plainly put, this type of collective project, involving hours of voluntary work, thus requiring a rather specific lifestyle and cultural capital of a certain kind, is not for everyone. Yet even taking into account traditional, large cooperatives, it seems crucial not to fall into the trap of expecting the third sector to act as an adequate substitute for the state with regard to extensive social tasks. Municipalities will still have a role to play in providing affordable and secure housing to large parts of the population. However, as we have attempted to demonstrate, it may in fact be a paradoxically appropriate strategy in "late liberal" capitalism for both government and civil society actors to secure common resources effectively and sustainably not by conventional public policies, which can quickly be overturned, but rather by contractual means, making clever use of the property rights toolbox. Or, as Marcuse states, "the existing range of alternatives in use in market economies suggests that the attempt to expand them even further might not be an entirely quixotic endeavor."[48]

Notes

1. Cf. for instance Dan Andrews and Aida Caldera Sánchez, "The Evolution of Homeownership Rates in Selected OECD Countries: Demographic and Public Policy Influences," *OECD Journal: Economic Studies* 2011, no. 1: 212.
2. Please see the introduction to this volume.
3. Andreas Exner and Brigitte Kratzwald, *Solidarische Ökonomie und Commons* (Vienna: Mandelbaum, 2012).
4. Silke Helfrich and Jörg Haas, "The Commons: A New Narrative for Our Times," in *Genes, Bytes and Emissions: To Whom Does the World Belong?,* Silke Helfrich, eds. (Berlin: Heinrich-Böll-Stiftung, 2009), 1–15.
5. Massimo De Angelis and Stavros Stavrides, "On the Commons: A Public Interview with Massimo De Angelis and Stavros Stavrides," *e-flux* 17 (2011): 1–17.
6. Andrej Holm, "Wohnen als soziale Infrastruktur," *Z. Zeitschrift marxistische Erneuerung* 95 (2013): 44–57.

7   Cf. for instance Lee A. Nicol. *Sustainable Collective Housing: Policy and Practice for Multi-Family Dwellings* (New York: Routledge, 2013), 26f.
8   Peter Marcuse, "Property Rights, Tenure and Ownership: Towards Clarity in Concept," in *Social Rented Housing in Europe: Policy, Tenure and Design,* Berth Danermark and Ingemar Elander, eds. (Delft: Delft University Press, 1994), 32.
9   Ibid., 25f. Following Wesley N. Hohfeld, *Fundamental Legal Conceptions as Applied in Judicial Reasoning* (New Haven: Yale University Press, 1916), Marcuse lists twelve key incidents of ownership with regards to housing, such as the "privilege to occupy and use for shelter" or the "right of profiting from a disposition."
10 This approach is partly based on Jean-David Gerber, Peter Knoepfel, Stéphane Nahrath, and Frédéric Varone, "Institutional Resource Regimes: Towards Sustainability Through the Combination of Property-Rights Theory and Policy Analysis," *Ecological Economics* 68, no. 3 (2008): 798–809.
11 Andrej Holm, "Wohnung als Ware: Zur Ökonomie und Politik der Wohnungsversorgung," *Widersprüche* 121 (2011): 20; author's translation (original: "Die Dekommodifizierung, also das Herauslösen der Wohnungsversorgung aus den Marktlogiken, kann dabei als Ziel und Maßstab für die Bewertung wohnungspolitischer Programme und Regelungen verstanden werden"); referring to Peter Williams and Neil Smith, "From 'Renaissance' to Restructuring: The Dynamics of Contemporary Urban Development," in *Gentrification of the City,* eds. Williams and Smith (Boston: Allen & Unwin, 1986), 204–224.
12 De Angelis and Stavrides, "On the Commons," 2; cf. the introduction to this volume.
13 Ibid.
14 Marcuse, "Property Rights," 26.
15 Ibid., 29.
16 Richard Arnott, "Housing Economics," in *International Encyclopedia of the Social and Behavioral Sciences,* Neil J. Smelser and Paul B. Baltes, eds. (Oxford: Elsevier, 2001), 6940.
17 John Doling, "De-commodification and Welfare: Evaluating Housing Systems," *Housing, Theory and Society* 16, no. 4 (1999): 161.
18 In Marxist terms, housing thus provides a poignant example for the 'dual character' of goods, having use-value as well as exchange value, cf. Holm, "Wohnung als Ware."
19 Andrews and Caldera Sánchez, "Homeownership Rates," 212.
20 Gøsta Esping-Andersen, *The Three Worlds of Welfare Capitalism* (Princeton: Princeton University Press, 1990).
21 On the Spanish case, cf. Melissa García Lamarca's chapter in this volume, and Melissa García Lamarca, "Resisting Evictions Spanish Style," *New Internationalist Magazine,* April 2013, http://newint.org/features/2013/04/01/sparks-from-the-spanish-crucible/ (accessed September 10, 2014).
22 https://ergebnisse.zensus2011.de/#dyntable:statunit=wohnung;absRel=anzahl;ags=11;agsaxis=X;-yaxis=eigentum; https://www.stadt-zuerich.ch/content/dam/stzh/prd/Deutsch/Statistik/Publikationsdatenbank/jahrbuch/2014/Tabellen/T_JB_2014_9_3.xlsx and http://www.statistik.at/web_de/statistiken/wohnen_und_gebaeude/bestand_an_gebaeuden_und_wohnungen/022985.html (all accessed September 8, 2014)
23 Cf. for instance Andrej Holm and Dirk Gebhardt, eds., *Initiativen für ein Recht auf Stadt: Theorie und Praxis städtischer Aneignungen* (Hamburg: VSA, 2011).
24 *Kosten der Unterkunft* ('housing costs') paid in addition to the *Regelbedarf* ('regular demand') as part of the *Arbeitslosengeld II* ('unemployment money II'), colloquially known as "Hartz IV" in Germany; *Wohnkosten* (also translatable as 'housing costs') paid in addition to the *Grundbedarf* ('basic demand') as part of the *Sozialhilfe* ('social welfare') in Switzerland.

25 E.g. Andrej Holm, "Kosten der Unterkunft als Segregationsmotor: Befunde aus Berlin und Oldenburg," *Informationen zur Raumentwicklung,* 2011, no. 11, 557–566.
26 Iris Marion Young, *Justice and the Politics of Difference* (Princeton: Princeton University Press, 1990), 239; cf. contribution by Kip, this volume.
27 Ulf Torgerson, quoted in Michael Harloe, *The People's Home? Social Rented Housing in Europe and America* (Oxford: Blackwell, 1995), 2.
28 It would be beyond the scope of this chapter to go into the history of public and social housing in any depth, cf. Harloe, *People's Home* for an extensive international overview.
29 Björn Egner, "Wohnungspolitik seit 1945," *Aus Politik und Zeitgeschichte,* 2014, no. 20–21: 13.
30 Christian Donner, *Wohnungspolitiken in der Europäischen Union* (Vienna: Christian Donner, 2000), 200; cf. Andrej Holm, "Privatisierung des kommunalen Wohnungsbestandes", in *Jahrbuch StadtRegion 2007/08: Arme reiche Stadt,* Norbert Gestring, Herbert Glasauer, Christine Hannemann, Werner Petrowsky, and Jörg Pohlan, eds. (Opladen: Verlag Barbara Budrich, 2008), 102.
31 Egner, "Wohnungspolitik," 17.
32 Cf. Kotti & Co, Sozialmieter.de and Selbstuniversität e.V., eds., *Nichts läuft hier richtig: Informationen zum sozialen Wohnungsbau in Berlin* (Berlin: 2014) for an excellent overview of these shortcomings from a local tenant activists' perspective.
33 Lukas Bühlmann and Niklaus Spori, "Förderung des gemeinnützigen Wohnungsbaus mit raumplanerischen Mitteln," *Raum & Umwelt* 10, no. 1 (2010).
34 The paramount example in German-speaking Europe would be Vienna, where a quarter of the total housing stock is in the possession of the municipality and which we have therefore included in this overview in spite of otherwise omitting the Austrian case in this chapter.
35 Cf. Hartmut Häußermann, "Marktplatz oder Gemeinwesen? Der politische Inhalt der Verkaufspolitik und die Folgen für die Stadtentwicklung," *Forum Wohnen und Stadtentwicklung* 2006, no. 2: 159–163; Andrej Holm, "Der Ausstieg des Staates aus der Wohnungspolitik," *Planungsrundschau* 13 (2006): 103–113; Michael Voigtländer, "Die Privatisierung öffentlicher Wohnungen," *Wirtschaftsdienst,* 2007, no. 11: 748–753.
36 De Angelis and Stavrides, "On the Commons," 2; cf. above.
37 *Wohnbaugenossenschaften Schweiz – Verband der gemeinnützigen Wohnbauträger,* the larger organziation, representing the labor/social-democratic tradition, and *Wohnen Schweiz – Verband der Baugenossenschaften,* of a more liberal heritage.
38 *Charta der gemeinnützigen Wohnbauträger in der Schweiz,* http://www.wbg-schweiz.ch/downloads/171/gemeinsame_Charta_01_01_13_d_2877.pdf (accessed September 8, 2014).
39 The Federal Revolving Fund *(Fonds de Roulement)* which was funded by the Confederation and which the cooperatives' associations hold in trust, and the Bond Issuing Cooperative (BIC) for Non-Profit Housing *(Emissionszentrale für Gemeinnützige Wohnbauträger, EGW),* which borrows substantial means for cooperatives through the regular capital market with the Swiss Confederation acting as a guarantor; cf. Julie Lawson, "The Transformation of Social Housing Provision in Switzerland Mediated by Federalism, Direct Democracy and the Urban/Rural Divide," *European Journal of Housing Policy* 9, no. 1 (2009). In addition, the *Wohnbaugenossenschaften Schweiz* operates a fund of its own.
40 Volker Dorn, "Changes in the Social Rented Sector in Germany," *Urban Studies* 12, no. 4 (1997): 469.
41 A similar system was in fact in place in Germany during the Weimar Republic period, cf. e.g. Hartmut Häußermann and Walter Siebel, *Soziologie des Wohnens: Eine Einführung in Wandel und Ausdifferenzierung des Wohnens* (Weinheim/Munich: Juventa, 1996), 103ff.
42 We are indebted to Dubravka Sekulić for introducing us to this fitting metaphor.
43 Concerning these movements, an exemplary case study for Zurich was authored by Thomas Stahel, *Wo-Wo-Wonige: Stadt- und wohnpolitische Bewegungen in Zürich nach 1968* (Zurich: Paranoia City, 2006).

44 Cf. Stefan Rost, "Das Mietshäuser Syndikat," in *Commons – Für eine neue Politik jenseits von Markt und Staat*, eds. Silke Helfrich and Heinrich-Böll-Stiftung (Bielefeld: Transcript, 2012), 285–287; Stefan Rost, "Die beste Genossenschaft ist gar keine: Klaus-Novy-Preis 2012 für das Mietshäuser Syndikat," *Freihaus* 18 (2012): 7–9; Peter Ache and Micha Fedrowitz, "The Development of Co-Housing Initiatives in Germany," *Built Environment* 38, no. 3 (2012): 399.The *Syndikat* itself is again organized as another GmbH with just one shareholder, an association whose members are, in turn, the various inhabitants' associations along with individuals who support the network's basic idea.
45 Marcuse, Property Rights, 29.
46 Rost, Genossenschaft, 9.
47 Cf. also Stuart Hodkinson, "The Return of the Housing Question", *Ephemera* 12, no. 4 (2012): 423–444.
48 Marcuse, Property Rights, 29.

Sören Becker, Ross Beveridge, Matthias Naumann

Reconfiguring Energy Provision in Berlin. Commoning between Compromise and Contestation

1 Introduction

In recent years the term "commons" has developed into something of a 'catch-all' phrase to describe the range of attempts to achieve alternative forms of societal organization and practices, from urban gardening to open-source software, or even the revitalization of public space. Apart from being an increasingly important notion in governance and institutional research, the term has also become a normative political concept in the production or utilization of resources, material items, or immaterial phenomena by a clearly defined group of people.[1] Taken even further, the idea of the commons has become a source of inspiration for various alternative imaginaries emerging in opposition to the structures of everyday capitalism. While many sectors of economic activity have been subject to thinking about the commons and commoning, this chapter deals with the electricity sector in a major European city: Berlin.

The fact that energy is a core resource, fundamental to everyday life, should render it suitable to organization according to the principles of the commons. However, the reality of electricity provision is that it is characterized by large-scale development and dominated by state and private enterprises. User communities, cooperatives or energy-autonomous localities have long been an exception, restricted to remote mountain regions or islands not connected to central networks that span the metropolises.[2] Despite this pattern, according to which large corporate and state monopoly structures have prevailed for a long time, the onset of renewable energies has created momentum for a restructuring of the energy sector, at least in Germany. Here the promotion of decentralized electricity generation through a feed-in tariff system has provoked significant shifts in the ownership structures of electricity generation plants.[3] In effect, the German *Energiewende* (energy turnaround) is more than just a technological phenomenon. The coalescence of changing technology schemes, new ownership patterns, and new forms of organization in the German system of energy provision opens up new possibilities to think about commoning of the energy system.

This chapter will utilize the concept of the commons to analytically consider recent developments in the city of Berlin. Berlin is promising as a case study in a variety of aspects, not least because it has been the stage for one of the major conflicts about the organization of electricity in Germany. In Berlin, alongside a number of corporate actors, two citizen initiatives are active in the process of awarding a new network concession. While one initiative has organized a citizens' plebiscite to impel the local state to remunicipalize the electricity grid and to establish a participatory grid operator, the other seeks to attain shares of the grid operator as a cooperative. This co-existence of a remunicipalization movement and cooperative organization is unique among major European cities. It allows for a comparison of their shared and conflicting ideas of how energy should be provided in Germany's capital and also provides insights into the form a commons-based energy system might take. Beyond this, a discussion of the two initiatives, their ideas and strategies might also contribute to the debate about the emancipatory potential of commons and commoning in general. While the more antagonistic plebiscite narrowly failed in early November 2013, the cooperative is still active in their search for shareholders and donations to acquire a citizen share in the network. It should not be forgotten that these developments and the existence of various models for an alternative organization of the energy sector in public discourse not only stirred up debate but also led to a discussion that extended beyond the field of energy provision in a narrow sense and connected to larger questions about participation and even the right to the city.[4]

To better understand the different visions for an alternative mode of energy provision prevalent in Berlin, we discuss them in relation to the notion of the commons and consider them in terms of their embeddedness in a conflictive urban context. The chapter has the following structure: to give a brief impression of the context of ownership changes in the German energy sector, section two will explore the spread of energy cooperatives and remunicipalizations across Germany. Section three will contextualize the conception of the commons which is used to frame the empirical analysis in this chapter. A discussion of the various actors, the different proposed organizational models, and the question to what degree they relate to our understanding of commons will be at the heart of section four. Section five provides a short conclusion.

2 Public and cooperative ownership in the German energy sector

In the 1990s and early 2000s, waves of privatization and market concentration as a result of liberalization[1] shaped the economic and institutional underpinnings of the electricity sector in Germany. Former state monopolies were replaced by an oligopolistic ensemble of the so-called "Big Four," those major electricity companies that had the majority market share around 2005.[6] Against this, one can observe a recent and increasingly strong development throughout Germany: municipalities and citizens trying to regain control of both electricity production and distribution facilities.

The numbers are impressive at first glance: 650 newly established energy cooperatives between 2000 and the end of 2012[7] and more than 120 newly founded public energy utilities since 2005.[8] Nevertheless, it is worth noting that these numbers capture newly founded utilities that might be active in either network operation or electricity generation, or simply selling energy packages bought on the stock market. Additionally, both numbers are based on legal registration, so they give no account of technological or commercial data such as generation capacity, membership or client numbers, and so on. Despite this advisable caution, one can argue that, together with so called "prosumers" – who generate the energy they require personally, e.g. with the help of a photovoltaic system on the rooftop of their private residential building – public utilities and energy cooperatives are significantly changing the structure of the German energy market.

Strictly speaking, neither of them is a new model. In the early years of electrification, a collective development of installations was one of the few viable alternatives in many remote regions that were not connected to networks supplying the industrialized metropolises.[9] Subsequently, hydropower cooperatives were established in the alpine and sub-alpine regions of Europe. Today energy cooperatives exist across the country, but they are unevenly distributed with clusters in southern and northwestern Germany.[10] With a total membership of 136,000 at the end of 2012, energy cooperatives are a key means of ensuring citizen participation in electricity generation.

Municipal energy suppliers share a similar origin, yet a different history. While for a long time they were protected by legislation that foresaw a patchwork of local and regional monopolies of energy provision executed by municipal or regional utilities, there was a widespread fear that they would be the first victims of market liberalization in the late 1990s.[11] However, history proved the "Dying Stadtwerke"[12] thesis wrong, and yielded an unexpected growth in numbers. A key reason for this was the almost simultaneous termination of many concession contracts with private suppliers. Some municipalities have seized this window of opportunity and have taken back the operation of the electricity networks in their territory, a development that some authors see as part of a general "renaissance of the municipal economy."[13] Remunicipalizations of this kind have been driven by dissatisfaction with the results of privatization as well as a general distrust of the neoliberal market-based financial model in Germany.[14] Other sources mention the increased economic capabilities of many municipalities as a driver for remunicipalization and, in the energy sector, the unwillingness of the big private energy companies to fund the transition to renewables.[15] While there are some widely known and highly conflictive cases of remunicipalizations, such as the formation of *Hamburg Energie* and the successful referendum to remunicipalize electricity, gas, and district heating networks in the city of Hamburg, the largest number of remunicipalizations has taken place in small and medium-sized towns in western and southwestern Germany without much public debate.[16] Both new public enterprises and energy cooperatives challenge the privatized mode of energy provision as such. When complemented with participatory measures, it is in the context of these trends to reverse privatization in energy that the idea of commons enters the realm of infrastructure.

3 Coming to terms with the commons: Critical and energy perspectives

The idea of commons and questions of their governance has become an important point of reference, one that implies a complex body of research. We will not follow the traditional strands of economic or institutional economic approaches to commons but will delve into what Moss et al.[17] have identified as the third, and most recent, strand of thinking about commons. This is put forward by mainly Marxist and Post-Marxist scholars, who conceive commons as an entry point to think about new, post- or non-capitalist forms of ownership and production.[18] This line of thought distinguishes commons from "enclosures" and "commodities," which are seen as crucial conditions for capitalist accumulation and valorization.[19] Against this backdrop, commons are positioned as a "promissory" term,[20] engendering alternatives to capitalism and neoliberalism:

Commons suggest alternative, non-commodified means to fulfil social needs, e.g., to obtain social wealth and to organize social production. Commons are necessarily created and sustained by communities i.e. by social networks of mutual aid, solidarity, and practices of human exchange that are not reduced to the market form.[21]

Compared with the traditional and the institutional economics strands of commons research, there are three main conceptual shifts within this third strand. In short, these encompass, firstly, a view that commons themselves are produced by the practice of "commoning," defined as creating a relationship towards a resource or an "aspect of the environment" that is "both collective and non-commodified – off limits to the logic of market exchange and market valuation."[22] Secondly, commons are seen to produce a "commonwealth" that is more than just a commonly governed resource.[23] In this sense, commons produce an added value, though one that resists an a priori definition across different possible practices of commoning. Thirdly, the production of commons is highly conflictual, "contradictory and always contested."[24] Commoning involves certain social and political interests, opposes and forecloses others. As a consequence, the practice of commoning is in line with the forms of contentious, antagonistic politics which several thinkers have proposed to counter consensual "postpolitics."[25] While there has already been normative work and research on the possibilities of interpreting local, autonomous, and/or small- to medium-scale energy systems as commons,[26] critical understanding has yet to be fully developed, i.e. an approach to commoning as a form of contestation and of creating alternative forms of organization that differ from commonplace privatized resource use or provision.

This is not to say that research on commons and energy does not cover alternative forms of organization that translate decentralized technology options into decentralized ownership patterns. Wolsink focuses on smart grids governed by a community;[27] Lambing speaks of a combination of production and consumption of energy in a commons-like governance structure[28] – most likely a cooperative – while Byrne et al. argue that a "sustainable electricity utility" could combine market incentives with community participation and could lead to a post-"cornucopian" energy regime.[29] While each accounts for conflicts in their proposal, none of them considers what we have identified as the three critical dimensions – the practice of commoning, the creation of a commonwealth, and the contested character of commoning – at the heart of their concepts. This is what we aim to do in our discussion of developments in Berlin.

4 Berlin: Different strategies for and notions of urban energy commons, or the struggle between state and cooperative ownership

The end of a long-term concession contract between the city of Berlin and the Swedish state electricity corporation Vattenfall at the end of 2014 has not only aroused the interest of private suitors, it has also led to the creation of two different citizens' initiatives that take contrasting approaches to influencing the Berlin senate's decision on the future concession for the Berlin energy network. The Berlin Energy Roundtable *(Berliner Energietisch)* is pushing the senate to remunicipalize the grid, which provides 3.5 million inhabitants with electricity through 35,000 km of distribution lines, and to establish a participatory municipal enterprise. The energy cooperative Citizen's Energy Berlin *(Bürger Energie Berlin)* acts primarily as a socio-economic actor and aims to buy a share of the future municipal or private grid operator. While the Roundtable has used the plebiscitary element of a referendum to pressure the senate legally, the cooperative, thus far, has followed a strategy of persuasion.

In this section, we compare these two initiatives in terms of a) the actors that constitute the two initiatives, b) the organizational model they propose for the city's grid, c) their references to the practice of commoning and their ideas about a commonwealth, and d) a short assessment of the degree of contention they pose to the city's debate on the future of the electricity grid. The empirical basis is provided by the method of process tracing[30] and three interviews conducted in August and September 2013.

a) New actors challenge urban energy policy

Not only has the organization of a referendum been a new tool for urban energy policy in Berlin and beyond, the processes in Berlin have also brought to light new civic actors seeking to influence urban energy governance. With some overlap in supporters, both initiatives have placed their members and activists more generally at the heart of urban energy politics.

In the summer of 2011, the *Berliner Energietisch* was founded as an organizational platform for different initiatives that support a full remunicipalization of Berlin's energy grid. Earlier in 2010, a small group of activists from the Berlin branch of the alter-globalization movement *attac*, the nationwide initiative *BürgerBegehren Klimaschutz* (Petition for Climate Protection), and the small NGO *PowerShift* had published a first concept paper on the formation of a possible new municipal utility, outlining that it should both produce from renewable energy sources and provide participatory structures (see below).[31] In the run-up to the referendum, the *Berliner Energietisch* grew considerably, numbering around forty groups encompassing a wide range of actors from large environmental organizations to small NGOs, leftist activist groups to anti-gentrification initiatives, and some professionals from the field of renewable energy.[32] As with its predecessor the Berlin Water Roundtable,[33] this constellation of actors within the Energy Roundtable thus reflected various factions of the city's social movements that, in this case, gathered around the issues of participation in and the right to infrastructure.[34] Political parties were not granted the opportunity to become official supporters of the Energy Roundtable, though the Left Party, the Greens and the Pirate Party supported the collection of signatures to satisfy the required quota before the referendum could occur.

The membership structure of the cooperative is less transparent when compared with the Energy Roundtable, as public acts of support and statements of solidarity are not as central to their strategy. Thus, beside the number of 2,300 members, little is known about the social structure of its membership. A representative spoke of members being mainly recruited from people genuinely interested in energy issues, spanning various social groups like students, freelancers, employees, and pensioners.[35] To become a member, you have to buy five shares at €100 each, which is seen as "a greater commitment" than signing a petition.[36] There is no local membership restriction, so people from other parts of the country may become members of the cooperative as well.[37] Altogether the cooperative collected a capital stock of €10.3 million by July 2014. This results in an average of about €4,400 in capital contributions per member, a number which is hard to interpret due to single large-scale donors and possible support from commercially very successful rural energy cooperatives. The cooperative also allows for donations and for buying multiple cooperative shares.[38] Additionally, to adjust to the high price of buying the network and the technological complexity, it has entered into a strategic cooperation alliance with another municipal energy supplier from southwestern Germany.[39]

b) Different models of organization

Both initiatives were founded in 2011 with the beginning of the concession-awarding process in sight. Both approaches drew their inspiration from already successfully implemented projects. While the Berlin Energy Roundtable, both in terms of organization and process, relied on an earlier successful referendum to disclose secret contracts between the city government and the then-privatized water utility in 2009, the cooperative looked to different cooperative electricity grid projects that have spread in medium-sized towns and rural Germany. However, both also developed their own particular characteristics that this section is devoted to.

In contrast to small towns or rural areas, the cooperative in Berlin only aims to acquire a share of the network operating utility. Their central goal is to gather enough capital to become part of a cooperation model in which a municipal (or "in a worse-case scenario" private) utility holds a majority share of the grid operator and the cooperative controls up to 49 percent,[40] though they have excluded the possibility of cooperation with any enterprise that promotes nuclear energy.[41] Additionally, 10 percent of the revenue should flow into a fund for the promotion of renewable energy installations in the city and its hinterland.[42] However, although cooperation is necessary for *Bürger Energie Berlin,* the core organizational principles of a cooperative remain authoritative. These are centered on the notion of membership according to the requirements outlined above. Each member would then be co-owner of the cooperative according to the part of the grid the cooperative has acquired. Within the general assembly, each member has one voice which is counted equally irrespective of the capital invested. In effect, those citizens who have become members would co-own their electricity grid and collectively have a say about business practices and network politics.

In fundamental terms, the model of the Berlin Energy Roundtable is more universalistic. It envisions a municipally owned network utility that is complemented by participatory procedures. This reflects ambivalent experiences with traditional municipal energy suppliers in the past. Firstly, although publicly owned, these were criticized as operating in a way indistinguishable from private utilities. Secondly, there was often a certain proximity between local government and the utilities, made most apparent in elder politicians becoming the heads of the utility from time to time. Thirdly, the idea was to actually prevent a future privatization by giving the citizens a direct say.[43] As a consequence, the Roundtable's model combines state ownership with a number of stipulations for embedding a strong participatory approach in a *"Bürgerstadtwerk"* (Citizens' Power Utility). These feature public meetings at a borough level, an extended advisory board with directly elected citizen representatives, and demands for transparency where core documents are to be made publicly accessible.[44] The nexus of transparency, participation, and control is central to their understanding: "You cannot order a subscription [of politicians and managers] to the public interest by law. Only control can secure it."[45] Beyond this there was also some discussion about social tariffs and the promotion of renewable energy within the Energy Roundtable. In contrast to the cooperative, however, the local state would remain the owner of the utility operating the power grid and the recipient of the revenues in the Roundtable's municipal model.

c) The Berlin energy initiatives – commoning and creating a commonwealth?

Having presented the plans for the future organization and ownership of the network utility envisioned by the two initiatives, we will now turn to discussing their ideas in relation to the commons perspective. Before we do this, we stress that caution is required. Neither the Roundtable nor the *Bürger Energie Berlin* actually use the term commons in their internal and external communication. Both tend to prefer arguing for public service *(Daseinsvorsorge)* and public interest *(Gemeinwohl)*, notions that have a longer history in the German discourse on infrastructure.[46] In rough terms, the idea behind this concept is that the provision of core infrastructures should not be led by market incentives, but should be provided for the good of society as a whole. However, there are considerable overlaps with the critical commons conception referred to in this paper. Our intention is, thus, not to rewrite the Berlin initiatives' ideas into a commons narrative, but rather to utilize the commons concept as an analytical frame to understand developments. By bringing public interest and commons into conversation, an analytical deepening of both concepts might be possible. Therefore, we will discuss aspects of commoning and a commonwealth in relation to the ideas of the two initiatives in Berlin.

The practice of commoning can be assessed from two viewpoints. First and ex-ante, one can focus on their ideas for the future electricity system; second and to a certain extent ex-post, one can also consider the degree to which they have already contributed to commoning the city's energy provision in the process so far.

From the ex-ante perspective, both conceptualizations of the future organizational model depict a break from private (and former public) network operation within the city and posit the replacement of the latter with forms of citizen involvement and participation. However, the community of the commoners would differ in each organizational model. Within the cooperative's solution, the commoners would consist of the sum of cooperative members – irrespective of their location or the amount of capital they have provided. Thereby, the practice of commoning could be translated into legally owning some part of the network.

In the Roundtable's version, the practice of commoning has a more indirect character. In reality, it would have been mediated through state ownership. The consequences are twofold. Firstly, one could argue that Berlin's entire citizenry would become stakeholders. This would, however, in legally correct terms, exclude those inhabitants of the city who do not hold the right to vote. The Roundtable sought to circumvent such an outcome by proposing less formalized neighborhood or borough meetings that would include these "denizens"[47] as well. However, the Roundtable was unable to bring these initial plans into a legally workable proposal for a draft law. Secondly, it would be imperative to actually make use of the opportunities for participatory procedures to bridge the gap between state and single citizen. Nevertheless, any citizen could theoretically seize their right to articulate an interest without the barrier of acquiring membership shares.

While these arguments point to an as yet unknown future, it is evident that both initiatives have already set off a process of commoning to some extent. Concerning the cooperative this is obvious. As their formal procedures and their model of membership participation are already in place prior to any potential partial acquisition of the network operator, their commoning activities are already obvious. Since the Roundtable lost the referendum in early November 2013, it is less apparent how they might contribute to future commoning. Still, in one respect, however, the entire process of coalition-building and preparing for the referendum could be seen as commoning as well. The Roundtable was an organizational platform for different initiatives supporting a full remunicipalization of Berlin's energy grid (see above). The internal structure of plenary meetings was defined by grassroots participation and consensus decision-making. It was within this structure that the draft formulating the organizational model above was devised; this came as a result of the process of balancing different, partly conflicting, factions and opinions within the Roundtable.[48]

Another factor that should not be underestimated is how the Roundtable was able to raise awareness and make people, not only citizens, think about the nature of energy provision in the city. The extent of this ideational commoning becomes visible in the numbers of signatures gathered in the process of preparing for the referendum. This course of action was deliberately chosen to involve as many people in the discussion as possible.[49] The Roundtable was highly successful in gathering over 270,000 signatures, the last step before the referendum, well in excess of the quorum of 173,000 signatures.[50] This specific combination of discursive intervention through campaigning and a participative internal structure could have led to a legally binding law ensuring even more participation in the future.

The question as to how the two initiatives and their visions could contribute to the creation of a commonwealth directs us to the ecological and social stipulations and goals that add to the participatory provisions. We have already mentioned the fund the cooperative foresees for installing solar and co-generation plants in the future. Beyond this, it is noteworthy that both initiatives subscribe to the aim of electricity provision from 100 percent renewable sources. Socially fair pricing schemes played an important role in the communication strategy of the Roundtable and their attempts to convince voters.[51] In contrast, the issue is less prominent in the campaign by the cooperative, which argued mainly in favor of cost reduction through energy saving and efficiency measures.[52] Although the social dimension was less institutionalized in the Roundtable's draft law due to legal restrictions,[53] it still envisioned, for example, energy consumption counselling for economically disadvantaged households. In purely monetary terms, one can argue that the revenue to be distributed among the cooperative members clearly defines a commonwealth here. In turn, as the local state would profit from gains from a municipal power utility, the pecuniary commonwealth in the Roundtable's vision is of an only indirect character.

d) Contestation and conflict – the public debate on energy in Berlin

In the beginning we stated that the establishment of commons and the practice of commoning, when it is directed to de-commodification and de-commercialisation, are both a contestation of a given order and one that is in turn contested, given that it would be expected to spark resistance from those actors who profit from the status quo. We now provide a very brief evaluation of this critical aspect of de-privatizing energy provision in the city of Berlin. In terms of the creation of a public debate, an aim of both initiatives, they have clearly succeeded. There was vast press coverage during the time of the signature gathering and in the run-up to the referendum, and most political actors and organizations adopted a position with regard to remunicipalization. Taking a closer look at this debate, this section assesses the contentious character of the two initiatives, seen in terms of the third pillar of our critical reading of the commons literature.

Again, both initiatives pushed for a democratization of Berlin's energy provision and called into question the current concessionaire Vattenfall. Consequently, they claimed to break with post-political, managerial styles of policy-making through their different stipulations for participation.[54] While access to the spaces of control is central to the Roundtable's concept, the cooperative also does not want to be "a silent shareholder."[55] They want to form a platform to involve "the active citizen currently so feared by politics"[56] in energy issues. This reflects a growing popular sentiment for more transparency, which came as a result of Vattenfall's politics and "dirty sale deals" in the privatization of 1997. The cooperative's spokeswomen Arwen Colell speaks of the threefold reconstruction the cooperative is aiming for: "firstly, it is a technical reconstruction. [We want] the grid to be a network of renewable energy. Then, it is a political reconstruction. We want to change the power structures that control electricity. And, it is a social reconstruction. We want to utilize the money that runs from energy in a different way."[57] But she does not want to see the cooperative solely as an act of contention: "it is more than attacking urban politics, because it is directly showing what we want. It goes beyond criticizing political organs or trying to change political institutions. Instead you say: I want this and that."[58] Despite these ambitious aspirations, the cooperative is welcomed by all political parties in Berlin's parliament. Their approach obviously does not create the same level of demarcation as that of the Roundtable, perhaps due to their reluctance to institutionalize binding rules. Critics assume that this stance derives not from their public opposition to Vattenfall, but their continuing openness to cooperation with other private and public actors.

In contrast, the provisions of the Roundtable have undeniably brought more antagonism into Berlin's energy politics. Rooted in the context of the city's social movements, the Roundtable has not only directed its arguments against Vattenfall as incumbent concessionaire but also against the local government. Directly after the formation of a government not supportive of a remunicipalization in 2011, the Roundtable threatened that "if politicians don't act, we could also start a referendum movement."[59] However, the Roundtable also tried to integrate different external interests into their campaign for the referendum. This is obvious in the draft granting job guarantees for Vattenfall workers in order to help secure support from the city's trade unions for a possible remunicipalization.[60] The same alliance-building appears with the direct democracy movement and the not codified but visible intersections with other activist struggles in fields such as housing, a central part of the right to the city movement in Berlin.

Effectively, the Roundtable campaign appears to have been a more politicizing force, having provoked more conflict in city politics, than the cooperative. Not surprisingly, it has mobilized classical opponents of public ownership who combine financial and juridical arguments with a standpoint that private service provision remains more efficient. This position was exemplified by the Berlin Chamber for Industry and Commerce,[61] and the somewhat conservative energy and mining union IG BCE, which rejected the proposed remunicipalization outright.[62] More interestingly, a second group of individuals and groups became apparent, one that leaned in favor of remunicipalization, but was alienated by the far-reaching nature of the Roundtable's plans. Hence, the Berlin section of the public services union ver.di insisted: "remunicipalization: yes, but not as a burden on employees and the people of Berlin."[63] Despite the fact that the Roundtable's draft law guaranteed the employees of Vattenfall their jobs and wage conditions,[64] the trade union failed to fully engage in the debate and strongly articulate their position. This might have been a reaction to the proposal to increase citizen involvement in a future advisory board, a move which would have weakened trade union influence on the company's decisions.[65]

Thirdly, and perhaps most interestingly, this divide ran through the city's coalition government. Christian-Democrat Senator for Economy, Cornelia Yzer, publicly opposed remunicipalization calling it a "costly experiment" that would endanger "stable energy prices."[66] The Social Democrats, on the other hand, proclaimed the need for remunicipalization, without clearly supporting the Roundtable's referendum. Senator for Urban Development and the Environment, Michael Müller, argued that "only with municipal electricity and gas can the city influence prices and climate policy."[67] As even remunicipalization supporters in the senate envision an ecological, yet rather traditional, local utility *without* direct citizen participation, instead of finding a common position the senate obstructed the Roundtable. With their defeat in an earlier water referendum in mind, the Berlin senate attacked large parts of the draft for the plebiscite in a very critical statement.[68] In what can be seen as a blatant attempt to dampen interest, the referendum later was moved to early November 2013, instead of having it on the same day as the German federal elections in September. Further the senate even suggested that the city's population should not vote in favor of the Roundtable's draft[69] and rushed a legal initiative through parliament that allowed for the formation of a municipal energy supplier – though no explanation of its role vis-à-vis the concession or the wider issue of citizen participation was given.[70]

Effectively, the postponement of the election date and the fierce opposition of key players in Berlin politics limited the remunicipalization campaign's hopes of success. In the end, it narrowly failed to secure its objective, falling 21,000 votes short of reaching the required minimum of 625,000 votes, although a moral victory was achieved with a vast majority of 83 percent voting in favor of the proposals.[71] This has left the Roundtable and its campaign in the ironic position of having failed to directly achieve remunicipalization, but having clearly shaped the political discourse on energy governance, contesting the status quo, introducing alternatives, and mobilizing support. It remains to be seen how much of an influence this altered political context will ultimately have on the government's decision-making process.

5 Conclusion

Adopting a commons frame, this paper has set out to explain the current developments concerning a possible remunicipalization of the Berlin electricity grid. We emphasized three elements of such a perspective: the creation of a commonwealth, the practice of commoning, and the scope for contentious politics. These were applied to the recent attempts of two initiatives to reverse the 1997 privatization of the electricity network operator. It seems that the political success of commons initiatives that go beyond a limited community rest on their institutional form and how they are embedded in the overall political landscape of their specific field. The attempt at universalizing a non-private mode of electricity provision by law has failed due to strong opposition that, interestingly, did not engage substantially with the commons aspects of the endeavor. While much of the debate reproduces classical arguments about pros and cons of public ownership, when the new participatory aspects were considered, they appeared unattractive to actor groups that might have supported a traditional remunicipalization (e.g. trade unions). Additionally, while both initiatives depict different ideas on how to enact commoning and how a commonwealth could be created, it appears that, in the end, the level of contention might have led to the Roundtable's referendum failing.

The ideas and organization of the cooperative clearly challenge the current status quo of energy provision in the city, but do not relate extensively to other urban issues. In contrast, the Roundtable's ambitious political project was seen as a strategic intervention to intersect discourses on direct democracy, renewable energy, and social justice. We have termed both of them commons-oriented approaches as they reflect, to varying degrees, the three dimensions of our critical commons perspective.

The differences between the two initiatives might best be captured in their degree of antagonism. The cooperative was, perhaps, more successful in proposing a model that would enhance citizen participation but could also be combined with private majority ownership of the network. In contrast, it is probable that the highly contentious and antagonistic character of the Roundtable made it less likely to succeed. Clearly, all commons research could benefit from reflecting on the emancipatory scope of individual projects, their role in not only challenging but also changing neoliberal social relations. A lot could be gained from future research engaging with similar cases. A systematic application of the three strands of commoning, the creation of a commonwealth, and the level of contention could yield comparable results that, in turn, could be applied to political strategies in a range of places.

Notes

1. Elinor Ostrom, *Governing the Commons: The Evolution of Institutions for Collective Action* (New York: Cambridge University Press, 1990).
2. William J. Hausman, Peter Hertner, and Mira Wilkins, *Global Electrification: Multinational Enterprise and International Finance in the History of Light and Power, 1878–2007* (New York: Cambridge University Press, 2008).
3. Timothy Moss, Sören Becker, and Matthias Naumann, "Whose Energy Transition is it, Anyway?," *Local Environment* online first (2014).
4. Peter Marcuse, "From Critical Urban Theory to the Right to the City," *City* 13, no. 2–3 (2009): 185–197.

5   Heinz-J. Bontrup and Ralf M. Marquardt, *Kritisches Handbuch der deutschen Elektrizitätswirtschaft: Branchenentwicklung, Unternehmensstrategien, Arbeitsbeziehungen* (Berlin: Edition Sigma, 2010).
6   Ibid. and Jochen Monstadt "Urban Governance and the Transition of Energy Systems: Institutional Change and Shifting Energy and Climate Policies in Berlin," *International Journal of Urban and Regional Research* 31, no. 2 (2007), 326–343.
7   Deutscher Raiffeisen- und Genossenschaftsverband (DRGV): *Energiegenossenschaften: Ergebnisse der Umfrage des DRGV und seiner Mitgliedsverbände* (Berlin, 2013).
8   Kurt Berlo and Oliver Wagner, *Stadtwerke-Neugründungen und Rekommunalisierungen. Energieversorgung in kommunaler Verantwortung: Bewertung der 10 wichtigsten Ziele und deren Erreichbarkeit* (Wuppertal: Wuppertal Institut für Klima, Umwelt Energie, 2013).
9   Hausman et al. 2008, *Global Electrification*.
10 Lars Holstenkamp and Jakob R. Müller, *Zum Stand von Energiegenossenschaften in Deutschland: Ein statistischer Überblick zum 31.12.2012* (Lüneburg: Leuphana Universität, 2013), 8–9. The main areas of newly established energy cooperatives are Baden-Württemberg and Lower Saxony, while in sub-alpine Bavaria there is a large stock of traditional energy cooperatives.
11 Bontrup and Marquard, *Kritisches Handbuch der deutschen Elektrizitätswirtschaft*.
12 "*Stadtwerke*" translates into municipal electric company.
13 Hartmut Bauer, "Zukunftsthema 'Rekommunalisierung'," *Die Öffentliche Verwaltung* 65, no. 9 (2012), 329–338, here 329.
14 Ibid., 335; Claus Matecki and Thorsten Schulten, "Zwischen Privatisierung und Rekommunalisierung: zur Entwicklung der öffentlichen daseinsvorsorge," in *Zurück zur öffentlichen Hand? Chancen und Erfahrungen der Rekommunalisierung*. Claus Matecki and Thorsten Schulten, eds. (Hamburg: VSA, 2013), 8–17, here 12.
15 Felix Höffler et al., "Rekommunalisierung: Renaissance öffentlicher Unternehmen?," *Wirtschaftsdienst* 93, no. 2 (2013), 71–86.
16 When counting the registration of new enterprises with municipal ownership in the field of energy, cf. Ivo Lormes, "Von der Renaissance der energiewirtschaftlich tätigen Kommune," *Presentation*, 20 June 2014. Cf. Tadzio Müller, "Effizienz und Demokratie: was bei der Rekommunalisierung der Energienetze unverzichtbar ist," *RosaLux*, no. 1 (2014), 12–13.
17 Moss et al., "Whose Energy Transition is it, Anyway?"
18 Karen Bakker, "The 'Commons' Versus the 'Commodity': Alter-Globalization, Anti-Privatization and the Human Right to Water in the Global South," *Antipode* 39, no. 3 (2007), 430–455; Massimo De Angelis. "Reflections on Alternatives, Commons and Communities," *The Commoner* 6 (2003), 1–14; Michael Hardt and Antonio Negri, *Commonwealth* (Cambridge: Belknap Press, 2009); Peter Linebaugh, *The Magna Carta Manifesto: Liberty and Commons for All* (Los Angeles: University of California Press, 2009).
19 David Harvey, *Justice, Nature and the Geography of Difference* (Cambridge: Blackwell, 1996).
20 Midnight Notes and Friends, "Promissory Notes: From Crisis to Commons," in *Sparking a Worldwide Energy Revolution: Social Struggles in the Transition to a Post-Petrol World*, Kolya Abramsky, ed., 32–59 (Oakland: AK Press, 2010).
21 De Angelis, "Reflections on Alternatives," 1.
22 David Harvey, *Rebel Cities: From the Right to the City to the Urban Revolution* (London: Verso, 2012), 73.
23 Hardt and Negri, *Commonwealth*.
24 Harvey, *Rebel Cities*, 71.
25 Chantal Mouffe, *On the Political* (London: Routledge, 2005); Jacques Rancière, *Hatred of Democracy* (London: Verso, 2009); Erik Swyngedouw, "The Antinomies of the Postpolitical City: In Search for

a Democratic Politics of Environmental Production," *International Journal of Urban and Regional Research* 33, no. 3 (2009), 601–620.

26   Julio Lambing, "Stromallmende: Wege in eine neue Industriegesellschaft," in *Commons: Für eine neue Politik jenseits von Markt und Staat,* Silke Helfrich and Heinrich-Böll-Stiftung, eds., 479–486 (Bielefeld: transcript, 2012); Maarten Wolsink, "The Research Agenda on Social Acceptance of Distributed Generation in Smart Grids: Renewable as Common Pool Resources," *Renewable and Sustainable Energy Review* 16, no. 1 (2012), 822–835; John Byrne, Cecilia Martinez, and Colin Ruggero, "Relocating Energy in the Social Commons: Ideas for a Sustainable Energy Utility," *Bulletin of Science, Technology & Society* 29, no. 2 (2009), 81–94.

27   Wolsink, "The Research Agenda on Social Acceptance."

28   Lambing, "Stromallmende."

29   Byrne et al., "Relocating Energy in the Social Commons."

30   Alexander L. George and Andrew Bennett, *Case Studies and Theory Development in the Social Sciences* (Cambridge, MA: MIT Press, 2005).

31   Attac Berlin, BürgerBegehren Klimaschutz and PowerShift, *Neue Energie für Berlin: Netze in Bürgerhand.* (Berlin, 2011).

32   Interview with an Activist of the Roundtable, August 28, 2013.

33   Ross Beveridge and Matthias Naumann, "The Berlin Water Company. From 'Inevitable' Privatization to 'Impossible' Remunicipalization," in *The Berlin Reader: A Compendium on Urban Change and Activism,* Matthias Bernt, Britta Grell, and Andrej Holm, eds. (Bielefeld: transcript, 2013), 189–203.

34   Alberto Corsín Jiménez, "The Right to Infrastructure: A Prototype for Open Source Urbanism," *Environment and Planning D* 32, no. 2 (2014), 342–362.

35   Interview with Arwen Colell, Bürger Energie Berlin, September 2, 2013.

36   Ibid.

37   Ibid.

38   Ibid.

39   Sebastian Puschner, "Da hat's gefunkt. Im Kampf um das Stromnetz holt die Genossenschaft Bürgerenergie die Stadtwerke Schwäbisch Hall ins Boot," *die tageszeitung,* April 23, 2013.

40   Colell, *Interview.*

41   Ibid.

42   Ibid.

43   Interview with Stefan Taschner from the Energy Roundtable, August 27, 2013 and Activist, *Interview.*

44   Berliner Energietisch, *Entwurf eines Gesetzes für die demokratische, ökologische und soziale Energieversorgung in Berlin: EnergieVG* (Berlin, 2012).

45   Taschner, *Interview.*

46   Ibid. and Frank Hüesker, *Kommunale Daseinsvorsorge in der Wasserwirtschaft: Auswirkungen der Privatisierung am Beispiel der Wasserbetriebe Berlins* (Munich: oekom, 2011).

47   Thomas Hammar, *Democracy and the Nation State: Aliens, Denizens and Citizens in a World of International Migration* (Aldershot: Avebury Press, 1990).

48   Activist, *Interview.*

49   Ingo Stützle, "Knapp daneben ist auch vorbei. Für einen Erfolg des Berliner Volksentscheids fehlten 20.000 Stimmen," *ak. analyse und kritik* 588, November 19, 2013.

50   Landesabstimmungsleiterin Berlin, *Volksentscheid „Neue Energie" am 3. November 2013: Ergebnis des Volksentscheids,* https://www.wahlen-berlin.de/Abstimmungen/VE2013_NEnergie/Ergebnisprozent.asp?sel1=6052&sel2=0798 (accessed December 15, 2014).

51   Taschner, *Interview.*

52   Colell, *Interview.*

53 Activist, *Interview*.
54 Swyngedouw, "The Antinomies of the Postpolitical City."
55 Colell, *Interview*.
56 Ibid.
57 Ibid.
58 Ibid.
59 Energy Roundtable spokesman Stefan Taschner in Svenja Bergt, "Rekommunalisierung der Energieversorgung: Bürger wollen ins Netz," *die tageszeitung,* June 9, 2013.
60 Taschner, *Interview*.
61 Industrie- und Handelskammer Berlin (IHK), *Garantie für Klimaschutz und sinkende Preise? Die Rekommunalisierung der Energieversorgung in Berlin im Faktencheck* (Berlin, 2013).
62 There are a number of reasons for this positioning of the trade union alongside industry representatives, landlord associations, and others. First of all, they account for a high percentage of the organized members among the employees of Vattenfall, the current concessionaire (this is also due to the large open-cast mining facilities Vattenfall operates in the Lusatia region southeast of Berlin). Remunicipalising the network operation in Berlin would not only push a corporation out of the city within which the union is strong, it would also transfer the network operation to public services, for which, according to the German sector-oriented trade union system, another union is responsible. Thirdly, and more indirectly, in the past the IG BCE has been more conservative relative to other German trade unions, showing considerable reluctance to engage with topics such as climate change, environmentally benign production, and strikes.
63 Bezirksvorstand ver.di Berlin, *Aktualisierte Positionen zum Thema Rekommunalisierung* (Berlin: ver.di, 2013).
64 Claudia Falk, "Bedeutung von Gewerkschaften und Betriebsräten im Prozess der Rekommunalisierung," in *Zurück zur öffentlichen Hand? Chancen und Erfahrungen der Rekommunalisierung*. Claus Matecki and Theodor Schulten, eds. (Hamburg: VSA, 2013), 120–139.
65 Ibid.
66 Alfons Frese, "Wirtschaftssenatorin Yzer will kein Stromnetz," *Der Tagesspiegel,* July 13, 2013.
67 Michael Müller, "Kommunale Energieversorgung: Berlin braucht ein Stadtwerk," *Der Tagesspiegel,* June 10, 2013.
68 Berliner Senat, *Stellungnahme des Senats zu dem Volksbegehren "Neue Energie für Berlin – demokratisch, ökologisch, sozial"* (Berlin: Abgeordnetenhaus, 2012).
69 Ulrich Zawatka-Gerlach, "Der SPD den Stecker gezogen: Die CDU setzt sich bei der Energiepolitik durch. Die Koalition empfiehlt nun beim Volksbegehren ein Nein," *Der Tagesspiegel,* August 30, 2013.
70 Sabine Beikler and Sidney Gennies, "Senat gründet Stadtwerk kurz vor Volksentscheid," *Der Tagesspiegel,* October 23, 2013.
71 Landesabstimmungsleiterin Berlin, *Volksentscheid "Neue Energie."*

AK Thompson

The Battle for Necropolis:
Reclaiming the Past as Commons in the City of the Dead

Considered from the standpoint of the commodity form's totalizing reach, the enthusiasm for the commons expressed by contemporary radicals suggests that fundamental social change may once again be on the agenda. Nevertheless, the celebration of the concept's promise has thus far tended to coincide with an eschewal of the difficult practical demands that it also entails. Consequently, many 'actually existing' experiments in commoning have contributed more to the edification of their minuscule participant bases than they have to the eradication of capitalist enclosure. To be sure, such experiments can be valuable sources of information. However, when conceived as ends in themselves, they risk becoming a sideshow to the struggle demanded by the concept that animated them. It is in opposition to this tendency that we must commit to the battle for necropolis.

On the surface, referring to our struggle for the commons as a 'battle' (describing it in the language of territorial war) seems at odds with the practical character of most contemporary campaigns. Indeed, many of these seem more concerned with finding reprieve in the cracks opened by neoliberalism's overreach than at provoking direct confrontations with power. Meanwhile, even our most promising experiments in (for instance) urban agriculture suggest that the struggle for the commons is currently motivated less by concerns with production per se than by the urge to recover neglected aspects of our humanity. Here, the inconsequential yields of our harvests are nothing when compared with the genuine relations we cultivate despite living in a time when such bonds have, for the most part, gone fallow.

But if the longing for human connection underwriting the commons' current allure makes the language of 'battle' seem dubious, matters are made still worse by my insistence that the terrain for which we must fight is necropolis – the city of the dead. Surely, some might say, such a claim can be nothing more than a symptom of the pop fixation on the imminent zombie apocalypse. And, indeed, evidence is everywhere; one need only to think of the stunning set-piece in the recent cinematic adaptation of *World War Z* (in which a zombie horde overruns Jerusalem by crashing down its historic walls) to see that this is the case.

But while the call to wage a battle for necropolis may seem on first blush to be little more than the *cri de coeur* of a science fiction shut-in (and while it may seem inimical to that species of sober analysis demanded by situations such as ours), it is precisely to the themes of *politics as war* and the *persistence of the dead* that we must turn if we hope to advance our struggles for the commons beyond their current state of wishful anticipation – a state that stimulates our longing for social transformation even as it thwarts the realization of our aims.

When pushed to its logical conclusion, the tension between the commons as wish-fulfilling image and the commons as unrealized practical accomplishment is enough to provoke a reckoning with the more basic (but also more brutal) connection between sovereignty and war. And though it is normally conceived as pertaining to territory, the struggle for the commons reveals that this war must necessarily involve a struggle for *the past* as well. As some readers may already have suspected, my analysis in these matters is indebted to the insights of Walter Benjamin. Familiar to many as a theorist of capitalism's dreamscapes and urban environments, I demonstrate how Benjamin might also be read as a compelling and provocative theorist of the commons. However, because I may have courted naysayers by conceiving of my subject in these unorthodox terms, let me begin by seeing what I can do to show that the premise is not as eccentric as at first it might seem.

The dead among us

What, then, is the connection between the commons and the city of the dead? Let's begin by considering the "right to the city," a slogan first coined by Henri Lefebvre in 1968 and subsequently popularized by groups struggling to derail capitalist efforts to militarize urban spaces and turn cities into theme parks for the rich. Picking up where Lefebvre left off, David Harvey has recently argued that the meaning of such an unwieldy collective "right" boils down to "greater democratic control over the production and use of the surplus" or, more precisely, "democratic control over the deployment of the surpluses through urbanization."[1] In these formulations, cities are posited as both the practical manifestation of a society's accumulated surplus and as a force in the further development of the surplus itself.

According to Harvey, the city fosters the production of social surplus by way of both its historical aggregation and consequent intensification of the productive forces.[2] At the same time, and at the other end of the production cycle, it serves as a catalyst enabling the realization of surplus value through the market. As a terrain of intensified consumption (for individuals, markets, and means of production), the city facilitates the reabsorption of the very surplus it helped to generate through its own intensification of the production process. For this reason, capitalists rely heavily on urban expansion to ensure that the value of commodities does not depreciate through crises of over-accumulation or the failure to reinvest. Consequently, as Harvey notes, the "history of capital accumulation" is ultimately inseparable from the "growth path of urbanization" itself.[3]

In order to understand what this has to do with the dead, it's necessary to ask: what is the social surplus? Returning to Marx's *Capital,* we discover that, along with being the concrete form taken by surplus value immediately prior to its realization through exchange on the market, social surplus is also the practical objectification of dead or expended labor. Indeed, for Marx, "capital *is* dead labour."[4] This sounds menacing, and Marx stokes our fear by adding that, like a vampire, capital: "only lives by sucking living labour, and lives the more, the more it sucks." But while skeptical readers might dismiss these lines as poetic indulgence, it's important to note that – in the immediately preceding passage – Marx gives his vampires a concrete dimension. "Capital has one single life impulse," he writes. And that impulse is: "to make its constant factor, the means of production, absorb the greatest possible amount of surplus labour."[5]

Here, the means of production become visible in their status as fixed or constant capital, the concrete form through which the social surplus is produced (i.e. extracted from living labor) and ultimately reabsorbed (e.g. through reinvestment, expansion, etc.). Since capitalists perpetually revolutionize the means of production to gain advantage on the terrain of relative surplus value, the ever-changing "fixed" aspect of capital[6] becomes the concrete repository (the tomb, the mausoleum) of dead labor. Moreover, since the production process relies on constant capital (i.e. as means of production) to extract surplus labor and thus to produce social surplus through the contractually concealed exploitation inherent in the working day,[7] such capital also "produces" dead labor on a daily basis. As a result, capitalism pits living labor in the present against the historically accumulated dead labor entombed in constant capital.

From the *Economic and Philosophic Manuscripts of 1844* right through to the exposé of commodity fetishism in *Capital,* Marx makes clear that the estrangement yielded by this relationship is immediate. The worker feels it whenever she confronts the object she created as an alien force. However, by speaking of the aggregate of this dead labor as a social "surplus" (by highlighting its subsequent transposition back into the ever-expanding realm of fixed capital), we are alerted to the fact that the practical manifestations of alienation accumulate over time as well. Conceived in this way, social surplus comes into view as the form taken by the historical *accumulation* of dead labor. This accretion can be traced concretely by considering how, as Benjamin noted, the railway track heralds the subsequent development of the steel girder – which in turn yields the skyscraper, the aesthetic emblem of an alienation accumulated to the point of becoming sublime.[8]

As a social form, the city is a monumental accomplishment. It is built over generations, and each generation inherits both the practical accomplishments of its predecessors *and* the accumulated estrangement that made those feats possible. Ralph Chaplin, author of the famous American labor anthem "Solidarity Forever" (1915) knew this estrangement well. In his account, "It is we who plowed the prairies, built the cities where they trade; / Dug the mines and built the workshops, endless miles of railroad laid." Nevertheless, as a result of the wage relation, capitalism leaves us to "stand outcast and starving midst the wonders we have made." As a popular retelling of Marx's labor theory of value, Chaplin's anthem is without equal – and it's for precisely this reason that he refuses to leave matters as he found them. Consequently, each verse of his battle hymn concludes with the reminder that, despite our outcast status, "the union makes us strong."

Canonized and subject to turgid recitation by today's staid labor movement, the incendiary dimensions of "Solidarity Forever" are now difficult to perceive. It is therefore necessary to retrace its lines in the interest of salvaging their neglected implications. Immediately, we discover that the "we" and the "us" that Chaplin invokes are clearly temporal ones, since no single generation of workers accomplished the various discrete stages of urban-industrial development he describes (the plowing of prairies, for instance, generally predates and enables the subsequent building of "cities where they trade"). Consequently, the "we" that stands outcast and starving is comprised of both the living and the dead. Furthermore, since the surplus labor of dead generations is trapped within the social surplus, the dead themselves are in some way concretely present in the "wonders" being contemplated (the

Hugo Gellert, "Karl Marx, Capital in Pictures", 1934.

workshops built by the historic "we," for instance, become a site for the extraction of dead labor in the present). In the final instance – and as the WPA-era communist artist Hugo Gellert knew well – these wonders include the city itself.

If there is a union, then, between the living and the dead (a union that will make both groups strong), the practical task falling to the living is to free the dead from the social surplus so that their estrangement might come to an end. Concretely speaking, this involves learning how to dismantle and reconfigure (rather than merely repossess) the accumulated matter of the built environment so that it might finally coincide with the will of those who produced it. No small task, to be sure. But even if the living rise to the occasion and commit to reconfiguring the social surplus, we must still determine what sort of earthly task can be assigned to the dead. One answer is this: we must allow, and even insist, that the dead remind us of the desire that animated their efforts while alerting us to the many ways that such desires have historically been susceptible to capture and recuperation.

According to John Berger, capitalism's strength can be measured by the degree to which it managed to break the interdependent bond between the living and the dead. Nevertheless, and despite this new disconnect, "the dead inhabit a timeless moment" that amounts to a "form of imagination concerning the possible." Consequently, Berger enjoins us once again to establish a "clear exchange" across the "frontier between timelessness and time."[9] Only then, he insists, might we benefit from the guidance of dead compatriots who never got to see their dreams fulfilled. Similarly, for Walter Benjamin, "there is a secret agreement between past generations and the present one. Our coming was expected on earth."

> Like every generation that preceded us, we have been endowed with a *weak* Messianic power, a power to which the past has a claim. That claim cannot be settled cheaply.[10]

Aligning Chaplin with Berger and Benjamin in this way may lead skeptics to claim that I'm taking liberties with "Solidarity Forever" and its current adherents. Nevertheless, living-dead alliances of the sort I've described featured prominently in the radical working-class culture of Chaplin's time. In Earl Robinson's famous "Ballad of Joe Hill" from 1936, for instance, the narrator learns in a dream that, although he was executed by firing squad in 1915, the eponymous Swedish-American labor organizer and songsmith lived on wherever there was struggle: "From San Diego up to Maine, / In every mine and mill / Where working men defend their rights / It's there you'll find Joe Hill." Drawing on similar themes, Chaplin concluded his own anthem (penned the year that Hill himself was executed) by reminding us how "we shall bring to birth a new world from the ashes of the old." Finally, the two anthems converge when we recall that (according to movement folklore) the ashes from Joe Hill's cremation were distributed among representatives of the international working class to be scattered worldwide.[11]

By reducing the social surplus to ash, the union of the living and the dead prepares the way for a new world to be born. Indeed, it was not romanticism alone that led anarcho-syndicalist icon Buenaventura Durruti to proclaim in the midst of Spain's civil war that, since workers had built the palaces and cities being razed in the conflict, they were "not in the least afraid of ruins." Seeming to riff on Chaplin directly, Durruti concluded his commentary by observing that, while "the bourgeoisie might blast and ruin its own world before it leaves the stage of history," it did little to change the fact that "we carry a new world here, in our hearts."[12] Whether by ruin or refurbishment, the tremendous accumulation of dead labor in the social surplus furnishes the energy to realize the promise trapped in the city to which we claim a right.

I will concede that setting down the rudiments of a political theology in trochaic tetrameter may seem like a hazardous undertaking.[13] Nevertheless, the conclusion to Chaplin's "Solidarity Forever" makes clear that, to the extent that the social surplus ever constituted a "wonder," its value owed not to the objectified form through which it first found expression but rather to the accumulated aspirations trapped within it as dead labor. Given this fact, the struggle for the urban commons must inevitably be a battle for necropolis.

Benjamin's common

For readers familiar with Walter Benjamin's work, the arguments rehearsed above will likely sound familiar. At the same time, however, the association may seem strange. After all, even prodigious eclecticism was not enough to lead Benjamin to include the commons among his various themes. Be this as it may, a careful reading suggests that the commons did feature in his work as an *implicit* reference. In order for it to be made explicit, we must first review his more direct engagement with the dead.

In his famous essay on the concept of history, Benjamin outlined how the human struggle for happiness was emboldened by the efforts of past generations, whose own struggles remained unfulfilled. The relationship becomes especially acute when people realize they are, "about to make the continuum of history explode." Consequently, according to Benjamin, Maximilien de Robespierre viewed ancient Rome as "a past charged with the time of the now" and "the French Revolution viewed itself as Rome reincarnate."[14]

But while the past can stimulate people's desire for social change, there's nothing inevitable about this outcome. Just as the oppressed clamor to lay hold of the past to advance their struggles, history's victors use it to substantiate the myth of progress that justifies their power. Although he does not use the term, Benjamin's account of the ensuing struggle suggests that the past itself is best understood as a commons forever in danger of enclosure. Indeed, according to Benjamin, "only a redeemed mankind receives the fullness of its past – which is to say, only for a redeemed mankind does the past become citable in all its moments."[15] Nevertheless, this same past is forever in danger of "becoming a tool of the ruling classes" by being subjected to (enclosed within) a narrative "conformism that is about to overpower it." Consequently, *"even the dead* will not be safe from the enemy if he wins."[16]

In the hands of the victors, the past becomes a catalogue of "cultural treasures" ("wonders," in Chaplin's sense) that get passed from ruler to ruler. And just as each treasure bears the mark of the barbarism that underwrote its creation, "barbarism taints also the manner in which it was transmitted from one owner to another." As indexes of desire, such treasures are distorted. They become symptomatic expressions of the historical enclosure that enabled their production and transmission. For this reason, Benjamin maintained that they should be considered with "cautious detachment."[17]

At the same time, however, these treasures also contain the promise of *another* outcome, since – like the social surplus more generally – they contain the unrealized aspirations of those generations trapped within them as dead labor. With minimal extrapolation, it becomes clear that *this promise* is the common inheritance that Benjamin enjoins us to actualize in its "fullness." Since they are both its stewards and its prisoners, claiming this common in the present requires that we forge an alliance with the dead.

By bringing the past into contact with "time filled by the presence of the now,"[18] such an alliance enjoins us to "awaken the dead, and make whole what has been smashed."[19] The spatial dimension of the common thus proves to be a transtemporal one, with past and present intermingled in an explosive admixture. Given the alliance of the living and the dead upon which it is founded, the institutional arrangements that might prevail in such a common remain difficult to imagine. Nevertheless, as Benjamin maintained, our capacity to realize common dreams is a power upon which the past lays a claim – and "that claim cannot be settled cheaply."[20]

Few will doubt the desperate elegance of Benjamin's formulation. Nevertheless, even the most compelling of arguments requires evidence if it is to be believed. For this reason, it's important to recall those events that can help to emancipate the battle for necropolis from the register of metaphor. Considering the problem from the standpoint of constituted power, one might be reminded of the hundred-plus workers who died during the construction of the Hoover Dam. A "wonder" of anthropocenic proportions set into operation the year Durruti perished, folk wisdom suggests that many of the workers who died building the dam became entombed in the concrete construction itself. Despite the intuitive logic to such claims, the likelihood that bodies disintegrate within the national infrastructure remains small; nevertheless, this does not mean they escaped being trapped in it by other means. One such means is commemoration. If we were to believe Oskar J. W. Hansen's monumental plaque erected at the site, these workers gave their lives "to make the desert bloom." In all probability (and if their situation had allowed it), the workers themselves would have disagreed.[21]

Oskar J. W. Hansen, *Hoover Dam Memorial* (1936)

Even the dead are not safe from the victor if he wins. As the past succumbs to historical enclosure, the social surplus becomes tightly bound to the myth of progress. America is a nation of monuments, thought Alexis de Tocqueville. What, then, do these monuments tell us about America? Even the Boston Tea Party becomes an amusement park under the weight of commemoration. Indeed, a recently opened memorial site in Boston Harbor left one reporter marveling at how "the live actors, replicas, artifacts, holography, and … commentary" sprinkled throughout the exhibit "create an environment that is as much theme park as it is museum."[22] How could it be otherwise? America cannot soberly acknowledge the violence that heralded its emancipation from colonial rule without conceding that those it now holds in thrall may be justified in following suit.

Such examples provoke feelings that oscillate between incredulity and vertigo; however, it's important to recall that the dead are not always given up without a fight. In its most rudimentary form, the impulse to wrest the fallen from the powerful finds expression in counter-commemoration. More ambitiously (and taking a page from *Antigone*), history turns its floodlight on those who have struggled to defend the bodies of their fallen kin directly. Historian Ruth Richardson reminds us that, toward the end of the Georgian era, working-class communities in England organized to protect deceased loved ones from grave robbers who sold corpses to anatomy schools in what she called "a pitiless example of free trade."[23]

In response to such thefts, these communities formed what amounted to impromptu graveyard defense leagues and often rioted against anatomy schools and other targets. According to Richardson, such organizing was motivated by the feeling that those who robbed graves "were the agents of social injustice, and their trade in corpses made a mockery of the meanings and values popularly invested in customary death practices." Moreover, since the "bodysnatchers" tended to emerge from the ranks of the communities they attacked, they "betrayed the deepest sentiments of their own class by their ruthless trade in human flesh."[24] Reporting on a riot against an anatomy school in Aberdeen in January of 1832, Richardson writes:

> A crowd gathered swiftly, and before long the school was invaded … The crowd shouted encouragement to those inside in their effort to set the building alight, while at the back some enterprising rioters began an attack on the rear wall, simultaneously undermining its foundation and battering its fabric. In a short time the entire wall collapsed, while the fire inside the building took hold … The school was fully demolished by eight o'clock, and the town was quiet by ten in the evening.[25]

By alerting contemporary readers to the central role played by the dead in shaping visions of justice, such struggles are reassuring in their concreteness. At the same time, they highlight the degree to which the dead themselves are most easily comprehended in their status as *bodies*. But while this dimension cannot be overlooked, it's important to recall that the dead are present in the Hoover Dam whether or not they are buried in it. Meanwhile, the struggle against the grave robber is not enough to release the dead from the cultural treasures they haunt as anonymous, toiling echoes. It's easy to perceive bodies as concrete, corporeal presences. Social relations are similarly concrete; however, their translocal and transtemporal dimensions make them more difficult to perceive (let alone grasp) directly. As in other cases where the gap between what can be sensed and what can be stated compels us to resort to mythological resolutions, the battle for necropolis shifts to the field of the wish image.

Common dreams

According to Benjamin, wish images arise when people begin anticipating the future by recalling a past whose promise has yet to be fulfilled;

> In the dream in which, before the eyes of each epoch, that which is to follow appears in images, that latter appears wedded to elements from prehistory, that is, of a classless society. Intimations of this ... mingle with the new to produce the utopia that has left its traces in thousands of configurations of life, from permanent buildings to fleeting fashions.[26]

In seeking a connection between the wish image and the commons, one might be reminded of how it has recently become fashionable for coffee shops in gentrifying neighborhoods to arrange their enterprises around a large common table rather than many small ones. This table (sometimes referred to as a "harvest table") is generally perceived to add value to the coffee-shop experience by encouraging forms of conviviality that would otherwise be impossible. For shop owners, the arrangement makes infinite sense: not only does it intensify the allure of the commodity by infusing it with the ambient promise of community, it can also help to maximize the number of paying customers.

But while we might condemn hipster coffee drinkers for trying to find community through the market (and while we might condemn them for their complicity in gentrification, which is itself a mode of enclosure), it's important to acknowledge that the problem lies not with the desire per se but rather with the insufficiency of its posited object resolution. Meanwhile, indulging in a little *recherche du temps perdu* makes clear that the search for community (and even for revolutionary alliance) in coffee shops might not be so outrageous after all.

According to urban sociologist Ray Oldenburg, "third places" like coffee houses are best understood as "levelers." As points between home and work that are distinct from both, third places allow for people to come together across social divisions on the basis of common interests. Connecting the "leveler" concept directly to the peasant insurgents who operated under the same name, Oldenburg notes that coffee houses established in the seventeenth century were themselves "commonly referred to as levelers, as were the people who frequented them."[27] Moreover, the rules posted inside the doors of London coffee houses during this period "enforced the leveling of coffee house visitors."[28] According to Oldenburg, it was a rule that patrons were happy to oblige.

In addition to providing "neutral ground upon which men discovered one another apart from the classes and ranks that had earlier divided them,"[29] third places like coffee houses provided patrons with warmth. "Warmth," writes Oldenburg, "radiates from the combination of cheerfulness and companionship, and it enhances the sense of being alive."[30] Already by the nineteenth century, however, the warmth had begun to fade. This was because "the openness and equality of the original establishments gave way to partitioned seating and single, large tables were replaced by strategically placed smaller ones."[31] Consequently, "community has become elusive"[32] and contemporary patrons "seeking to gain respite from loneliness or boredom ... manage only to intensify those feelings." Little wonder, then, that we should find them sitting "spaced apart from one another ... hunching over some invisible lead ball of misery."[33]

Based on Oldenburg's account, it's possible to see how (despite its obvious profit-maximizing function) today's harvest table might help patrons to recall a time when community seemed inseparable from leveling. In this way, it might even sharpen visions of a future happiness by furnishing them with a positive content. By themselves, however, wish images say nothing about *the means* by which that happiness might concretely be realized. As a result, such images tend more regularly to refurbish the status quo by infusing hollow commodities with a new vitality than they do to become dynamos propelling social change. Such ambivalence highlights a challenge that has affected movement-based struggles for the commons as well.

According to Silvia Federici, the commons were so important to the "struggles of the medieval rural population that their memory still excites our imagination, projecting the vision of a world where goods can be shared and solidarity ... can be the substance of social relations."[34] But while such visions can help to convince us that arrangements of this kind might be possible once again, it's important to recall that the medieval commons existed alongside private ownership – and that it was *this* form of ownership that made it valuable from the standpoint of social reproduction. As Federici notes:

> the commons were essential to the reproduction of many small farmers or cottars who survived only because they had access to meadows in which to keep cows, or woods in which to gather timber, wild berries and herbs, or quarries, fish-ponds, and open spaces in which to meet.[35]

More bluntly, we can say that the commons were by no means antithetical to private property. Instead (and regardless of the degree to which claims on the commons were secured through struggle from below), the commons themselves were an externality that was nevertheless factored into the productive calculations of feudal landowners, who (for their own reasons) did not want their cottars – their source of labor power – to die. Given this arrangement, there's little reason to idealize life on the peasant commons. Nevertheless, as Federici points out, the commons also yielded a remarkable degree of freedom. In her account, "besides encouraging collective decision-making and work cooperation, the commons were the material foundation upon which peasant solidarity and sociality could thrive."[36]

With the advent of enclosure, the bonds of social solidarity fostered by the commons led peasants to fits of riotous excess and to their subsequent denunciation as levelers. By the mid-seventeenth century, this "leveler" tendency became associated with conspiratorial dreams of regicide and declarations of popular sovereignty. But while such developments suggest that the promise inherent in the commons had led levelers of all sorts to confront the profane demands of politics, it's important to recall that (with the notable exception of the landholding class themselves) claims on the commons were rarely issued directly in the name of those who asserted them.

Sovereignty as wish…

Even as enclosure intensified, the overwhelming tendency among outcast forces was to frame their struggles as attempts to restore conditions thought to have been prescribed by God. In 1649, a group of peasants in Surrey came together under the banner of the Diggers. Outraged at enclosure and motivated by a peculiar reading of Christian scripture, they occupied wastelands, denounced landlords, and struggled to find their way back to Eden. According to the group's leader, Gerrard Winstanley, "they that are resolved to work and eat together, making the Earth a Common Treasury, doth joyn hands with Christ, to lift up the Creation from Bondage, and restore all things from the Curse."[37] The scene is well known, and the outcome is as tragic as the Digger's efforts were courageous. What's less often noted, however, is how Winstanley's experiment could not be carried out in the name of the earthly force that stood to gain from it. Instead, the action proceeds under the watchful eye of Christ, with whom the Diggers imagined they had joined hands. The weight of sovereign responsibility is thus transposed, and profane self-interest is glossed in transcendental conceit.

We can hardly blame them. It's hard to assume the burden of sovereignty, and movements in the present have on the whole fared no better. Moreover (and even after the disenchantment of the world heralded by capitalism's triumphant ascent), Christianity remains an amazing compendium of wish images. Winstanley's reading of scripture was unorthodox, to be sure; however, it doesn't take much to find evidence of a communist tendency guiding the Christians of biblical times. Consider, for instance, the *Acts of the Apostles,* where it is written:

> And the multitude of them that believed were of one heart and one soul: neither said anything of them that aught of the things which he possessed was his own; but they had all things in common ... Neither was there any among them that lacked: for as many as were possessors of lands or of houses sold them and brought the prices of the things that were sold, and laid them down at the apostles' feet: a distribution was made unto every man as he had need.[38]

According to Karl Kautsky, early Christian communism operated primarily through interventions at the level of consumption. For this reason, work and families (not to mention possessions) were denounced in an effort to circumvent worldly concerns and forge a brotherhood in Christ.[39] As the sect grew and began attracting "wealthy and cultured persons," however, Kautsky found that "many a Christian propagandist began to feel the need of putting the Christian doctrine more amiably in order to attract these people."[40] This revisionist impulse is most evident in the Gospel of Saint Matthew, where an "astute spirit of revisionism has wiped out every trace of class hatred."[41] Nevertheless, even today, the fraternal bonds forged by the Apostles persist in their allure. As Kautsky notes, "however much certain influential circles of the Christian congregation ... sought to obliterate its proletarian character, the proletariat and its class hatred were not obliterated thereby."[42] And even as the church evolved into a menacing force looming over the medieval era, the saintly renunciation of earthly property persevered as a compensation, a supplement, and – as Winstanley's legacy attests – a spur to action too.

As wish image, the Christian common was already inseparable from the necropolis in ancient Rome, where believers who had not yet overcome their status as a marginal cult began carving out catacombs to bury their dead. Interpreted by nineteenth-century Romantics as a kind of conspiratorial underground, the Christians of the catacombs were said to congregate, say mass, and make arrangements for their mutual safety. In *Martyr of the Catacombs,* an anonymous novel penned at the height of the Romantic era, the seductive allure of nocturnal necropolitan conspiracy is indulged to what may be an unhealthy degree. According to the author, "the vast numbers who dwelt below were supplied with provisions by constant communication with the city above. This was done at night. The most resolute and daring of the men volunteered for this dangerous task."[43]

Marveling at the catacombs themselves, the author recounts how the Christians descended willingly into their depths, "carrying with them all that was most precious to the soul of man, and they endured all for the great love wherewith they were loved."[44] In this way, they forged a connection with the dead as well. "Witness these gloomy labyrinths," the author enjoins, "fit home for the dead only, which nevertheless for years opened to shelter the living." In addition to this alliance, the catacombs also provided a means for the past to make its way into the present. For the author of *Martyr*, the results are nothing short of inspiring.

> The walls carry down to later ages those words of grief, of lamentation, and of ever-changing feeling which were marked upon them during successive ages by those who were banished to these Catacombs. They carry down their mournful story to future times, and bring to imagination the forms, the feelings, and the deeds of those who were imprisoned here. As the forms of life are taken upon the plates of the camera, so has the great voice once forced out by suffering from the very soul of the martyr become stamped on the wall.[45]

Predating Benjamin's observation that wishes leave their mark on "thousands of configurations of life" by more than half a century, the account of history as resonant image conveyed by this passage is nothing short of extraordinary. Still, it's important to recall that the anonymous author of *Martyr* was not alone in having succumbed to the seductions of those "tender greetings of affection, of friendship, of kinship, and of love" that "arose amid the moldering remains of the departed."[46] Indeed, similar sentiments found compelling visual expression in the paintings of the neoclassically trained Romantic Jean-Victor Schnetz. A student of Jacques-Louis David, Schnetz's *Funeral of a Young Martyr in the Catacombs of Rome* (1847) splits the difference between the enthusiasm that led him to lionize the fighters of the July Revolution in a work that rivaled Delacroix's own submission on the theme[47] and the neoclassicism of his teacher (whose *Serment des Horaces* stimulated Jacobin sentiment in its own special way).

Jean-Victor Schnetz (1787–1870). *Funeral of a Young Martyr in the Catacombs of Rome during the Time of Persecutions,* 1847. Oil on canvas, 338 × 382 cm. Inv. 1173.

Distorted by their transposition into the hagiographic register, contemporary readers can be forgiven for doubting the historical accuracy of these Romantic glosses on catacomb life. Nevertheless, few can doubt that the idea of the commons as an *underground* (existing within and alongside, but also beneath the established world) has persisted as an enduring wish image. Indeed, versions of it can be seen in sources as varied as St. Augustine's *City of God* and Victor Hugo's *Hunchback of Notre Dame*. In the latter work, hallucinogenic recollections of the medieval commons are enlisted as a kind of antithesis to – and compensation for – the bourgeois world despised by the Romantics. In the novel's Court of Miracles, conceptual distinctions are torn down with the same enthusiasm that toppled fences and hedges during the enclosure riots. For Hugo, the Court of Miracles was "a city of thieves, a hideous wart on the face of Paris; a sewer, from which escaped every morning … that stream of vices … which always overflows in the streets of capitals." Meanwhile, it was also "a lying hospital where the bohemian, the disfrocked monk, the ruined scholar … were transformed by night into brigands."

> The limits of races and species seemed effaced in this city, as in a pandemonium. Men, women, beasts, age, sex, health, maladies, all seemed

to be in common among these people; all went together, they mingled, confounded, superposed; each one there participated in all.[48]

Hugo's description allows us to witness the ease with which the Romantics fused their love of the medieval commons to the promise of political conspiracy. From this volatile admixture sparked wishful anticipations of a triumphant underground – a zone marked indelibly by social dissolution and, ultimately, by signs of death. *Hunchback* was penned nearly two centuries ago. Still, Hugo's sensibility (like that of the Romantics more generally) continues to find expression in the countless celebrations of the common-as-underground that infuse today's radical counterculture with mythic significance. To get a sense of this dynamic, one might recall the protest encampment described in *Expect Resistance*, CrimethInc's swashbuckling homage to those who live like they mean it:

> When I showed up the occupation was already in full swing. It looked like the outpost of a medieval army: banners painted with inscrutable proclamations, cauldrons of stew steaming over an open fire, sooty-faced barbarians conferring in the crisp morning air. It seemed inconceivable that something like this existed in my own century, let alone my zip code.[49]

Such accounts are inspiring. Not only do they stimulate the imagination and provoke our longing for happiness by bringing the mythic past into the present, they also provide a concrete vision of what might be accomplished in the small autonomous spaces we carve out of the hostile enclosures in which we find ourselves trapped. But while our struggles are often animated by recollections of the mythic past, such recollections do little to clarify how the desired outcome is to be practically achieved. Indeed (and as was mentioned previously), the wish image's indeterminacy makes it highly susceptible to capture.

To get a sense of this dynamic, one might recall the degree to which ancient Rome spoke to the Romantics as they launched their rebellion against capitalist ascent. Percy Shelley made his indebtedness clear when, in an 1818 letter to Thomas Love Peacock, he recounted how Rome was "a city ... of the dead, or rather of those who cannot die, & who survive the puny generations which inhabit & pass over the spot which they have made sacred to eternity."[50] The trick, as Shelley saw it, was therefore to forge an alliance with the dead so that we might overcome our puniness and potentially become sacred once again.

Fully a generation earlier, Rome had been a wish image for the Jacobins, who zeroed in on its republicanism as a model for their own aspirations. Considering the "conjuring up of the dead of world history," Marx recalled how the heroes of the French Revolution "performed the task of their time ... in Roman costumes and with Roman phrases."[51] This dramatic citation, however, did not exhaust Rome's wish-image scope – or its political range. In the 1930s, dead Romans were once again invoked, this time by the Nazis, as they slouched toward Germania. In the hands of Albert Speer, the Pantheon became the model for the *Volkshalle*.

In the face of such indeterminacy, it's important to consider what must be done to push our struggles beyond wishful anticipation. How shall the dead be freed from the social surplus, and how shall they be spared from perpetual induction into armies whose mythologies are at odds with their interests? How, following Benjamin, shall we awaken the dead and make whole what has been smashed? Such questions require programmatic answers; however, before such answers can be devised, it's necessary for matters to be clarified conceptually. And this means returning once more to the problem of sovereignty.

... And as profane necessity

What, then, is the relationship between sovereignty, the commons, and the city of the dead? In order to answer this question, it's useful to return to *Rebel Cities* where, in an oblique attack on the Romanticism that dominates contemporary Left scenes, Harvey proposes that the common is best understood as "an unstable and malleable social relation between a particular self-defined social group and those aspects of its actually existing or yet-to-be-created social and/or physical environment deemed crucial to its life and livelihood."[52] Although he evades direct reference, this definition betrays a significant indebtedness to the concept of the political outlined by Carl Schmitt. Indeed, Harvey's account of the "self-defined social group," its "physical environment," and those aspects deemed "crucial to its life and livelihood" neatly reiterate Schmitt's insistence that politics arises from the relationship between a people, a territory, and what he called its form of life or "mode of existence."[53]

Given this congruity, it's not surprising that Harvey's account also reiterates Schmitt's friend-enemy distinction. For Schmitt, politics presupposes a "distinction of friend and enemy" in which the political enemy is "existentially something different and alien, so that in the extreme case conflicts with him are possible."[54] As a result, politics itself requires that the enemy be "repulsed" so that one might "preserve one's own form of existence."[55] Here, the collective subject constituted through the friend-enemy antagonism preserves its form of existence by repulsing the enemy in order to secure control of contested terrain. Only then is it possible to determine which social relations will prevail therein. Standing at the opposite end of the political spectrum, Harvey adopts a nearly identical position when he notes how, "at the end of it all, the analyst is often left with a simple decision: whose side are you on, whose common interests do you seek to protect, and by what means?"[56]

Answering such questions demands that we determine who we are, where we operate, and what kinds of social relations we would like to see prevail within our territory. To the extent that we find ourselves plagued by the vampirism of constant capital, "we" are none other than the living in league with the dead. Although our territory is not yet defined, we know that it is potentially as expansive as the planet and as microscopic as the finest machined parts in the wonders against which we're pitted. Since we are not yet sovereign, we know that our enemy has determined the social relations that prevail in our territory. As a result, we, the living, are pitted against the dead as a mortal adversary – but it doesn't have to be that way.

Along with its *Trauerspiel*-like frisson, one practical implication of this assessment is that the question of territory reveals itself to be necessarily *prior* to considerations regarding the mode of production. As a result, our prefigurative experiments in commoning are likely to amount to nothing if we don't control the territory upon which they occur. From this realization arises a second, more challenging one: enclosure is not the antithesis of the commons as we often posit it to be. Rather it is the practical means by which the commons can be achieved in a world populated by enemies. As Harvey notes:

> In the grand scheme of things (and particularly at the global level), some sort of enclosure is often the best way to preserve certain kinds of valued commons. That sounds like, and is, a contradictory statement, but it reflects a truly contradictory situation ... The production and enclosure of non-commodified spaces in a ruthlessly commodifying world is surely a good thing.[57]

Our opposition, then, should not be to enclosure per se, but rather to the fact that the world's existing enclosures were not erected by us or in our interests. Our struggle for the commons, then, presupposes the constitution of a political "we" capable of fighting for the control of territory. Only then does it become possible to consistently intervene at the level of social relations. And only then does it become possible to break apart and reconfigure the built environment so that the aspirations of the dead might finally be fulfilled.

"How does one organize a city?" Responding to his own question, Harvey is unequivocal: "we simply do not know."[58] The scale and the social fragmentation of contemporary urban environments exacerbate the problem, to be sure, and the fratricidal rivalries of Left forces don't help much either. But if Harvey's impasse suggests the need for further investigation, it also encourages us to consider what we might learn by forging an alliance with the dead. At the very least, our counterparts in this union can tell us what *didn't* work – and what they had most longed for before being interred in the surplus.

Notes

1. David Harvey, *Rebel Cities: From The Right to the City to the Urban Revolution* (New York: Verso, 2012), 22, 18.
2. And here we must include both the machinery and infrastructure required by capital-intensive production as well as the concentrated labor power made available through the process of urbanization itself.
3. David Harvey, "The Right to the City," *New Left Review* 53 (Sept–Oct 2008): 24.
4. Karl Marx, *Capital, Volume 1* (Moscow: Progress Publishers, 1977), 224 (emphasis added).
5. Ibid.
6. As fixed or constant capital, the "means of production" most obviously include machines; however, it is important to remember that they also include buildings and other "externalities" like roads, sewers, and electricity grids that are not necessarily factored directly into the production costs of individual capitalists but nevertheless play a fundamental role in the generation of surplus value. This dynamic is emphasized in the work of Autonomous Marxists who have foregrounded the importance of the "social factory."
7. As Marx explains in Chapter IX of *Capital Volume 1*, the extraction of surplus value is possible to present as a consensual arrangement on account of the specific attributes of the commodity labor power. In particular, he notes how payment for the working day, which is indexed to the cost of the daily reproduction of the commodity labor power, is less than the value of the product produced through the consumption of the commodity labor power itself.
8. To get a sense of this sublime alienation, one could do no better than to consider Spike Jonze's recent film *Her* (2013), in which a lonely guy falls in love with his computer's operating system while perched in a glass tower overlooking a near-future Los Angeles played by a present-day Shanghai (currently the largest city in the world). For Benjamin's discussion of the steel girder, see "Paris, Capital of the Nineteenth Century" (1978).

9   John Berger, "Twelve Theses on the Economy of the Dead," in *Hold Everything Dear: Dispatches on Survival and Resistance* (New York: Pantheon Books, 2007), 3–4.
10   Walter Benjamin, "Theses on the Philosophy of History," in *Illuminations* (New York: Schocken Books, 1968), 254.
11   Jared Davidson, *Remains to be Seen: Tracing Joe Hill's Ashes in New Zealand* (Wellington: Rebel Press, 2011).
12   From an interview with Pierre van Paassen published in *The Toronto Daily Star*, August 5, 1936. Durruti died three months later on November 20, 1936 after being shot while trying to defend Madrid from Fascist incursion.
13   Then again, maybe not – after all, Walter Benjamin himself noted that one eyewitness to the July Revolution "may have owed his insight to the rhyme" when he recounted in verse how, in the moment of insurrection, street fighters fired upon clock towers to stop time itself (1968: 262).
14   Walter Benjamin, "Theses on the Philosophy of History," in *Illuminations* (New York: Schocken Books, 1968), 261.
15   Ibid., 254.
16   Ibid., 255.
17   Ibid., 256.
18   Ibid., 261.
19   Ibid., 257.
20   Ibid., 254.
21   Although it is difficult to know whether any of the workers who died building the dam felt a strong mythological bond to the national project (as soldiers sometimes do in their final moments), the objective conditions of Depression-era America suggest that they were probably motivated by more pedestrian concerns. As soon as the project began in 1931, both the dam site and the nearby town of Las Vegas became overrun with unemployed workers looking for relief. By some estimates, their numbers reached 20,000. See Andrew J. Dunar and Dennis McBride, *Building Hoover Dam: An Oral History of the Great Depression* (Reno: University of Nevada Press, 2001). The timing of the project suggests that at least some of these workers may have had Robinson's "Ballad of Joe Hill" on their lips as they trudged from camp to work site. Meanwhile, to get a sense of the properly mythological dimension of the Hoover Dam commemoration plaque's claim, it's useful to recall the oblique Biblical reference (Isaiah 35) upon which it relies. This same reference can be found underwriting the historic conquest of Palestine, as Zionists following Herzl's proclamations in *The Jewish State* (1896) sought to make a supposedly uninhabited desert bloom: "The word 'impossible' has ceased to exist in the vocabulary of technical science. Were a man who lived in the last century to return to the earth, he would find the life of today full of incomprehensible magic. Wherever the moderns appear with our inventions, we transform the desert into a garden. To build a city takes in our time as many years as it formerly required centuries; America offers endless examples of this…" (Rockville, MD: Wildside Press, 2008), 115.
22   "Modern History: Revolution and Innovation Intersect at The Boston Tea Party Museum" (*The Voice of Downtown Boston,* December 10, 2013), http://www.thevoiceofdowntownboston.com/modern-history-revolution-and-innovation-intersect-at-the-boston-tea-party-museum/ (accessed November 19, 2014).
23   Ruth Richardson, *Death, Dissection, and the Destitute* (Chicago: University of Chicago Press, 2000), 90.
24   Ibid.
25   Ibid., 91.
26   Walter Benjamin, *Reflections* (New York: Schocken Books, 1978), 148.
27   Ray Oldenburg, *The Great Good Place: Cafés, Coffee Shops, Community Centers, Beauty Parlors, General Stores, Bars, Hangouts, and How They Get You Through The Day* (New York: Paragon House, 1989), 23.

28 Ibid.,186.
29 Ibid., 24.
30 Ibid., 41.
31 Ibid., 192.
32 Ibid., 32.
33 Ibid., 34.
34 Silvia Federici, *Caliban and The Witch: Women, The Body and Primitive Accumulation* (New York: Autonomedia, 2004), 24.
35 Ibid., 71.
36 Ibid.
37 Andrew Hopton (ed), *Gerrard Winstanley: Selected Writings* (London: Aporia Press, 1989), 19.
38 Acts of the Apostles, 4:32, *King James Bible,* http://biblehub.com/acts/4-32.htm (accessed November 19, 2014)
39 Karl Kautsky, *Foundations of Christianity* (New York: Monthly Review Press, 1972), 345–354.
40 Ibid., 329.
41 Ibid., 330.
42 Ibid., 331.
43 Anonymous, *Martyr of the Catacombs: A Tale of Ancient Rome* (Grand Rapids, MI: Kregel Classics, 1990), 79.
44 Ibid., 84.
45 Ibid., 87–88.
46 Ibid., 90.
47 Jean-Victor Schnetz, *Combat devant l'hôtel de ville* (1830).
48 Victor Hugo, *Notre Dame de Paris* (New York: The Riverdale Press, 1903), 88.
49 CrimethInc, *Expect Resistance: A Field Manual* (CrimethInc Collective, 2008), 71.
50 Cited in Jonathan Sachs, *Romantic Antiquity: Rome in the British Imagination, 1789–1832* (Oxford: Oxford University Press, 2010), 153.
51 Karl Marx and Friedrich Engels, "The Eighteenth Brumaire of Louis Bonaparte," *Selected Works, Volume 1* (Moscow: Progress Publishers, 1969), 398.
52 Harvey, *Rebel Cities*, 73.
53 It's noteworthy that, while Schmitt's analysis presupposes the nation state as the primitive, mythological, unit for the elaboration of forms of existence, his category can be applied equally well – and perhaps more accurately – to contests *within* the nation state. Here, the most extreme form of friend-enemy antagonism is civil war. By dispensing with Schmitt's fascist mythology, it becomes clear that the most universal contest between different "forms of existence" concerns class war. Indeed, Schmitt refers to this possibility directly in *The Concept of the Political* when he notes how "a class in the Marxist sense ceases to be something purely economic and becomes a political factor when it reaches this decisive point, for example, when Marxists approach the class struggle seriously and treat the class adversary as a real enemy and fight him … in a civil war within a state." (Chicago: University of Chicago Press, 1996), 37. This position holds regardless of the qualification Schmitt tires to establish in Note 9 where, following a distinction advanced by Plato in the *Republic*, he notes that "a people cannot wage war against itself and a civil war is only a self-laceration and it does not signify that … a new people is being created" (Ibid., 29).
54 Carl Schmitt, *The Concept of the Political* (Chicago: University of Chicago Press: 1996), 26–27.
55 Ibid., 27.
56 Harvey, *Rebel Cities,* 71.
57 Ibid., 70.
58 Ibid., 140.

Authors

Ivo Balmer graduated with an MA in sociology from the University of Zurich. He works as a doctoral researcher at the University of Bern department of geography. His dissertation project analyzes housing policy in Swiss municipalities. He recently co-founded a new housing cooperative in Basel.

Sören Becker is a human geographer and political scientist working at the Leibniz Institute for Regional Development and Structural Planning (IRS) in Erkner, Germany. His research interests are new forms of organization and ownership in the energy sector, local democracy, and socio-material change. He received his MA degree from the University of Potsdam (Germany) and also studied at the University of Kent (UK).

Tobias Bernet received his MA in anthropology and history from the University of Zurich. He now works as a doctoral fellow at the Max Planck Institute for Human Development in Berlin, where he is writing a dissertation on the history of cooperative housing projects in German-speaking Europe. He's a co-founder of one such project in Leipzig and a volunteer advisor to several others.

Ross Beveridge is a research fellow at the Leibniz Institute for Regional Development and Structural Planning (IRS). His research interests lie in the fields of urban and environmental governance, particularly the policies and politics of privatization/remunicipalization, climate change, and energy transitions. His current work engages with debates on de/politicization and new practices of democratic politics.

Dr. Dipl. Psych. Majken Bieniok completed a doctorate in psychology at the Humboldt University, Berlin, where she is also an associate researcher in the department of cognitive psychology and a founding member of the interdisciplinary Urban Research Group at the Georg Simmel Center for Metropolitan Studies. She is also a lecturer and program coordinator for psychology at the Touro College Berlin. Her current research focuses on concepts of cities and metropolises, favored urban sites, urban commons, and health and well-being.

Ignacio Castillo Ulloa is an architect with a MSc in urban management, and a PhD candidate in urban and regional planning at the Technical University Berlin. His research interests address uneven socio-spatial development and the alternative (local) practices that counteract it, focusing on the way discourses mediate power relations. He partook in the elaboration of a new regional plan for the Great Metropolitan Area of Costa Rica (funded by the EU) and the project "Improving Governance in Secondary Cities in Bangladesh" (sponsored by the former GTZ). His dissertation problematizes, within the scope of radical planning and through spatial analysis, how protest action of urban-social movements may turn out to be a valuable asset to set off local community self-development schemes.

Dr. Mary Dellenbaugh is an interdisciplinary urban researcher and a co-founder of the Urban Research Group at the Georg Simmel Center for Metropolitan Studies, Humboldt University, Berlin. After completing her BSc at the University of New Hampshire, and funded in part by a German Academic Exchange Service (DAAD) scholarship, she relocated to Germany in 2007 to pursue her MA in landscape architecture at Hochschule Anhalt. In 2013, she successfully defended her dissertation in cultural geography at the Humboldt University, Berlin. Her current work concentrates on post-socialist urban dynamics, European real-estate markets, holistic approaches to shrinking cities, and the symbolic and material changes in cities associated with the postmodern and post-industrial turns.

Melissa García Lamarca is a doctoral researcher in geography at the University of Manchester, and an associate fellow with the European Network for Political Ecology (ENTITLE). Her research untangles the relationship between the financialization of housing, the lived experience of mortgaged households facing foreclosure or eviction, and processes of subjectification that unfold through their engagement in housing rights struggles in the Barcelona metropolitan area.

Didi K. Han has been involved in various social movements in South Korea, primarily the anti-neoliberal globalization, migrant worker media activist, and direct action for democracy movements. She is currently researching neoliberal urbanism and the urban commoning movement in South Korea at Simon Fraser University, Canada.

Hajime Imamasa studied sociocultural anthropology at the department of anthropology at the University of California, Los Angeles (PhD candidate). He has been a member of a para-academic commune "Suyu plus Trans" and an occasional "guest" at *Bin-Zib*. His area of interest includes modes of collective memory in Korea and Japan as well as sites of commoning and dissent, particularly home and school.

Angela Jain (PhD) has an academic background in spatial planning. Since 2007 she has been head of the division 'Infrastructure and Society' at the Nexus Institute, Berlin (www.nexusinstitut.de). From 2009 until 2013 she worked on the Indo-German research project "Sustainable Hyderabad" funded by the German Federal Ministry of Education and Research (BMBF). In 2012, she also supervised the project "Governance and Participation in the Telangana Region" with focus on scenarios for water governance, which was funded by the Foundation Friedrich-Ebert-Stiftung (FES) India. Her research focuses on social-science oriented sustainability research, citizen participation in urban development and local governance in the South Asian context.

Markus Kip is a PhD candidate in sociology at York University in Toronto. His dissertation deals with practices of labor union solidarity with undocumented migrant workers in Germany. Markus is a co-founder of the Urban Research Group at the Georg Simmel Center, Humboldt University, Berlin. Besides labor solidarity and transnational migration, his research interests are urban theory, socialist urbanism, modernism and postmodernism, and the sociology of law.

Brigitte Kratzwald is a social scientist and commons activist dealing with currently arising new forms of collective production and bottom-up strategies of reorganizing the society in a way conducive to both, human beings and our non-human environment. She holds lectures and workshops about related issues and has published several articles in this field. She is part of various teams organizing events dealing with social transformation, e.g. the German Commons Summer School in Thuringia (Germany) and the Elevate Festival in Graz.

Tobias Kuttler studied geography, European ethnology and urban planning in Berlin. Study and research visits took him to the US, Spain, India, and South Korea.

His focus is on social and cultural aspects of sustainable urban development and participatory approaches to urban planning. His recent work in Hyderabad and Chennai, India, investigates how urban dwellers organize their daily survival by appropriating the built environment, drawing attention to practices of everyday infrastructure-making. This approach seeks to challenge dominant notions of infrastructure and contributes to a better understanding of the complexities of spatial planning in South Asian megacities.

Manuel Lutz is PhD candidate in political geography at the Center for Metropolitan Studies, Technical University Berlin. He studied spatial planning at the Technical University Dortmund (Dipl. Ing.), including extended research stays in Russia and North America. His research focus is on poverty governance and homelessness, urban informalities, urban planning, urban movements, and local hegemony.

Agnes Katharina Müller is an architect and PhD candidate in urban planning at the Technical University Berlin. Her dissertation analyzes the change of work and its socio-spatial and structural influences on the city. She is a co-founder of the interdisciplinary Urban Research Group at the Georg Simmel Center for Metropolitan Studies, Humboldt University, Berlin. Her research interests include postindustrial cities, participatory planning, urban commons, the city and digital media, and global networks within a sustainable urban development.

Matthias Naumann is a human geographer and research fellow at the Leibniz Institute for Regional Development and Structural Planning (IRS) in Erkner. He also works as a visiting lecturer at the Brandenburg University of Technology Cottbus and at the Free University Berlin. His research interests include urban and regional development, infrastructure governance, and critical geography.

Dr. Daniel Opazo is an architect and researcher based in Santiago, where he is an assistant professor at the department of architecture, faculty of architecture and urbanism, Universidad de Chile. His research focuses on the relationship between architecture, the city, and the political, with emphasis on the production of public spaces. Currently he is developing a research project on how different traditions of participatory design deal with political conflict and collective imagination.

Dr. Martin Schwegmann is an urban researcher, urban designer, and architect. He is a co-founder of the Urban Research Group at the Georg Simmel Center, Humboldt University, Berlin. He is currently program manager for Actors of Urban Change, a joint program of the Robert Bosch Foundation and MitOst e.V. Here his focus centres on sustainable urban development through cross-sector collaboration and participatory approaches. His wider research focus is on temporary uses, urban social movements, urban commons, social innovation, and transition management.

AK Thompson is an activist, writer, and social theorist. Regularly featured as a speaker in both movement and scholarly settings, Thompson has taught at the CUNY Graduate Center, Brooklyn College, and Fordham University. His publications include *Black Bloc, White Riot: Anti-Globalization and the Genealogy of Dissent* (2010) and *Sociology for Changing the World: Social Movements/Social Research* (2006). Between 2005 and 2012, he served on the editorial committee of *Upping the Anti: A Journal of Theory and Action*.

Picture credits

Seizing the (Every)Day: Welcome to the Urban Commons!
Figure 1: Photo: Markus Kip
Figure 2: Photos: Majken Bieniok and Agnes Müller
Figure 3: Photo: Lars Zimmermann, CC by 2.0, https://www.flickr.com/photos/larszi/9293597797/in/photostream/

Defending Space in a Changing Urban Landscape – A Study on Urban Commons in Hyderabad, India
Figure 1: Photo: Tobias Kuttler
Figure 2: Source: Own graphic, based on GHMC Draft Master Plan
Figure 3: Photos: Tobias Kuttler

Overcoming Privatized Housing in South Korea: Looking through the Lens of "Commons" and "the Common"
Figure 1: Photo: SuhWon, reproduced with permission

Uncommon Claims to the Commons: Homeless Tent Cities in the US
Figure 1: Photos: Lutz
Figure 2: Photos: Lutz

Creating and Appropriating Urban Spaces – The Public versus the Commons: Institutions, Traditions, and Struggles in the Production of Commons and Public Spaces in Chile
Figure 1: Source: Daniel Opazo
Figure 2: Source: Daniel Opazo

From Urban Commons to Urban Planning – or Vice Versa? "Planning" the Contested Gleisdreieck Territory
Figure 1: Reproduced with permission of the Aktionsgemeinschaft Gleisdreieck e.V.
Figure 2: Actual park design, Gleisdreieck Park 2014. Reproduced with permission of Atelier Loidl

Insurgent Acts of Being-in-Common and Housing in Spain: Making Urban Commons?
Figure 1: Source: Naredo et al., 2008, compiled from National Statistics Institute (INE), Ministry of Development and Ministry of Housing sources. Updated by Naredo to include figures until 2011. Reproduced with permission

Housing as a Common Resource? Decommodification and Self-Organization in Housing – Examples from Germany and Switzerland
Figure 1: Source: own work
Figure 2: Source: own work
Figure 3: Source: own work. Data Sources: Zensus 2011 – Gebäude und Wohnungszählung [Germany]; Volkszählung 2000 – Gebäude- und Wohnungsstatistik; Statistisches Jahrbuch der Stadt Zürich 2014 [Switzerland]; Statistik Austria – Registerzählung 2011 [Austria])
Figure 4: Source: own work
Figure 5: Source: own work

The Battle for Necropolis: Reclaiming the Past as Commons in the City of the Dead
Courtesy of Mary Ryan Gallery, New York. Reproduced with permission.
Courtesy of US Department of the Interior –Bureau of Reclamation. (Photo: Alexander Stephens, reproduced with permission)
Photo: Gérard Blot, Musée des Beaux-Arts, Nantes, France. © RMN-Grand Palais/Art Resource, NY, reproduced with permission

Bauwelt Fundamente (selected titles)

1 Ulrich Conrads (ed.), Programme und Manifeste zur Architektur des 20. Jahrhunderts
2 Le Corbusier, 1922 – Ausblick auf eine Architektur
4 Jane Jacobs, Tod und Leben großer amerikanischer Städte
12 Le Corbusier, 1929 – Feststellungen
16 Kevin Lynch, Das Bild der Stadt
21 Ebenezer Howard, Gartenstädte von morgen (1902)
41 Aldo Rossi, Die Architektur der Stadt
50 Robert Venturi, Komplexität und Widerspruch in der Architektur
53 Robert Venturi / Denise Scott Brown / Steven Izenour, Lernen von Las Vegas
118 Thomas Sieverts, Zwischenstadt
126 Werner Sewing, Bildregie. Architektur zwischen Retrodesign und Eventkultur
127 Jan Pieper, Das Labyrinthische
128 Elisabeth Blum, Schöne neue Stadt. Wie der Sicherheitswahn die urbane Welt diszipliniert
131 Angelus Eisinger, Die Stadt der Architekten
132 Wilhelm / Jessen-Klingenberg (ed.), Formationen der Stadt. Camillo Sitte weitergelesen
133 Michael Müller / Franz Dröge, Die ausgestellte Stadt
134 Loïc Wacquant, Das Janusgesicht des Ghettos und andere Essays
135 Florian Rötzer, Vom Wildwerden der Städte
136 Ulrich Conrads, Zeit des Labyrinths
137 Friedrich Naumann, Ausstellungsbriefe Berlin, Paris, Dresden, Düsseldorf 1896–1906.
138 Undine Giseke / Erika Spiegel (ed.), Stadtlichtungen.
140 Yildiz / Mattausch (ed.), Urban Recycling. Migration als Großstadt-Ressource
141 Günther Fischer, Vitruv NEU oder Was ist Architektur?
142 Dieter Hassenpflug, Der urbane Code Chinas
143 Elisabeth Blum / Peter Neitzke (ed.), Dubai. Stadt aus dem Nichts
144 Michael Wilkens, Architektur als Komposition. Zehn Lektionen zum Entwerfen
145 Gerhard Matzig, Vorsicht Baustelle!
146 Adrian von Buttlar et al., Denkmalpflege statt Attrappenkult
147 André Bideau, Architektur und symbolisches Kapitel
148 Jörg Seifert, Stadtbild, Wahrnehmung, Design
149 Steen Eiler Rasmussen, LONDON, The Unique City
150 Dietmar Offenhuber / Carlo Ratti (ed.), Die Stadt entschlüsseln
151 Harald Kegler, Resilienz. Strategien & Perspektiven für die widerstandsfähige und lernende Stadt
152 Günther Fischer, Architekturtheorie für Architekten.
153 Bodenschatz / Sassi / Guerra (eds.), Urbanism and Dicatorship

All titles are available as well as e-book.
More Bauwelt Fundamente on: degruyter.com

Harald Bodenschatz, Piero Sassi, Max Welch Guerra (eds.)

Urbanism and Dictatorship

A European Perspective

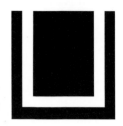

Urban design under European dictatorships in the first half of the twentieth century must be considered in an international context, as the professional and cultural exchange between European countries was – beyond conflicts and political orientations – very intensive. This European perspective is likewise an expression of our culture of memory: our ability to recognize old and new forms of dictatorship!

248 pages, 100 b/w-illustrations, softcover
(BWF 153) ISBN: 978-3-03821-660-5
Urbanism